Part of the 1845 Henfield Tithe Map
with selected locations and homes.
Scale 12 inches to mile (approx).

Henfield's 19th Century Egg Basket

E. J. Colgate

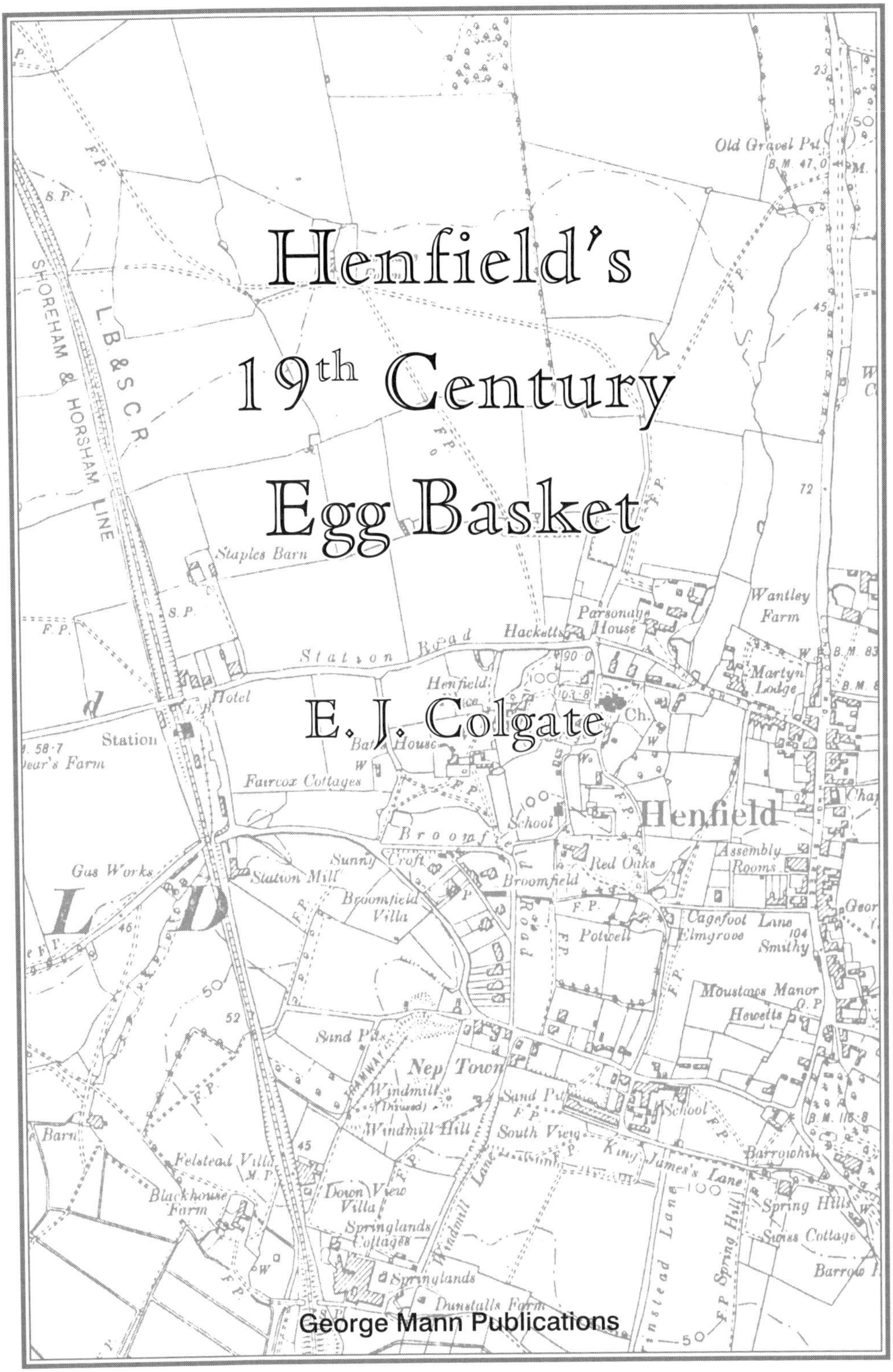

George Mann Publications

Published by
George Mann Publications
Easton, Winchester,
Hampshire SO21 1ES
01962 779944

A CIP catalogue record for this book
is available from the British Library

ISBN 9781907640223

Printed in England

By the same author:
Falling Off a Horse in the Falkland Islands ~ ISBN: 9780954163426
The Power and The Poverty ~ ISBN: 9780955241567
Henfield's Wonderful Railway ~ ISBN: 9781907640148

Further copies of this book may be obtained from:
E. J. Colgate, 7 Southview Terrace, Henfield, West Sussex BN5 9ES
Tel: 01273 494584

George Mann Publications

Contents

Introduction v

Acknowledgements vii

Glossary viii

1: The Village – River Adur barges – The Workhouse 1

2: Friendly Societies – Tanyard odours – Broadmare Common 9

3: Invasion threat – A village school – Southdown Sheep 14

4: 5% loans – The debtor's prison – A Woolwich hulk 21

5: Bankrupt pub – A well of good water – An attractive barn 31

6: Wage demands – Timber for sale – Violating manor law 37

7: A journeyman tailor – Triplets – Unwanted family 44

8: New Poor Law – A workhouse mill – Pauper confrontation 50

9: Workhouse riot – Midnight fire –Tempting reward 56

10: Corn-mill strike – Union Workhouse – Cricket Club 64

11: Horse thieves – High Street oil lamps – Threatening drunks 75

12: Emigration – Midnight mutton – Transportation 86

13: A gunshot - Workhouse life - A mother seeks justice 93

14: Village farms – Ploughman's whip – Haymaking frolics 99

15: High Street traders – Gamekeepers – Poachers 107

16: A warm rabbit – Pigeon egg hailstones – Mustard poultices 114

17: Corn Law opinions – A new map – A skeletal beggar 120

18: Hungry visitors – A bargee's booty – The Sparrows Club 129

19: Starving immigrants – Cholera – Round frock missionaries 135

20: New-shop dispute – Outlaw Lake – Deserting sailor 140

21: The Henfield Band – A fire engine – The village omnibus 146

22: Horse cruelty – Petition to Her Majesty – The missing ring 153

23: An outlaw's Mecca – Baccy & a pint – Basket makers' strike 161

24: The ploughing match – A horse race – Harriers and hares 170

25: Gingerbread scrambles – Violin variations – Sleepy carter 177
26: Why the heathen rage – Railway promise – Dishonest miller 182
27: Smithfield heifer – Christmas tree lamps – Taxation debate................. 194
28: Disappearing onions – Failing barges – The Rifle Corps 205
29: School inspection – Stoolball – Ginger beer & a dud shilling............. 212
30: Riding a windmill – Mercury for geese – Wait for the Wagon 222
31: Easter battle – Food adulteration – 'Rough Music' 230
32: The telegraph – Special Train – The Bank of Engraving 236
33: Magic lantern – A dirty narrow lane – Brickbats and tiles.................. 244
34: An arsonist – The Prosecuting Society – A ferocious bull 252
35: A maimed dog – School treat – The excise officer intervenes 258
36: Gas lighting – A General Election – Cattle murrain........................... 267
37: Pig in a bag – Lottery luck – The lights go out.................................. 278
38: 4.00 a.m. bugle blast – Government grant – Kiss in the Ring 288
39: The Snake House – 'Spinning Jenny' – Smallpox 295
40: Night attack – Roman candles – A missing ramrod............................. 302
41: H.M.S. Minotaur – The bag in a pond – 'Snow black' night 308

References 317
Index 319
- General 319
- Henfield Locations 321
- People 322
- Other Places 324

Illustrations

1813 OS map (1857 proposed railway in red) .... front cover
The carpenter's shop beyond Golden Square .... front cover
The Henfield Omnibus .... back cover
Henfield Common Windmill above Barrow Hill .... back cover
1845 Henfield Tithe Map showing selected locations and homes .... front endpaper
1895 OS map showing the development of the village .... back endpaper
Eight for thought – up on the Lydds south of Henfield Common v
The cottage and village pound by the Town Field 2
George Lock's Service Certificate 3
The Windsor Coach 4
Cock Fighting at the Plough 9
Henfield cricket at the Sussex Pad 16
Barrow Hill House 17
Southdown Sheep for sale 19
Percy Gregory gains a strip of land 23
The Nep Town Windmill 24
The new buildings on the Haycroft 34
1845 Tithe Map; Mr. Borrer's barn, William Ede's house and Windmill Lane 60
Mr. Borrer's church extension for the schoolchildren 65
Workhouse Food Tender advertisement 66
Sheep on Henfield Common Cricket Pitch 73
A Muzzall wagon at the carpenter's shop 75
1845 Tithe Map; Horn Lane and Oreham Common with landowners 77
The White Hart 83
New Inn and Rye Farms for Sale 100
North end of High Street 109
The Henfield Band 147
Eastbourne versus Henfield 148
The Henfield Omnibus when taken over by Edward Pattenden 152
Mr. Tobitt takes over the BALDWIN & GARRETT emporium 164
Broadmare Common with copyholders' cattle 166

'Sunny' Woolgar's bill to Rev. J. Goring of Wiston House near Steyning....... 168
The Henfield Common Windmill from Broadmare Common 190
Henfield v Steyning on Henfield Common 196
The old house beyond Nep Town Windmill.. 201
The Infants' School Inspector's Report 213
Percy Gregory's property up for sale 214
Crouch Hill Toll House 220
The rebuilt George Inn.. 222
The old houses by Church Street.. 224
"Wait for the Wagon" chorus... 228
A Telegram for Henfield.. 236
The Portsmouth Special Train 237
Henfield Prosecuting Society.. 254
The Schoolboys at their best.. 259
Henfield Place, near the church 261
The Cowfold/Henfield Turnpike Trust annual account................................. 267
The joy of owning a bat – cricket at the Boys' School 275
Henry Fair's 'Best Cultivated Garden' card of merit 276
Martyn Lodge 285
The church galleries 292
Mr. Cooper's yard beside the Congregational Church 305
The church rebuilding under way, 1870 308
The rebuilt St.Peter's of 1871 with its medieval chapel of stone walls 309
The 'Penny Readings' programme.. 313

Introduction

This is a book about the people of Henfield in Sussex during the19th century – an egg basket of good and bad times in their many guises.

Life for the ordinary family was tough. Poverty was endemic, welfare support minimal and punishments for minor discretions harsh.

People sought relaxation in sport, concerts, summer fetes and flower shows. Friendly Societies gave working men an annual day of pleasure.

The village moved forward with the times as education embraced more children, barge and stagecoach gave way to the railway, lighting and sanitation were gradually improved and the machinery of justice was kept well oiled by neighbourly disputes and some surprisingly wicked events.

Eight for thought – up on the Lydds south of Henfield Common [1]

Each character's features are best recreated by using a potion of imaginative thought because few helpful pictures of the time survive.

Many Henfield fields have disappeared beneath two centuries of new housing.

Old farms and labourers' homes have gone too.

There is nothing to see at Pokerlee way out where the railway used to be.

Tiny Dogham Place is a roofless ruin hidden among trees at the back of the common.

The plate glass windows of the big High Street grocer/draper's shop have transformed into the village supermarket.

The daily Brighton stagecoach is now a half hourly bus across the common where village people still enjoy family or social occasions and sometimes watch the cricket; just as they did when Napoleon threatened our shores.

Henfield in the good(?) old days.

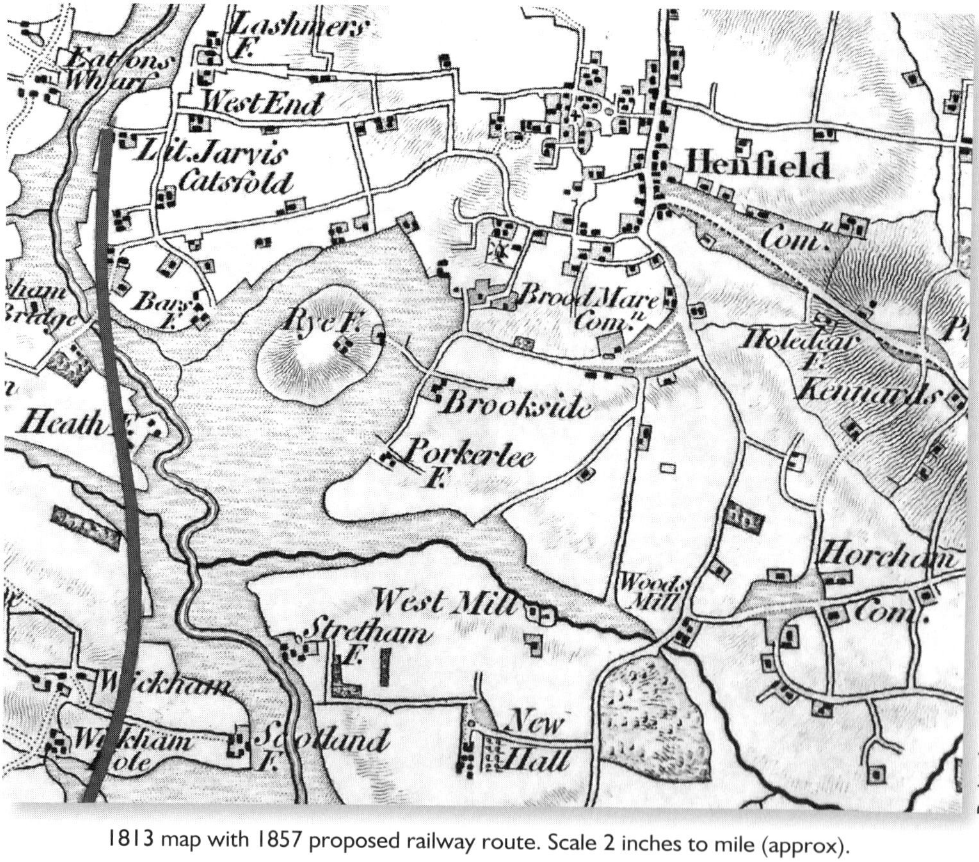

1813 map with 1857 proposed railway route. Scale 2 inches to mile (approx).

Acknowledgements

Major sources are West Sussex Records Office in Chichester, East Sussex Records Office at Brighton Keep, Henfield Museum and the National Archives at Kew.

Brighton Keep's newspapers have village 'stories' hidden away amongst microfilm copies of 19th century Sussex and Brighton editions.

Some of the adverts in those papers are intriguing; the cock-fight at The Plough Inn, the 1844 Rye Farm livestock auction, workhouse food and clothing tenders and the 1848 cricket team playing at Eastbourne.

Chichester has the Parish Records and signed depositions of witnesses, victims and suspects made prior to Quarter Sessions trials.

Henfield Museum includes excellent indexed copies of censuses from 1841; a ten yearly record of each inhabitant - age, home and occupation.

Kew houses the railway and Steyning Union Poor Law records.

The many people involved at those places have been exceedingly kind in giving all the help possible.

Most particularly, my very sincere thanks go to my publisher for his expertise and patient guidance turning my script into this book.

It is dedicated to my long suffering brothers, sisters, children and their spouses for showing great patience when being told how the book is getting on – and to all my fantastic grandchildren.

Glossary

This glossary provides background and explanations for terms used throughout the book..

Henfield

Henfield is almost in the middle of Sussex and eight miles from the sea. The village's attributes, or lack of them, are listed in the 1820's and 30's Pigot and Co. Directories:

> "HENFIELD ... a neat and pleasant village ... forty-four miles from London, eleven from Brighton and Horsham, five from Steyning ...pleasantly situated on the navigable River Adur ... the country around is replete with rural beauty ... not a place of trade or manufacture nor anything of curiosity or interest ... about 1,000 inhabitants."

Parish Vestry

Consisted of the vicar, the churchwardens and the overseers. Any paid-up rate payer could participate. It dealt with parish affairs, particularly law and order, Poor Law and Parish Roads.

Parish rates were raised on property. Poorest householders were exempt.

Two overseers and two waywardens were chosen for the year. Each carried out his duties in addition to his daily work.

During the Napoleonic Wars an annual list of male parishioners was sent to the Quarter Sessions for the compulsory draw for service in the militia.

OVERSEERS dealt with the bulk of parish business.

PARISH CONSTABLES were paid for each type of task carried out.

WAYWARDENS were responsible for Parish Roads (wider than farm lanes but not part of a Turnpike Trust's toll-road).

Poor Law

Required a parish to provide help for anyone in real need, particularly those with a legal 'Settlement' in the parish.

SETTLEMENT was where a person belonged; initially the parish of their birth except for an illegitimate baby who had the mother's.

The 'Settlement' changed if property was bought elsewhere or a work contract of over a year's duration was completed there.

THE WORKHOUSE kept people unable to maintain their home.

Stretham Manor

Was the Bishop of Chichester's Manor including much of Henfield. Tenants were subject to the manor's Customary Laws.

[The 19th century Manor Roll scribes wrote Streatham with an 'a' and Tipnoke without an 'a' which is followed in the book.]

COPYHOLD gave the tenant Commoners' Rights on the manor commons to graze livestock, dig mould or collect fuel; but not to cut timber.

COPYHOLD ACT 1852 allowed holdings to be enfranchised by the tenant paying the lord an agreed sum to be independent of the manor.

FREEHOLD gave the tenant the right to vote in a general election.

HERIOT was the payment to the manor made at every change of tenant; a throwback to when the tenant had to return armour lent him by his lord. The customary 'heriot' was the best cloven footed beast but was often a money payment as in this house sale:-

HENFIELD, SUSSEX
TO BE SOLD BY PRIVATE CONTRACT
All that house converted into, and occupied as two separate tenements
with wood-house and other buildings, and the large productive
GARDEN AND ORCHARD,
containing together about three quarters of an acre,
possessing a long frontage to the public road, near the church in the
parish of Henfield formerly the property of the late Mr. G. Vinall.
The premises are copyhold of the manor of Streatham,
subject to a QUIT RENT, the HERIOT sixpence certain,
and are now let to a respectable tenant at £20 per annum.
£200 may remain on mortgage, if desired, by the purchaser.
Apply to Mr. Lawrence Smith, Solicitor.

House sale with quit rent and heriot payments due

QUIT RENT replaced the medieval compulsory work service for the lord.

THE MANOR COURT was held twice a year. Court proceedings were written up on the manor roll; most importantly any property held on Conditional Surrender as security for a loan to the tenant.

THE REEVE was responsible for the smooth running of manor affairs.

In Henfield it was local man, Percy Gregory, a grocer, small landowner and village goods carrier to London.

Significant Calendar Dates

Lady Day; 25th March

Michaelmas; 29th September.

The Petty Sessions Court

Tried alleged misdemeanours and crimes. Justices of the Peace dealt with minor offences.

COUNTY ASSIZES or QUARTER SESSIONS dealt with serious crimes.

PETWORTH HOUSE OF CORRECTION was the prison. It had a notoriously hard regime.

Money

2.4d = 1p …1s = 5p...

A sovereign = £1 = 20 shillings (s) … 1 shilling = 12 pence (d) …

A guinea = £1 1s 0d.

A ½d is a halfpenny (*hay'pny*) … ¼d is a farthing (as in 'then').
£8 5s 9¾d reads 8 pounds, 5 shillings and 9 pence 3 farthings;
3s 6d as 3 shillings and 6 pence. 2½d as tuppence hay'pny!

In 1800: a farm worker earned 10s 0d a week; beef cost from 6d per lb (5p per kg), Dutch cheese and sugar each cost 8d per lb (7p per kg); butter was 1s 1d per lb (11p per kg); and a pair of sheets under £1.

Measurements

These are near equivalents:-

LENGTH: mile = 1½km; yard = 1m; foot = 30cm; inch = 2½cm.
WEIGHT: ton = 1016kg; hundredweight = 51kg; stone = 5kg;
pound (lb) = ½kg; ounce = 30g; drachm (dram) = 5g.
CAPACITY: WET; gallon = 4l; quart = 1l; pint = ½l.
DRY; bushel = 40kg; gallon = 5kg.
AREA: acre = 0.4 hectare.

Chapter 1

The Village – River Adur barges – The Workhouse

The 19th century opened with Britain and France at war.

A tax of 2d in the £ was introduced on any annual income over £60. Parliament ordered a census to be taken to ascertain every inhabitant. All men were liable for service in the home defence force, the County Militia.

The census showed Henfield to have 1037 inhabitants in 127 dwellings.

The parish church, St. Peter's, stood on a commanding knoll in the centre of the village. To the east was the High Street. South was the sandstone ridge of Nep Town; beyond and to the west lay the brooks – the low lying fields around the River Adur. North were the stiff clays of the Weald.

The High Street's eastern side was lined by shops and houses from the White Hart Inn and close neighbour Plough up the hill to the George and down the far side to Golden Square.

There the Brighton Turnpike Road turned sharp left across the common leaving the old parish road to wend its way towards Shoreham. Between the two stood Prospect Cottage, home of spinster Ann Gander, friend of anyone in need.

The other side of the street was mainly grass apart from a cluster of old houses each side of the turning into Church Street. From opposite the White Hart, the Hay Croft meadow stretched almost to the brow of the hill where Cagefoot Lane led to the Tanyard. From the lane to Golden Square was the Town Field; the venue for many outdoor social events.

Midway along it, stood the only building, a minute cottage owned by manor reeve, Percy Gregory, and occupied by one of the village blacksmiths. Beside it were the village pound, for strayed animals, and the parish stocks for straying villagers.

The cottage and village pound by the Town Field

By the road junction was James Patching's 'Bee Hive' brewery, possible source of much straying.

Along the far side of the Town Field a bridleway led into Nep Town.

There the village mill faced the prevailing westerlies in a field beside aptly named Windmill Lane leading down to the brooks.

The miller, Robert Loase, also ran a farm. His wife, Mary, was in charge of the dairy and earned the farm a good name in the neighbourhood for its high quality milk.

At Nep Town's highest point, Burning Mountain, (just 125 feet above sea level) people could gaze across the Adur Valley to the ruins of Bramber Castle, once the seat of Norman overlords, and to Steyning's Norman Church set against the South Downs.

Steyning was the location of the Petty Sessions Court. It was also the market town for local farmers and the mail centre for Henfield. Collections and deliveries were made three times a week by the postboy with a small cart pulled by two dogs.

It was the two dog mail cart that brought the printed form from the Quarter Sessions requiring the vestry to inform James Hedgecock, George Lock and David Penfold that they had been drawn to serve for the parish in the Sussex Militia.

James Hedgecock was landlord of the White Hart. He considered himself far too old for soldiering and intended staying at home with his family.

The one alternative to service was finding somebody willing to be a paid substitute.

James set about finding his substitute. Producing money for the payment was far preferable to being marched around in any uniform.

Unemployed Richard Blower, a married man over 20 miles away in East Sussex, had a different view; being marched around as a soldier was far preferable to having nothing to provide for your wife and children.

He became James' substitute, glad to be earning money again.

In addition to the militia allowance, his wife received 4s 6d weekly relief from Henfield vestry because he was serving for one of their men.

James Hedgecock continued to serve his customers at the White Hart.

Day labourers George Lock and David Penfold had to accept the luck of the draw. They underwent four weeks' training in Brighton before being marched off to serve their time.

At the end of it, each came home with a certificate stating him to be in actual service. They presented them to the vestry for payment.

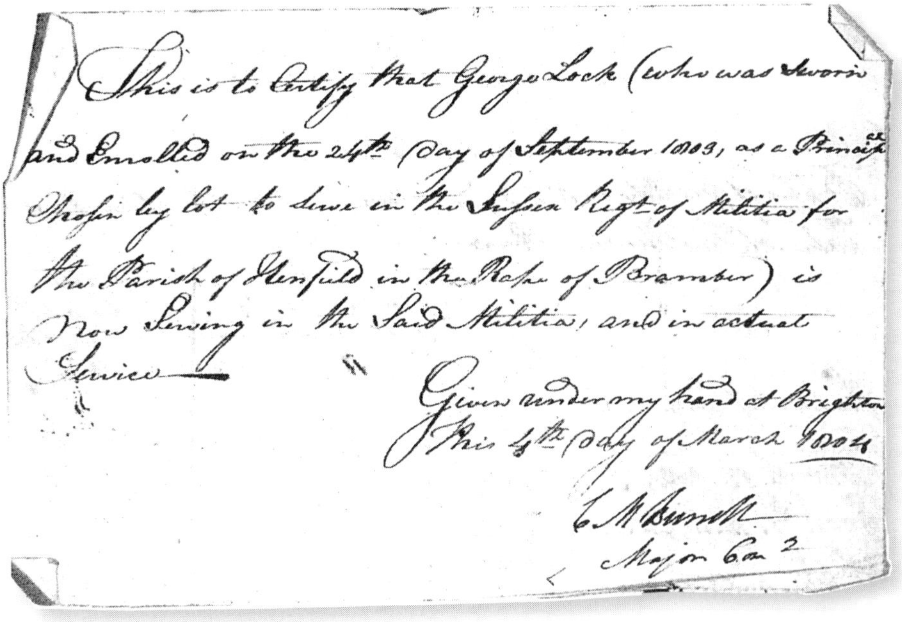

This is to Certify that George Lock (who was Sworn and Enrolled on the 24th Day of September 1803, as a Princip[l] Chosen by lot to serve in the Sussex Regt of Militia for the Parish of Henfield in the Rape of Bramber) is Now Serving in the Said Militia, and in actual Service

Given under my hand at Brighton This 4th Day of March 1804

C M Burrell

Major Com 2

George Lock's Service Certificate

Richard Pattenden, one of the overseers for the year, accepted the certificates and gave the men their allowance amongst his other payments.

Rd Pattenden Overseer

March 9th	*Paid to James Lelyett the water carriage of 1 chaldron of coal for the poorhouse*	*3s 6d*
16th	*I paid to George Lock for the milishar*	*£7 10s 0d*
22nd	*for licker at the meating*	*£1 10s 0d*
	a saylor on the road with a pass	*1s 0d*
Apr 9th	*A old woman*	*1s 0d*
	For Lent wine and bread	*£2 4s 0d*

Richard Pattenden was a man of independent means owning a four horse post-coach on the Brighton to London run.

Often he or his son drove it coming from Brighton Mondays, Wednesdays and Fridays over the Dyke, down past Saddlescombe and Poynings, across Henfield Common and round the tight turn into the High Street.

The coach was brought to a halt beside the George Inn to change horses.

As soon as the fresh team was in place, the driver set off again heading for Horsham down the hill and out into open country to cross the parish boundary at Mock Bridge.

It was the route for the two summer coaches as well; to Oxford changing teams at the George and to Windsor favouring the White Hart.

BLUE COACH OFFICE, BRIGHTON.

WINDSOR COACH.

THE Public are most respectfully informed, that the WINDSOR COACH will commence running, for the SUMMER SEASON, on Monday, 9th of May, and will leave the above Office throughout the season, every Monday, Wednesday, and Friday mornings, at nine o'clock; and will leave Windsor every Tuesday, Thursday, and Saturday, at the same hour.

CROS WELLER & Co, Proprietors.

ROUTE.—*Henfield, Horsham, Crawley, Guildford, Chertsey, and Egham.*

The Windsor Coach

Mock Bridge spanned the River Adur where wharves, cut back into the banks, marked the limit for Henfield's other transport system, the six barges that plied down river to Shoreham Harbour.

The Adur Authority was improving the river by straightening some of the worst meanders to aid drainage and ease the way for boats. Chalk from the pit in the Downs at Beeding was being used to strengthen the banks. On top of them were the tow paths.

The improvements were good news for barge owners.

James Lelliott owned two, Lion and Stag, taking timber and farm produce down to Shoreham and bringing back light items of merchandise or bulk loads of chalk, roofing slates, gravel for the toll road or coal for his coal merchant's business.

The haulage prices were set by the bargemen along the river villages consulting together. They announced that 'by the dearth of the times' an increase in charges was necessary of 6d for all goods, wares and merchandise upstream of Old Shoreham Bridge. The price to Eton's Farm by the confluence of the two river branches would be 3s 0d. To Mock Bridge it would be 3s 6d. [3]

The Adur Authority increased river tolls to help cover costs.

Richard Woolven and John Hughes, the proprietors at Mock Bridge, put their wharfage charges up for timber and chalk.

John Hughes lived close by the river there with a private wharf for his profitable malt house brewery and the coal business he ran in competition with James Lelliott's.

Cargoes of coal arrived at Shoreham Harbour almost daily from Newcastle or Sunderland to be discharged onto the river banks ready for merchants to collect.

Henfield men shovelled the coal onto their barge and waited for the incoming tide to ease the horse's ten mile tow up river.

At Mock Bridge they offloaded at the wharf close to the road.

The merchants used wagons with six-inch wide wheels that eased the work for the horses and caused less wear and tear on the roads than narrower wheels thus having the minimum charge of 4d a horse at the Crouch Hill toll gate.

Customers were charged around £2 a ton, far too expensive an item for day labourers earning just 10s 0d a week.

Poor village households used faggots, the bundles of hedge and tree cuttings, or furze.

Some families relied on an allowance of faggots as part of their Poor Law Relief. The number allowed depended on the size of the family. Single people had very few.

Spinster Mary Barnett used the last of her wood in July. It would have been disastrous in winter but no wood meant no fire whatever the season and no fire meant no hot food.

Mary went out and helped herself to enough faggots for her needs. When the owner found out, she finished up in Petworth House of Correction.

She did not see Henfield again until October when autumn's colder weather was making the need for faggots even greater.

Each autumn the number of requests for Poor Relief rose as farm work slackened and men not on a fixed contract were laid off. Food, clothing and shoes were most in demand.

Provided the applicants were considered of good character, they were allowed sufficient to keep their home intact and avoid the workhouse.

The workhouse was feared by everyone.

The building was almost a hundred years old, sited in Nep Town well clear of the main population.

There were four ground floor rooms, smaller rooms above and two garrets; home for around 40 reluctant parish paupers.

The governor and mistress were Thomas and Ann Cain, themselves once in need of parish aid.

The vestry allowed Thomas just 2s 9d a week for each inmate.

He occasionally earned small additions to his pay.

To Thom Cain

Dec 12th	*for swiping 2 chimneys*	*1s 6d*
20th	*for killing the hog*	*1s 0d*[4]

Ann gained an income making shirts, breeches, waistcoats, frocks and gowns for the inmates.

She earned an extra 10d for each day's laundry she did; a tedious task using wood ash in the water to loosen the dirt before setting to with brown soap, starch and blue.

The women span wool and linen to be woven into cloth for shirts and sheeting. Wool was plentiful but the flax tow and tire had to be brought down from Horsham.

Bt of Ed. Booker 1 doz tire 15s 0d, 1 doz tow 15s 0d[4]

The men planted the large garden with potato, cabbage, pea, bean, carrot, onion and parsnip tending the growing plants carefully to ensure crops were as good as possible.

	To Thom Cain	
March 10th	*2 ozs Carriett seed*	*3s 3d*
14th	*3 ozs Parsnip seed*	*9d*
	2 ozs Onion seed	*1s 0d*
	½ gallon Beans	------
17th	*200 of cabbage plants*	*2s 3d* [4]

Pigs were reared in the yard ready to become pork. The weight of hogs killed in the Poorhouse

1st hog 28 stone - 2nd 35 stone 1lb
3rd 41 stone - 4th 31 stone 6lbs [4]

Cheap cuts of mutton and beef came from the butchers.

	To John Cornford	
Nov.	*A neck of mutton 4½lbs*	*2s 10d*
	12 lbs mutton at 8d	*8s 0d*
	24 lbs beef at 6d	*12s 0d*
	2 lbs suet at 8d	*1s 4d* [4]

Millers supplied 2nd grade flour.

	To R Loase	
Jan 9	*4 bushels flour*	*£1 10s 8d*
	1 bushel bran	*1s 0d*
	To J Botting Woods Mill	
May 8	*bush flour, 2 bush fine pollard*	*£4 12s 0d*
	24 bush seconds	*£3 10s 8d* [4]

John Hughes provided malt and hops from his Mock Bridge malthouse.

Nov.	*1 pound of hops*	*1s 4d*
	2 bushels malt	*17s 6d* [4]

Village shops took turns in providing clothing and 2nd or 3rd quality groceries.

March 1st.	*Mr. Richard Pattenden to George Vinall for the Poorhouse*	
	1lb Candel Grease 1 lb Rushes	*2s 3d*
	8lb Butter at 13d & 4lb Dutch Cheese at 8d	*11s 4d*
	2lb Sugar at 8d 2 oz tea at 5d 3lb sope at 10d	*4s 8d*
	1lb currants	*10½d*
	1 dish 6d & 2 broms at 2½d	*11d*
	6 chamber pots & I bedpan	*2s 5d*
	2 oz tea 1 brom 2 oz allspice	*1s 2½d*
	1 brom wrighting paper	*6d*
	1 pair of sheets 14s 6d 1 blanket 10s	*£1 4s 6d*

All the cooking was done at the kitchen coal range. Meat was roasted on spits in front of it. Vegetables and puddings were cooked in pots hooked above the fire. A large kettle of hot water was kept beside it.

For meals, the inmates sat at a variety of chairs and benches round the table. The food was served on wooden dishes and eaten with wooden spoons and a knife. Tin pint-pots held the drink.

Workhouse lighting was by dip-candles. The inmates made the candles by melting the grease into a mould and putting a rush pith in for the wick.

Night perhaps offered most warmth. The shared beds had sacking nailed to the frame to support a chaff or feather mattress with two sheets, a blanket, a coverlet and bolster.

To Thom Cain

For nails for nailing a sacking bottom to a bedstead os ½d

Beneath the bed was the shared brown chamber pot.

Only the utterly destitute moved into the Workhouse willingly.

Chapter 2

Friendly Societies – Tanyard odours – Broadmare Common

Many men guarded against hard times by joining a Friendly Society. All three of the High Street inns had one, self financing, to give each member cash payments in times of sickness or need.

Anyone aged less than 41 'able to get his own bread' could become a member. If it was later discovered he already had an infirmity when joining, he was expelled, 'no money returned'.

The most poignant occasion was at a member's death. Everyone had to attend the funeral with black gloves and hat band. The deepest sympathy was expressed for the widow. In practical terms it amounted to a small regular payment.

The society's quarterly club night provided the opportunity for members to enjoy themselves a full two hours provided they kept to the rules. Good manners and tolerant behaviour were demanded.

At the White Hart, swearing at or disobeying the chairman brought a 3d fine; quarrelling or fighting, 6d; calling for a drink or tobacco without leave, 6d; upbraiding a fellow member receiving benefit, 7s and not leaving the room within five minutes if told, £1. [1]

The Plough had a greater attraction for its wider clientele in cock-fighting.

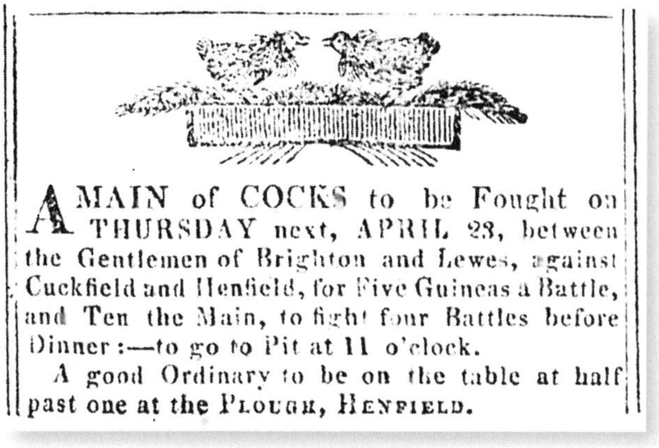
A MAIN of COCKS to be Fought on THURSDAY next, APRIL 23, between the Gentlemen of Brighton and Lewes, against Cuckfield and Henfield, for Five Guineas a Battle, and Ten the Main, to fight four Battles before Dinner:—to go to Pit at 11 o'clock.

A good Ordinary to be on the table at half past one at the PLOUGH, HENFIELD.

Cock Fighting at the Plough

The gentlemen of Brighton and Lewes brought their birds over for a match against the gentlemen of Henfield and Lindfield at five guineas a battle and ten guineas the match.

The first pair of birds faced each other, claws tapered to kill. When their owners released them, battle began in a flurry of feathers and flying blood to the delight or despair of the encircling betting men.

At 1.30 the match stopped for the good Ordinary; the landlord's set-price dinner and correct strength beer to ensure their afternoon's sport.

After dinner, cocks were set in the pit again. More money changed hands.

The victors departed with surviving birds and their share of the prizes. Henfield spectators returned home to await the next month's fixture.

Brighton and Lewes again formed the opposition with Cuckfield joining Henfield as hosts.

The first birds were scheduled in the pit at 11 o'clock as usual with four battles being fought before the good Ordinary which would be on the table at 1.30 p.m. as usual. Prizes remained the same.

Spectators arrived in time to enjoy a drink and to bet if they wished.

The pub clock showed the hour; 11.00 a.m. Feathers and blood flew as furiously as ever, money changed hands and victors crowed the prowess of their birds.

At the end of the day the outright winner was the landlord; his coffers were more or less full.

Up at the George there was a sobering event in the passing of the landlord who had run the inn for more than 40 years. It remained shut awaiting sale.

During that time the quarterly meeting of the George Friendly Society became due. It was the occasion when members owing any money to the society were required to settle their account – usually from incurring a fine for breaching club rules.

The George Society stewards arranged for their important meeting to take place at James Hedgecock's White Hart. The clerk, school master Mr. Matthew Phillips, drafted an advertisement for the Sussex Advertiser informing all members. He was fully aware that possibly the majority of them were illiterate or could barely read and that had he been able to give the time he could help them.

Only one meeting was necessary at the White Hart before the George was bought by Richard Pattenden; a purchase which forged a firm link between the two inns because his son Richard had married James Hedgecock's daughter, Elizabeth.

Mr. Phillips could concentrate on his Elm Grove Academy that he had taken over from his father at the end of Cagefoot Lane.

The school catered for Young Gentlemen. Particular attention was paid to English and Latin Classics, the French language, Navigation preparatory for naval situations, and to Surveying and Arithmetic suitable for any Commercial Line, the Counting-house or Shop; all at fees as moderate as the current high price of provisions admitted.

Although the curriculum was far reaching, the school itself was small – stated on the Manor Roll as a tenement with two buildings, one used as a Schoolroom and the other as a Coach house, and one walled court ... part of land called Potwell. [3]

Young Ladies were catered for at Mrs. Hunter's Boarding School in the High Street. She assured families of repute that she gave the greatest attention towards the improvement of her pupils in ensuring they received an excellent education. The English and French languages were taught with grammatical precision. Geography and History were both studied and the useful and ornamental kinds of Needlework perfected. The most approved Writing, Music and Dancing Masters attended.

What neither school did was to offer reading, writing or arithmetic for young children of labourers. That was the role for a Dame School or the good offices of the Established Church.

Children at outlying farms were unlikely to attend any Dame School.

Regular education through the offices of the Church did not happen. St. Peter's had a particular difficulty in fulfilling its duty within the parish.

The vicar, Rev Guy, was also rector of West Stoke beyond Chichester. Because he found his commitments as rector too time consuming for regular visits to Henfield, he appointed a curate to minister there.

A curate's stipend was low. It meant just one Sunday service. Ancillary duties in the parish were stunted.

The vestry endeavoured to provide education by appointing William Beard to teach parish children as an addition to his main occupation:

Monthly Account July	*Wm Beard for teaching*	*1s 0d*
	a Spelling Book by William Beard	*1s 2d* [4]

Some learnt to read, sign their name and write with the aid of a spelling book but for most families the education essential for their child was learning the skills to earn a living.

Elm Grove Academy gained new next-door neighbours at Potwell House when the owner, William Borrer, broke his tenuous link with Henfield by moving his family to Hurstpierpoint where he became a man of note – High Sheriff of Sussex.

His move may have been partly prompted by the odiously smelly Tanyard just across the lane.

Its pond was fed by underground water from Nep Town. The pond fed the tan hole where oak bark was soaked to provide tan for the tan pits.

Thomas Lanaway had taken over the Tanyard with over 30 hides and 100 calf skins plus a thousand horns from past animals.

Each hide became two backs for the long and tedious preparation process.

It was odorous from the start. The tanners received skins from the butcher's slaughterhouse, cleansed them of flesh and placed them in the lime pits. After the lime pits, the hair was scraped off and the backs were hung in the tan pits – each new pit a little stronger and smellier.

At the far end of the Tanyard, near Church Street, there was a Fellmonger's Yard where Jonathan Sowter produced more odours processing sheep hides for delicate articles, gloves and parchment.

Everybody used leather in one form or another. Trade was secure.

Thomas did have one morning of concern when fire broke out.

If the flames caught hold of the long shed full of his important store of oak bark they could have been disastrous. Fortunately his men noticed soon enough and managed to souse them with bucketfuls of water.

Thomas Lanaway chose to go into partnership with William Wisden from Patcham which worked well for a few years but terminated with a notice in the Sussex Advertiser explaining that the partnership was dissolved by mutual consent and that any person who had demands on it should send their account to Mr. W. Wisden.

At the next Streatham Manor Court, Thomas made over his land to William Wisden who now had sole control of Tan Yard odours.

Most traders kept clear of partnerships preferring to go it alone trusting in their own capabilities and endeavours.

Henfield's brick making industry was in sole charge of Thomas Bound who lived in Nep Town at the top of narrow Grinstead Lane which led steeply down to the Dag Brook fields by Broadmare Common.

His raw material was the clay of the common. The bricks were shaped behind the pond house there and when dried were fired ready for the builders.

Thomas Bound bricks became Henfield houses.

At his death, his house was put up for sale. [5]

To be SOLD by AUCTION
on Monday the 14th of April,
A FREEHOLD HOUSE and Premises,
Situate near the Poor-House at Henfield,
late the property of Thomas Bound, Brickmaker.
On the same day will be sold, on the premises,
the Household Furniture, at eleven o'clock.
The Freehold will be sold
at the White Hart Inn at three o'clock.

The furniture became dispersed about the village.

Dr. Charles Morgan bought the house and converted it to five tenements providing steady income from the rents. With the freehold he became worthy of casting a vote for his favoured candidate to be M.P.

The brickyard was left to Richard Pattenden to add to his London coach service and the George Inn; a successful business man. [6]

Broadmare Common also supported another business, basket making, carried on at a short row of ancient cottages owned by Percy Gregory at the foot of Barrow Hill. The buildings were so out of repair they seemed to prop each other up beneath ragged thatch.

The common provided raw material for both industries: shallow pits dug for brick clay; land left undisturbed for coppiced osier willows to provide the long shoots for basket-rods and wicker-work.

The competing interests sometimes led to fractious confrontation.

Chapter 3

Invasion threat – A village school – Southdown Sheep

Brick and basket disputes and smelly tanyards became nothing in 1803 when Napoleon Bonaparte massed his troops at Boulogne.

For England the threat of invasion was suddenly very real.

The Militia were put on full alert. Beacons were set up on the Downs to spread the signal of any landing. Detailed evacuation plans were made to move families to the north of the county.

Henfield had 54 wagons, three of them with a tilt cover against the weather, and 81 carts. People who needed transport – the old, the disabled and mothers with young children – were allocated to particular vehicles. The others would walk as they always did.

Livestock returns were made. Henfield farmers counted their beasts; 33 draught oxen, 115 fatting cattle, 190 cows, 179 young cattle and colts, 2405 sheep, 148 heavy horses and just 20 riding horses.

High on the numbers list were the pigs; 236 of them hogs, 52 sows and 165 young pigs; the poor man's meat supply. [1]

Henfield's evacuation plans never had to put in use but other people were travelling the country in bulk; battalions of infantry and cavalry from almost all the counties of England.

A Rifle Brigade moved through the village from Horsham on their way to Brighton.

The 55th Regiment of Foot marched from Canterbury to Brighton. Some of them were marched out again to be quartered in Henfield and the surrounding villages.

Soldiers were soldiers, smart in attractive uniforms whatever the regiment, and disciplined in their ways; upright and obedient to an officer, not always so upright with their admirers.

When the South Gloucester Militia arrived in Brighton, a local girl, Martha Ward, became very taken by one of them. Months later, Brighton vestry removed her to her settlement parish, Henfield. There she had to explain herself to the overseers. It resulted in a warrant being issued to the Henfield Constable of the Hundred of Tipnoke calling on him to arrest Private John Porter of the South Gloucester Militia as father of a child likely to be born to Martha Ward.

Private Porter was arrested and taken before the Justices of the Peace. He resolutely refused to pay for any child's upkeep.

Another warrant was issued and the constable conducted him to Petworth House of Correction to await judgement at the next Quarter Sessions.

The fate of Private Porter meant nothing to the genteel people of Henfield. Their concern was of yet another child to be cast on the parish by a wanton woman setting foot in church only to have her child baptised.

Private Porter found the rigid regime at Petworth House of Correction stimulus enough for a change of mind about fatherhood. Quarter Sessions intervention was not required.

Martha was attended for the birth of her child by Dr. Morgan. He delivered the baby safely and received his agreed fee from the vestry.

Dr. Morgan held the contract for treating the parish poor at twelve guineas a year. Attendance and treatment were extra. He charged half a guinea for each lying-in, a shilling for bleeding or for pills, powders and liniments. The successful reduction of a labourer's broken leg cost the vestry four guineas; for a boy kicked by a horse, 1s 6d.

Such cases could be treated with confidence, unlike the contagious killers tuberculosis with its lingering death or smallpox that struck and killed or disfigured the victim with scars. The fear of them was overpowering.

Thomas Ward, one of the church bell ringing team, had suddenly gone down with smallpox and was dead within days. They buried him beside the belfry tower late that same night, despite a heavy thunderstorm, to ensure the disease remained within the coffin. [2]

The one beacon of light was Dr. Jenner's cowpox vaccination. Doctors were gradually becoming more convinced of its efficacy. The scourge of centuries could be defeated.

One of Dr. Morgan's most professionally satisfying times came in the autumn of 1807 when smallpox again broke out in the parish.

The vestry considered the needs of the people as a whole. They ordered a general inoculation of cowpox vaccine. Dr. Morgan undertook the task.

The vaccine came from the pustule of someone already treated; a scratch on the arm and a drop of vaccine inserted. A week later came the check to ensure success – a newly raised pustule ready to provide more vaccine.

Within the week he had completed almost 300 vaccinations.

Pustules swelled. The outbreak was halted. People had a new respect for their doctor, a gentleman of great medical skill and propriety.

When the scare subsided, life returned to normal.

For the majority of labourers, normal life remained long hours of work with little or no leisure except their pub Friendly Society's Annual Day.

The White Hart's Day was Whit Monday, the working man's main holiday of the year. It saw the High Street transformed with stalls of gingerbread and trumperies, higglers offering cheap ware and haberdashery, sideshows, music for song and dancing; a holiday for all to enjoy. [3]

Henfield's elite society had more opportunity for leisure activities.

Cricket was one; definitely a gentleman's sport involving money.

C R I C K E T.

A GAME of CRICKET will be played at the Suſſex Pad Inn, near Shoreham Bridge, on Thurſday next, the 24th inſtant, between the Gentlemen of Henfield, Woodmancoat, Albourne, and Twineham, with one picked man, againſt the Gentlemen of Lancing and Sompting.

The Wickets to be pitched at ten o'clock.

N. B. A good Ordinary will be provided on the ground.

☞ On the Wedneſday following the Return Match will be played on Henfield Common, by the ſame Gentlemen.

Henfield cricket at the Sussex Pad

On Henfield Common, the Gentlemen of Shoreham River to Arundel River played the Gentlemen in the Weald of Sussex for 22 guineas. They started at 10 a.m and broke for a good Ordinary dinner provided at the ground by the landlord of the George.

The next month the gentlemen of Henfield, Storrington, Steyning, Ashurst and Woodmancote played against Horsham; this time at 20 guineas a side with yet another good Ordinary by the George landlord.

Others found more pleasure in following Mr. John Wood's Chestham Harriers. They had the thrill of hunting down ten hares on two successive weekends.

Social visiting was an important marker of a society family's position.

On the small rise behind Ann Gander's Prospect Cottage at Golden Square a new building was under construction overlooking the common.

This was no cottage of Broadmare brick. It spread high, wide and mighty to the demands of ex High Sheriff of Sussex, William Borrer – a father's wedding present to oldest son, William, and wife, Elizabeth.

William junior was 30, well educated, interested since childhood in botany and already a Fellow of the prestigious Linnean Society in London. Elizabeth was daughter of banker Nathaniel Hall.

Her father's house at Southwick had been their temporary residence but by Christmas 1811 their new home, Barrow Hill House, was ready.

Barrow Hill House

With its fine entrance porch, high ceilings, wide patio and balconies it stood supreme among Henfield homes. Families who considered themselves part of parish society were keen to become acquainted.

Families were also having to adjust to rising costs for their boys' education at Elm Grove Academy. Fees were raised to £27 per annum with French £6 and dancing a further £4; a total of at least £30 for any self-respecting father.

Just after Christmas, the Bishop of Chichester called a General Meeting of the Clergy to promote the National Society's Education of the Poor – the children of the £30 a year labourers and the village craftsmen. Their children's education, free of charge, would comprise the blessings of religion and useful knowledge.

Henfield responded with a committee led by William Borrer as secretary. Subscriptions were made by the Gentry along with farmers, shop keepers and newly widowed Elizabeth Hedgecock of the White Hart. Each would be able to recommend scholars.

Soon sufficient funds were raised to rent a cottage near the church with permission to alter it as necessary.

Inner walls and ceilings were taken out to make a single room and forms were fixed to the floor. The cottage was now a school.

The bishop's meeting had stipulated education should follow the Madras System formulated by Dr. Bell in India. Suitable equipment was purchased; reading cards and books, copy books, sand boards, slates, arithmetic tables and printed lessons to be hung from the walls.

A selection of Church publications was added; An Abridgement of the Bible, Prayer Book and The Catechism Broken into Short Questions. [6]

The school opened in August; Henfield education at last involving the boys from all walks of life.

The subscriptions from public spirited inhabitants were augmented by collections at occasional church services where the sermon was a rousing tug at heart and purse strings.

If sufficient funds became available, a school for girls would be provided.

William Borrer monitored proceedings with regular visits.

The teacher taught the lesson to the brighter pupils who each then instructed a small group. Learning was encouraged by a rewards system.

Boys who read well enough received a Bible and Prayer Book on the condition they attended church on Sunday until they were 13 years old.

The church pews were already allocated to families – apart from the back five near the windowless corner by the tower set aside for the workhouse paupers. Forms for the boys were provided in the nave risking the scuff of nailed boots on the brass memorials laid there.

That summer there was more Borrer news. John Hamlen Borrer, cousin of William, was giving up Parsonage Farm where he bred Southdown sheep. They were up for sale together with Thomas Coppard's flock.

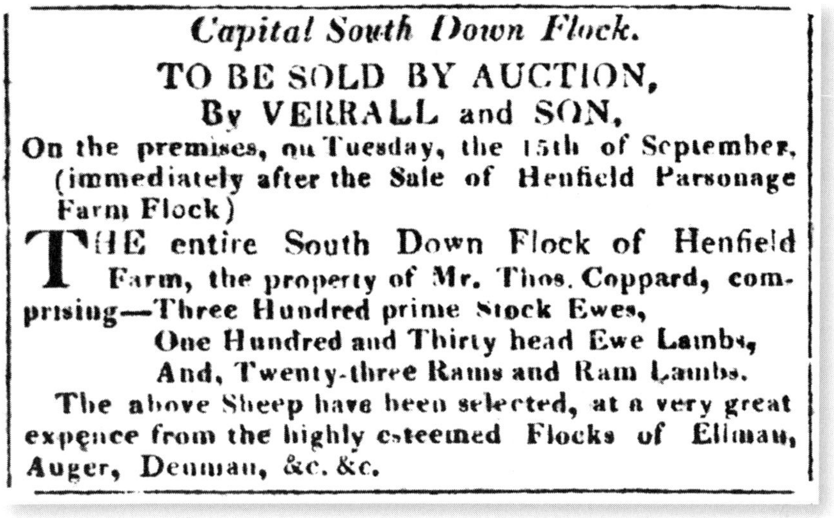

Capital South Down Flock.

TO BE SOLD BY AUCTION,
By VERRALL and SON,

On the premises, on Tuesday, the 15th of September, (immediately after the Sale of Henfield Parsonage Farm Flock)

THE entire South Down Flock of Henfield Farm, the property of Mr. Thos. Coppard, comprising—Three Hundred prime Stock Ewes,
One Hundred and Thirty head Ewe Lambs,
And, Twenty-three Rams and Ram Lambs.

The above Sheep have been selected, at a very great expence from the highly esteemed Flocks of Ellman, Auger, Denman, &c. &c.

Southdown Sheep for sale

The auctioneers assured gentlemen wishing to improve their own stock that no expense or pains had been spared in raising the sheep – a total of 650 prime ewes for breeding, 330 ewe and wether lambs and 35 ram or ram lambs. Anybody not present at 12 noon on the 15th September could find themselves too late, the start would be prompt. It was.

The next week was the annual show of the Bramber Agricultural Association at the White Horse in Steyning. The president praised his stewards Mr. J. H. Borrer and Mr. T. Coppard for their unremitting support. Prize-giving followed; elegant pieces of silver plate.

Mr. Coppard gained one with his three year old heifer. Mr. Borrer no longer had any beasts. For him the praise of the president was enough.

Another sale took place on the boundary of the parish with Woodmancote at Hole Farm where the tenant had notice to quit at Michaelmas. The farm was copyhold of Streatham Manor; 60 acres of arable, meadow and pasture land within a ring fence.

Amongst the sales news there was a brief reminder of the sufferings of war when people read that the latest list of 15000 English prisoners held by the French included 120 Sussex people. Among them were two Henfield names, John Liffen and his wife incarcerated at Valenciennes.[8]

Questions were raised in Parliament where it was explained that His Majesty's Government was doing all that it could for the prisoners but any present initiative was prevented by the state of affairs on the continent

– Napoleon Bonaparte was deep within Russia approaching Moscow with triumphal expectations.

The Liffens remained in France, Moscow blazed and Russia's bitter winter decimated French soldiers retreating through snow and ice. A defeated Napoleon was exiled to Elba.

None of it affected Henfield for several years until an overseer turned up with a woman and her two children plus a Quarter Sessions Removal Order dated 17th June 1815. It stated they were being legally removed from Hurstpierpoint to Henfield.

Henfield overseers accepted them and they were put in the workhouse; Isabella Godman, three year old Thomas and Margaret aged one.

The Removal Order clarified matters. Isabella Godman's husband was a gunner in the first battalion of the Royal Artillery stationed at Woolwich under orders of embarkation for a foreign land.

The foreign land had to involve Napoleon, on the loose after escaping from Elba and marching an intensely loyal army to regain lost glories. England had Wellington scrambling to oppose him. War would be bloody. A dead soldier's family could become a burden on parish rates. Hurstpierpoint had chosen to remove the danger posed by the Godmans.

The very next day, Sunday 18th, Wellington and Bonaparte clashed at Waterloo. Victory for the allied armies, exile to the South Atlantic for Napoleon and demobilisation for gunner William Godman whose battalion had never left Woolwich.

William Godman was reunited with his family in Henfield. There they stayed, convinced a loyal and disciplined soldier could secure his future.

Chapter 4

5% loans – The debtor's prison – A Woolwich hulk

Just a fortnight later, as if celebrating the great news of victory, Henfield's cricketers went down for a grand match against Brighton on the Prince Regent's Ground.

It was still a game for gentlemen at 20 guineas a team.

They made an early start with wickets pitched at 9.30 a.m., a mid match break for a good Ordinary dinner and an agreement to play into the evening to ensure a positive conclusion. [1]

Henfield's men were able to return home in good spirit.

Such was not the case for Matthew Phillips. His Elm Grove Academy was no longer the thriving school he had taken over. He was facing a serious funding crisis.

William Borrer eased the situation with a temporary loan of £400 at 5% interest.

When that became due for repayment, Matthew only managed it with extra help from John Longley, the High Street mercer.

William Borrer's acceptance that he had been repaid the £400 was entered on the Manor Roll but Matthew was now paying 5% on £600.

He decided on a different career, keeping a tavern in Brighton. Elm Grove was let to a new master seeking to establish himself.

For a while, Matthew's prospects seemed brighter until funds again ran short. Lack of ready money forced him to seek yet further help.

This time, a Brighton butcher, Harry Tuppen, came to the rescue with just £300 at 5%. Matthew was solvent; life was back on an even keel.

Six months later, the world came crashing down around him as butcher Tuppen began bankruptcy proceedings for a debt of £187 10s 6d.

At the end of tortuous meetings in London, the Comissioners of Bankrupt imposed a Bargain and Sale of the property.

Harry Tuppen bid £700 and Elm Grove was his.

Matthew Phillips was left flat on his back, cut down to size by a Brighton butcher.

William Borrer's £400 was soon in demand again. Robert Loase was finding life difficult at the windmill. He made a Conditional Surrender of the mill with his farmland, thankful to accept the money. Better times would see him on his feet again.

Richard Pattenden's expectations clouded a little at the George Inn.

A minor event was a storm in London that prevented his Brighton coach running. Two of his disappointed passengers who were booked for Horsham travelled by post chaise instead and demanded payment for the journey because of the cancellation of the scheduled service. It cost Richard £3 2s; unwelcome but an acceptable price for continued custom.

There was considerably more money involved when a coaching associate explained how he was strapped for immediate funds and was in desperate need of a little temporary help. Richard provided it.

The man's thanks were effusive – as had been the explanation of his needs – his future all due to Richard's kindness and generosity.

In London, Leicester, Loughborough and Horsham, 29 other people had been persuaded to assist a silver tongued coach master – horse dealers, corn dealers, upholsterer, tailor, linen draper, hosier, boot maker and hatter.

Months were to pass before any of them turned rising doubt into deed and began legal action against the man.

He was finally brought to justice with a long prison sentence but there was nothing for his creditors except the hollow reflection that the man's foreseeable future was undoubtedly secure.

Richard's darkest cloud was a Brighton proprietor's introduction of a new daily coach, the Royal Clarence, on the Henfield route calling at the White Hart for its change of horses. The White Hart was already the inn for the Brighton/Windsor route leaving only the Oxford coach using the George.

Income fell to such an extent that he decided to make a conditional surrender of his brick making land on Broadmare Common for a temporary loan of £200. He continued the business himself but if he failed to repay the money he would lose the lot.

Reeve Percy Gregory's father, Charles, was another obliged to raise money. He went to Elizabeth Hedgecock at the White Hart who obliged with £220.

At the next Manor Court, Charles Gregory made a conditional surrender to Elizabeth of his house, Forges, at Golden Square and three acres of marshland on Pokerlee Farm near the old Streatham Manor House.

Percy and another tenant were the two official manor representatives and Henfield's corn chandler Edward Verrall signed as witness.

Percy Gregory himself had business at the court. He presented a hand written document granting him 'a piece of land on the East Side of the Road on Broadmare Common' to link his row of tumbldown cottages with his Lydds field. 23 manor tenants, headed by Wm. Borrer and including both Richard Pattenden and Charles Gregory, signed the agreement.

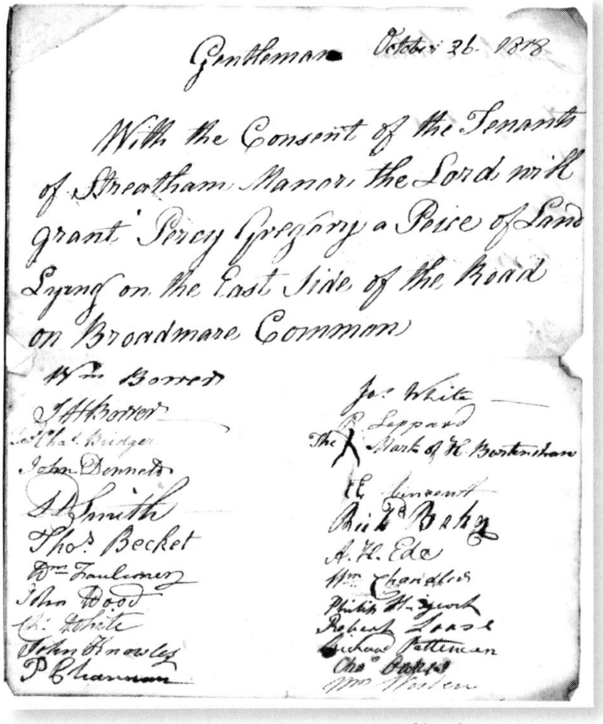

Gentleman October 26. 1818

With the Consent of the Tenants of Streatham Manor the Lord will grant Percy Gregory a Piece of Land Lying on the East Side of the Road on Broadmare Common

Wm Borrer

Thos Becket

John Wood

John Knowles

Jos White

A. H. Ede

Wm Chandler

Richard Pattenden

Percy Gregory gains a strip of land

Richard Pattenden was willing for Percy Gregory to gain a small piece of insignificant land. As regards his own ambitions, he had decided enough was enough. He put son Richard in charge at the George. The Royal Clarence was taking too much of his revenue.

Farmers, too, were losing revenue. A poor spring in 1816 became an inexplicably sunless summer with a disastrous harvest.

The Government's newly introduced Corn Law to protect home crops by restricting imports accentuated the problem.

Wheat was in desperately short supply. Bread prices rose, the staple food for the working man hit by a double whammy with the new Game Law preventing any but landowners from taking rabbit, hare, pheasant or partridge and making poaching punishable by transportation. Nep Town workhouse beckoned families across the parish.

For Robert Loase it was his worst season in 25 years milling. He was hard put to pay the annual interest on his loan from William Borrer.

The Nep Town Windmill

What made his plight worse was the knowledge of plans going ahead for a new windmill to be erected on Henfield Common.

Corn Chandler Edward Verrall's income virtually ceased as too many of his business dealings failed to materialise. Bills had to be put aside and he found himself sliding deeper into debt.

Suddenly creditors were pressing him for payment.

He was a confident man and knew his turnover would recover once the next harvest was cropped. He held out determinedly against threats of legal action.

When his creditors began bankruptcy proceedings he refused to pledge his property and risk losing everything.

To his dismay, the result was imprisonment in the debtors' gaol at Horsham.

Edward quickly regretted his decision. It was mid-winter with bitter January cold. Freezing damp penetrated everything.

Nights were worst, sleeping in a cell by himself where he was confined from early evening. A common-room provided company during the day, if only for mutual commiseration. Apart from cleaning the areas there was little to help pass time. Food was minimal for any who received no financial help from friends to purchase their own.

Unless money for his creditors was forthcoming he would remain there with only one chance of release, a petition through the court for insolvent debtors.

He made his petition and lived on hope.

Time dragged interminably until his chance came at a specially convened Quarter Sessions sitting at Horsham.

At the court, he readily agreed to pledge all his property and interest to his creditors; freedom was of far greater value.

Edward Verrall returned home a wiser man.

In the village the School Committee held a very important meeting. The General Visitor of the Sussex Society for the Education of the Poor had visited the school. His report was to hand.

Secretary William Borrer rose to read it out.

The Visitor praised the children of the top class. They had undergone the examination well except that they read too fast.

There the praise ended.

Progress in the lower classes was slow. The greatest complaint was the noisiness and disorder of the school. Although failures were partly due to the master, the room needed to be properly fitted out by making the benches moveable and leaving the centre part open for the classes to be gathered there.

The Committee – now strengthened by Lord de la Zouche of Parham House and the Brighton banker William Wigney – determined on an immediate improvement.

The school was reorganised and the master paid off.

Subscriber Mr. Nathaniel Hall, who had lately moved into the village to be near his daughter at Barrow Hill, named a man from Southwick as a probable replacement, Mr. William Godley – except he would need to be taught how to teach.

Mr. Godley was approached and agreed to take up an appointment on a temporary basis.

Arrangements were made for him to be trained, expenses paid, at the National Society's Central School in Gray's Inn Lane, London.

In April 1816, Mr. Godley commenced his training. In June he returned, fully qualified, ready to commence teaching. [3]

He proved conscientious and able enough to be given a permanent contract.

Most pupils achieved as much as they could under his guidance. Some were unable to overcome the pitfalls of reading. A few, like Charles Nathan Stoner, progressed enough to be considered potential monitors who would be instructed by Mr. Godley ready to repeat the lesson to the younger boys.

The school flourished and within two years the house near the church was no longer adequate; a purpose built school was needed.

The difficulty of a site was overcome when the Bishop of Chichester gave permission for the school to be built on the south side of the common as Copyhold of the Manor of Streatham with an annual quit rent of sixpence.

Funds were raised, plans prepared and building went ahead, "Henfield National School for Boys of the Poor", 60 feet by 20, fully adequate for the 137 pupils.

Parents would provide the small short-fall in funds through a quarterly payment of a shilling for each boy.

Children had to arrive ready for 9.00 a.m. with clothes as neat as circumstances permitted, clean skins and hair cut short and combed. Once inspected, they filed in to begin lessons.

The vacant house near the church was cleaned and renovated to continue as a Girls' School. More than 50 girls were ready to take advantage of it.

Mr. Borrer, becoming championed by many as 'Friend of the Village,' showed his concern for both boys and girls by providing shoes enabling each new pupil to begin with a comfortable walk to school.

Children on the farms beyond West End had the best part of two miles to walk.

Samuel Ward had less than 200 yards – perhaps too close for him and for his teacher. Samuel's father, Charles, had a reputation in the village. He was known as 'Lossam'; big and aggressive, teller of tall tales and accustomed to carrying a gun. If the school changed from encouragement by rewards to a more threatening environment, 'Lossam' was quite capable of intervening physically.

The Committee's attention was concentrated on providing a house for Mr. Godley beside his school. He was now married and his wife, Sarah, had borne him a son, John. The provision of proper accommodation for them was important.

Nathaniel Hall provided finance at a very low rate of interest. Local craftsmen competed for the contracts.

George Vinall built the walls and did the plastering for £55, William Martin undertook the carpentry and fenced the garden for £45 and John Nye, working hard to re-establish himself after bankruptcy, completed the painting and glazing for £7.

William Godley moved in, his rent at £5 a year from his £50 salary.

People were encouraged to become subscribers paying for their own children. Landlord of the George, Richard Pattenden, did so. The new governess at the workhouse, Widow Stringer with eight children to support, paid for her 10 year old – the Committee for her 12 year old. Ex workhouse governor Thomas Cain, now a shoemaker, paid for six year old Thomas.

The Committee paid where there was absolute hardship – Widow Cornford with nine children to support and Widow Chate with ten.

They also paid for Samuel Saunders' boys, James and William.

Samuel had started as a farm labourer down on Oreham Common with never a spare penny to his name.

He married when he was 21; Charlotte, just two years older than himself.

Their first baby was a girl, Eliza. When she was two they had James. Late in the following year Charlotte was again pregnant.

Samuel ensured she had sufficient good quality food to nourish her through the cold winter weather. Of especial importance was the mutton he provided; much of it made into a rich broth as she neared her time.

In early February she gave birth safely to another son.

On the 8th he was baptised William.

On the 19th, Samuel was detained on suspicion of stealing a sheep during the night of the 6th of November.

He was brought to trial at the next Assizes accused that 'he did kill with a felonious intent to steal and carry away the whole carcass of a ewe sheep of the value of thirty shillings belonging to William Goddard'. [4]

Among the list of jurors at the Assizes were twelve men from Henfield.

They would not be called for the case but the full story would carry back. Samuel made his plea, evidence was given and sentence passed – death.

Death at 25.

Samuel, dumbstruck and bemused, was returned to his cell.

The Assizes finished with the judge announcing that he had carried out his solemn duty of sentencing 19 men to death, one of them for attempted murder. The attempted murder sentence remained. The others he now commuted to transportation beyond the seas.

Samuel's thoughts were his own.

He was first moved to the Justitia prison hulk at Woolwich.

A year later he was still on the hulk and having a letter written home to Charlotte;

My Dear Loving Wife,

I received your kind affectionate letter dated 23rd May and likewise the one dated 19th April – and with the money order for wich I return you my sincere thanks for it gives me Great pleasure to hear that my Dear Children being well but must say I am much affected for to think that you are deprived of that Blessing of sight God trust will restore you Dear your age with time and patience will probably be the cure, I certainly shou'd a answered the first letter but supposing you might think that I had recea ...?... it or I shou'd a wrote to you again in your unhappy situation it must be impossible for you to Grant me this my request that by Going to J. Dennett Esq & the Rev Mr. Comyns and return them my grateful thanks for that kindness – on what they have don for me – and likewise to Mr. Goddard and I return him thanks for is forgiveness in one of the Greatest and Abominable Acts that a man was ever Guilty off and I hope God will reward him and I do further humbly beg and hope that the said Gentlemen will do what they possably can to restore me to my Dear and unhappy Children and if Please God I shou'd obtain such a Blessing no inducements whatever shall prevent me doing the Utmost in my Powers to support my Dear Wife and Family by Honesty and Industry – and become a good member of Society Dear Wife if you cannot possably Undertake this Business I do Beg and hope my Dear Mother and Sister will do it for me – Write to me again as soon as you can and give me every possible information respecting the same I have nothing more particular to Relate but must say that I am as well as my present situation will admit give my duty

to my Dear Father and Mother – and Blessing to my Dear Brother & sisters and may the Blessing of God attend you all
I am your ever loving Husband Sam Saunders. [5]

Samuel did not achieve his wish of being restored to his dear children, nor was he transported. He would serve his sentence on the Justitia hulk.

Charlotte and the children were moved into the workhouse. She adapted as best she could.

For the first year there were no insurmountable difficulties. In the second, Charlotte had an uncomfortable shock – she was pregnant.

She was not the only expectant mother there. Jane Golds, from her behaviour a simple minded girl, had been taken advantage of as a servant.

In September, Jane gave birth to a lusty son she named Henry.

Charlotte also gave birth to a son and chose to name him John.

Both babies were baptised by the curate at St. Peter's Church.

He left blanks in the register for the father's name – and everyone knew the significance – but there was a further label of disapproval for Charlotte in the added words; 'A married woman in the Workhouse'.

Charlotte, unable to read, was unaware of the slight. She returned to the workhouse and nurtured baby John.

When oldest son James was six he began school on the common, walking there each day with other Workhouse boys.

Two years later, William joined them.

Samuel continued convict life on the Justitia and completed his sentence. He made his way back to Henfield and was reunited with Charlotte.

He accepted toddler John and determined on a better future.

Finding work was not easy. He had to resort to parish relief; a monthly allowance of 5s 0d with casual aid as needed.

The next year saw great rejoicing, another son, Samuel, after his father.

Even greater rejoicing followed when Samuel gained employment and was able to move his family to Rye Island over a mile out from the village on slightly raised land among the brooks. The house was old and in need of attention but there he could prove his honesty and industry.

On the common, the Boys' School, with over 150 pupils, continued to flourish under William Godley. His promising student, Charles Nathan Stoner, now 13, was proving his worth as a reliable monitor.

The governors knew they had an excellent head teacher. They resolved that in consideration of Mr. Godley's meritorious conduct a gratuity of £5 be presented to him in addition to his £50 salary.

William's wife, Sarah, was nearing her time for their second child. Late in October she gave birth; a son, Henry, brother for two year old John.

In March, rejoicing gave way to great sadness. Baby Henry's short life was over.

Sarah never recovered and in the summer she, too, passed away.

William grieved again, obtained the help necessary for John and devoted himself to his child's welfare and giving the village boys a good education.

Chapter 5

Bankrupt pub – A well of good water – An attractive barn

In the cold of the following January, miller Robert Loase passed away at Nep Town.

In his will, the mill went to his daughter through her husband, James Embling of Petworth.

The £400 loan from William Borrer was still outstanding. Mrs. Loase took the one course open to her; put the dairy farm up for sale.

The sale went ahead. Mrs. Loase repaid Mr. Borrer and began a quieter life satisfied that the Nep Town Windmill itself was still in family hands.

The Pattenden family seemed in danger of losing its high standing in the village when a presentment was made at the April Manor Court implying objection to Broadmare clay becoming Henfield bricks;

> Also they present that Richard Pattenden senior a Copyhold Tenant of this manor hath for several years last past dug up the soil of Broadmare Common within this manor and converted such soil to his own use and carried the same off from the Manor to the damage of the Lord and his tenants having the Right to the Herbage of the said common. [1]

Invidious rumour gossip was also circulating the village that he was in serious financial difficulties.

Suddenly, vicious rumour became undeniable fact. Richard Pattenden, senior, was bankrupt.

Notices appeared in the London Gazette requiring all creditors to attend the Court of Commissioners of Bankrupt in the City of London to prove their claims.

At the next court, claims were proved.

Creditors converged on Henfield and met at Richard's own inn to decide on selling his property and determine whether or not he should be allowed to continue business until the time of sale.

Finally, adverts appeared in the Brighton newspapers:-

> To be Sold by Auction by Mr. Creasy, Thursday 29th March 1827 at Twelve for One o'Clock precisely. All those desirable FREEHOLD PREMISES called the GEORGE INN at HENFIELD with the stables and appurtenances .... on the most frequented London and Windsor roads and is resorted to by numerous visitors as one of the most delightful retreats in summer, and all the posting on this road runs to this house. [2]

On sale day it was not enfranchisement or the delights of a summer retreat that decided the outcome but simply the desire of the Brighton brewery, Tamplin's, to add yet another inn to its growing list of hostelries.

Henfield beer lovers may not have worried but one man did, James Patching. His 'Bee Hive' brewery, along with his grocery, was just down the other side of the road at Golden Square. Could the 'Bee Hive' survive against such opposition?

The following Wednesday the George stock in Trade and Household Furniture were sold.

Richard senior's downfall seemed complete when his butcher's property behind the George went under the hammer as well.

The buyers came and the property went. Richard Pattenden moved down the street to Widow Hedgecock in her cottage beside the White Hart.

One of the first overnight customers for the Tamplin's George was the Streatham Manor surveyor Mr. Florance.

Reeve Percy Gregory received a letter from the manor steward informing him Mr. Florance would arrive at the George on the Thursday evening of the following week to survey three properties being sold. Percy, as manor bailiff, was to be ready to receive him at his house the next morning.

First he had to inform others about the meeting: - Mr. Lawrence Smith and Mr. Hamlen Borrer as trustees of the late owner and Hamlen's relative, Nathaniel Borrer of Hurstpierpoint, the potential purchaser, in case they wished to attend.

Percy also had to find men able to ascertain exactly which fields and buildings belonged to each property because it had all been worked as a single unit. [3]

The surveyor was able to detail everything: - farm houses, cottages, barns and out buildings; the acreages of arable, meadow, pasture and marsh land; the heriot, '6 heriots of the best cloven-footed beast', and the 16s 6d quit rent.

Percy had proved himself the efficient servant – bailiff or reeve as the steward selected.

He also proved a good father at the marriage of his daughter, Harriett, when he and his wife made room in their house for the newly-weds. He also made over his grocer's shop to her which in effect made it the husband's.

In the next Sussex Directory the entry was Nathan Harwood, grocer and draper.

Percy no longer had an entry because his carrier's business changed hands, too, being taken over by another Nathan – Charles Nathan Stoner, ex pupil teacher, now an up and coming man determined to make his mark in life.

The younger Richard Pattenden was also determined. He bought a large plot of land in the Hay Croft almost opposite the White Hart and built up the family butcher's business again.

The butchery stretched back 70 yards. Fronting the road were the shop with a front parlour beside it. Behind, were a back parlour, kitchen, pantry, store room, wash house and cellar. Upstairs, were four bedrooms and two attics. There were coal and wood sheds and a good sized piggery. A variety of fruit trees grew in the walled garden. Right behind was meadow. There, Richard had a stable for six horses, a chaise house, his slaughter house and the bullock pound.

Almost of greatest value was his well of good water guaranteed never to fail. Without it there would be no butchery. [4]

A considerable amount of land round the parish was changing hands. Some was advertised as arable ideal for crops, some as good grazing ground or meadow for hay, some as land abundantly stocked with game and some as having thriving oak timber.

Several of the brooks were advertised for sale.

Smallest was part of Dag Brook where the land began to rise; a market garden including apple, plum, pear and cherry trees, gooseberries, currants and strawberries. Market gardens were becoming popular.

Percy Gregory sold the three acres of Pokerlee marshland his father had mortgaged. Elizabeth Hedgecock was repaid her money.

William Borrer had his eye on one of the brooks near Rye Island; 13 acres, part meadow, part arable with a thatched barn and open-fronted cattle hovel in a fenced yard. He considered it a good investment and went ahead with the purchase. The barn was of old weather boarding but on a brick foundation and had plenty of years use as an autumn store for wheat or barley ready for threshing.

The planned new windmill on the common had become fact, built and put for auction on the rising ground to the south with twelve acres of land.

Mr. Robert Stephens from Shiprods way out by Chestham made the best bid at £1430. [5]

He determined to provide a good service for village families, any of whom could go to the mill for small cash payment purchases – powerful competition for the Nep Town mill.

William Borrer provided the opportunity for resourceful men to further their ambitions when he put five roadside plots of the Hay Croft up for sale alongside Richard Pattenden's butchery.

Draper John Hickox bought the adjacent plot; a far smaller one.

The next ones went to John Bailey (the village's slightly eccentric watchmaker), plumber/glazier William Mason, shoemaker John Ware and Edward Pattenden who had made his name as a stagecoach driver on the fast Brighton to London runs up the Hickstead Road.

The plots were bought at a reasonable price. Building homes on them would need more money than some of the buyers possessed.

Within the year, five new properties graced the High Street.

The new buildings on the Haycroft

New as they were, each was subject to the custom of the manor in having to pay quit rent of a penny a year in lieue of service due to their lord.

Two properties were subject to conditional surrenders to the money lenders; draper John Hickox with £200 from William Wisden and William Mason with £200 from solicitor Lawrence Smith.

John Hickox had a double-fronted shop with a parlour, back kitchen and three bedrooms.

William Mason's skill as a craftsman handy with a paint brush enabled him to furnish his bedrooms with four-post mahogany stained and painted tent bedsteads, painted wash-basin stands and dressing tables. Downstairs, as well as painted parlour and chamber chairs he had claw and Pembroke tables, a Kidderminster carpet, chimney ornaments, a few prints, some books and a weather glass. It was a home to be proud of, especially as his wife had given birth to their first son, Walter.

The new house left sufficient room on the plot for a good size garden with a greenhouse and piggery. The family pig played a crucial role in the household economy. Kitchen refuse, hog-weed from the hedgerows and acorns won from the woods would become good pork and ham.

The next major sale caught out all the village pundits. Just two years after the auction of the George, the White Hart was put on the market under the hammer of Mr. Creasy:-

> On the premises, at Henfield, on Friday 4th April 1829 at Three for Four o'clock in the afternoon precisely.
>
> THE WHITE HART INN which has been established for many years and is in the best part of HENFIELD with many commanding advantages. The premises are FREEHOLD, and give the owner the right to Vote for Members of Parliament for the Rape of Bramber and for the County of Sussex.
>
> May be viewed on application to Mrs. Hedgecock at the White Hart.

Prospective purchasers were shown round the inn with its spacious Friendly Society Clubroom, the productive garden and the orchard.

The sale began at precisely 4.00 p.m. Bidding was brisk.

At its end, John Lloyd from out of the parish became the new owner. Henfield's coaching inns were no longer part of Hedgecock or Pattenden life.

Ex Life Guards Sergeant-Major Lloyd, survivor of the Battle of Waterloo, was inheriting a strong Friendly Society.

About 30 young men had joined that year bringing the membership to nearly 170. On their annual day they marched up to the church in fine style headed by the Henfield Band of Music. The afternoon's feasting and revelries were as good as ever but the ordinary man was hard put to find money for a pub evening with his mates. [6]

Chapter 6

Wage demands – Timber for sale – Violating manor law

The labourer's weekly wage had been static many years but the cost of food kept rising. Lack of sufficient money to provide the basic necessities of life led to rising discontent among the men.

The discontent became confrontational.

The Brighton Gazette reported tumultuous assemblies at Steyning and Shermanbury with men banding together to demand higher wages.

Steyning Petty Sessions magistrates issued a warning that such meetings were illegal. Every person attending, inducing others to attend or holding out threats to make others attend would be dealt with according to law.

Henfield labourers planned their own gathering to demand a decent wage.

JPs anticipated trouble and doubted the ability of the parish constables to maintain order. A number of ratepayers were summoned to be sworn in as special constables tasked to help deal with unlawful incidents.

The day before the workers' meeting, magistrates arrived to swear in the selected specials but encountered an unexpected difficulty. The men had no desire to act against fellow villagers. Of all those summoned, only four agreed to be sworn in. Those declining were warned they would be indicted for refusing to comply.

That evening a special meeting of the parish vestry was held to consider wages for the coming year. Everyone knew full well that the labourers had been preparing their own written demands. The vestry determined their terms. It was decided that men would be more willing to listen to vestry proposals if farmers attended the meeting. Nobody wanted trouble and a fair offer to the men should receive a fair response.

In the morning, labourers made their way to the common. By nine o'clock a reasonable number had gathered but it was nothing like the expected crowd. Groups were detailed to round up reluctant men. Someone set off for Woodmancote to seek support from there.

Numbers swelled. Confidence increased.

William Borrer monitored proceedings from his Barrow Hill mansion. At noon he joined with land owners and farmers and together they walked down onto the common.

The men formed a circle and the meeting began. William Borrer, very much the squire, explained that he would first read the vestry's resolutions of the previous evening;

> Able-bodied labouring men shall have from the present time to Lady-day 1831, weather wet or dry, 12 shillings per week.
>
> Lads 14 to 16 years of age will have 4 shillings; from 16 to 18, 6 shillings.
>
> Young men 18 to 21, will have 9 shillings.
>
> From Lady-day to Michaelmas, the days of more light and extra working hours, an extra shilling for men, sixpence for others, will be given.
>
> Families will have an allowance for their third child onward of one shilling and sixpence each from birth to 14 years old paid out of the poor rate.
>
> The vestry will provide employment for all unemployed labourers, whether married or single, at an equal scale of wages.
>
> If there is insufficient work in repairing the roads, land will be hired for cultivation by spade; that or other such work.
>
> No parish rates will be used to increase the wages of people employed by any individual.
>
> The sole use of rates money, apart from payment for men employed by the parish, is for helping the sick, the infirm and the young children.[1]

Mr. Borrer finished with his own note of warning; the parish would put down and punish to its utmost, any act of disorder or violence to either person or property.

The men's leaders replied with their own resolutions.

That done, negotiations began. The men waited.

Before long there was full agreement and everyone relaxed.

At that point, men appeared striding along the road from Woodmancote. When they arrived, John Hamlen Borrer assured them that agreement had been concluded and their own employers would fully support them.

The Woodmancote men promptly turned round and marched off home again.

For the Henfield men there were drinks ready on the Town Field opposite the George. In the evening the band struck up and led a celebratory parade through the High Street. Behind the band strode a marcher with a placard;

Happy day
thanks be to God
and the Gentlemen

Behind the placard three men were carried on chairs, one with a loaf, one with a cheese and one with a leg of mutton; behind them came the happy labourers.

The marchers halted. An announcement was made; William Borrer Esquire, 'Friend of the Village', and Mrs. Lucretia Wood of Chestham had each subscribed one hundred pounds towards a fund for financing labourers' employment.

Whole hearted cheers rang out with an extra three cheers for John Hamlen Borrer acknowledging his assistance in their cause and for Dr. Charles Morgan who had praised the honesty and industry of the parish labourer.

The delighted labourers returned home.

Special Constables for Henfield? Not that day.

Readers of the Brighton Gazette would see that William Borrer's benevolence was not restricted to Henfield. Authenticated letters from the south and west of Ireland had been published telling of the utmost distress prevailing there through a winter of famine, disease and death.

A relief fund was raised by the Brighton Library. William Borrer was amongst the Gazette's list of benefactors. For the starving Irishman, his contribution was £1. [2]

Lucretia Wood, leading lady among the Henfield elite, did not follow Mr. Borrer's meagre response, sensitive as she was to the needs of other people. There were more pressing matters to concern her.

Her late husband, John, had created Chestham Park with a new house on Crouch Hill, none of it subject to Streatham Manor Law. The house was built in eye catching Italianate style with five bays roofed with slate brought by barge from Shoreham.

Lucretia now had sole responsibility not only for the large house but also for a number of farms, amongst them the adjoining Mockbridge and Nymans, plus a wide variety of property within the manor. Some of it was desirable like James Patching's brewery with its two acre meadow by the High Street; some of it cheap tenements for labourers.

John Wood had developed his property as a game preserve with woodland shelter for pheasants. His gamekeeper and bailiff played crucial roles in breeding the birds and maintaining the woods.

Mature timber was a valuable commodity with its sale an important item in Chestham finances.

When 193 ash, 35 elm and four aspen trees were felled, they were advertised as of particular interest to coach makers and wheelwrights.

The sale took place on a February afternoon up in the village at the George Inn – far more appropriate than open fields for a winter's day. Bidding was brisk. The timber fetched a good price.

Chestham's most valuable trees were the oaks.

Lucretia Wood's bailiff marked 1413 for sale in nine separate lots.

The auctioneer's advertisement was bold. The sale would; 'include some of the finest and largest sized trees in the county of Sussex ...... standing on Chestham and Mockbridge Farms in the parish of Henfield (a part of the county so well known for the excellence of its timber) ...... oak timber such as is not to be obtained at any ordinary sale'. [3]

Once felled, the timber could be conveyed south by barge along the river to Shoreham or by wagon north on the Turnpike Road through Horsham.

Catalogues detailing the lots were made available up in London at Lincoln's Inn, at Lewes, Horsham and Brighton where the auction would take place.

The day of the great sale came – and proved a stunning anti-climax.

Just three lots went; 67 trees on Chestham's extensive lawn surrounding the house and 143 on the farm. The remainder would continue growing for another year.

The following March, Lucretia Wood's bailiff included more of her property beyond the parish and marked 1669 trees. The sale was again advertised in the newspapers but it would be by private contract without the involvement of an auctioneer.

The papers also carried notice that His Majesty's Navy were inviting tenders from merchants for the supply of 8000 loads of Rough Oak Timber, Oak Thick-stuff of 5, 6 and 10 inches and Oak Planks 3 inches thick for Woolwich, Chatham and Portsmouth.

The omens were good.

Chestham oaks sold well. The bailiff was satisfied. The merchants could sell the timber on to the Admiralty at profit as they pleased.

Streatham Manor tenants did not do so well from the timber on their land. It was the lord's timber. Without permission they could not fell it, let alone sell it.

Timber was essential to the maintenance of property. Anthony Ede felled four small oaks and six lesser trees that had been pollarded most years for firewood. The timber became post and rail fencing on his land. The fencing was sound but he had omitted to gain permission from the Manor Court. At the next sitting he was fined over £3; a hard lesson for the small tenant.

Lord de la Zouche who held Henfield Park and Parsonage did not have to worry about such things. His farm manager followed correct procedures and gained permission to fell 26 trees for estate repairs.

When John Woolven felled five trees along his hedgerow by the lane at Oreham Common, Percy Gregory queried the legitimacy of the felling. He wrote to the steward at Chichester:

> *Mr. John Woolven a Customary Tenant of Streatham Manor has cut five trees that stood in a lane adjoining his land and drawd them over the hedge into his field. Those trees are them that I Ask you if he might cut last year as thay stood on the waste land called a tenantry lane and you said you should send a person over to see what there was on the waste which I told him.*
>
> *Your answer will oblige. P. Gregory.* [4]

The reply put the onus on Percy as manor woodward. If the trees grew on manor land, he should deem them delivered up for use of the lord. If the man refused, another method would be taken to convince him of his error.

Percy Gregory was in an uncomfortable position – a village man wanting to live on good terms with others but also being the official having to ensure tenants respected Manor Law.

John Woolven was resolute. The trees would remain where they were until the next court when his friend would speak for him.

Percy Gregory did his duty and informed the steward.

Court Day eventually came at New Hall just down the road from Oreham.

Surrenders of property were recorded and tenant deaths proclaimed but the five trees dispute did not figure. John Woolven's timber was safe.

Before long, Dr. Morgan was breaching manor law. Percy Gregory wrote to the steward;

Sir, This is to inform you that Mr. Charles Morgan has Dug and Carried away from Henfield Common between 20 and 30 cart loads of Mould and I will thank you to inform me what is to be done as I told him it was not allowed to do so.

Percy Gregory. [4]

Again the answer was of no real help. The mould could not be recovered.

The doctor was not called upon to answer at the next Manor Court.

Within months there was yet another dispute. A tenant's gardener was removing turf from the common.

Percy wrote to the steward asking if permission had been granted. The steward wrote to the tenant who replied to the reeve;

Mr. Gregory, The Bishop of Chichester has allowed me to cut some turf on Henfield Common. He begged me to acquaint you with it, and that you would direct the gardener where he may cut it, he also begged me most particularly to tell you that having heard that there had been much turf cut and also some timber cut and sold, that he wished you to tell all his copyholders, that they must desist from laying waste his manor, and caution them against any further molestation of his property, and to keep strictly his manorial rights.

Yours most respectfully C Goring. [4]

Percy Gregory was incensed. The man was telling him to accuse his neighbours of violating Manor Law. He took pen and paper;

To William Leeves Esq Chichester Henfield Jan 12/30

As the Revd. Goring left me this letter yesterday I will thank you to inform me what steps is to be taken as I have not any knowledge of any timber been cut or sold as he says in his letter. I should like for him to say who the person is as the tenants and myself does not like to have the Name of selling the Lord's Timber nor they will not allow him any more turf on the wastes of Streatham Manor.

Your answer will oblige. P. Gregory. [4]

The next month, Rev. Goring visited the reeve personally to inform him of the circumstances regarding the bishop's sanction.

Percy Gregory's reply was blunt; even if the bishop had given permission, Revd. Goring had no right to turf from the common.

Two more letters went off to Mr. Leeves. Percy Gregory wrote stating how he had told Rev. Goring he would take no notice of the claim until the steward or the bishop told him. Rev. Goring had already made one falsehood. Now turf was being dug by another tenant and he did not know what was to be done in it.

Rev. Goring wrote thinking it proper to inform the steward of the insulting reply his application had been met with and how the reeve called in question the bishop's authority. Turf cutting had been suspended. He would thank the steward to communicate with the reeve to remedy the matter.

Percy Gregory, as reeve, had done his best to preserve the integrity of the tenants but the Bishop of Chichester and his clergy seemed all powerful.

Chapter 7

A journeyman tailor – Triplets – Unwanted family

The curate wielded the power in purely parish matters although influenced by the larger landowners.

This was especially so at the annual Easter Vestry Meeting where they selected the overseers for the coming year.

By 1832 the workload of overseers had become too great an addition to their daily occupation. An assistant overseer was needed.

The vestry considered they had the very man for the post, William Godman, the Royal Artilley gunner from Woolwich who had almost fought at the Battle of Waterloo.

Godman had been appointed Governor of the Workhouse and had proved very efficient over the previous three years supported by his wife Isabella as matron. He happily accepted the extra work.

One of his new responsibilities was to ensure that everyone liable paid their poor rate.

The vestry calculated the total cost of providing for the parish poor that year and set the rate at 1s 0d in the £ on the rental value of property.

It proved adequate until the winter when farm labourers were laid off work.

By January 1833 the vestry had insufficient Poor Relief money left. A new rate was needed. They set it at 2s 6d.

Expenses kept rising.

In April the rate was increased to 4s 0d; a 400% increase in twelve months. [1]

Landowners and people with large properties had sufficient capital to grumble and accept the rises.

For many poorer families living day by day, the shilling rate was a burden. The four shilling rate meant real hardship.

It certainly did to William Vinall.

William was a fully qualified journeyman tailor whose income depended on work coming in from a shop or a village family.

He had recently married and moved into a tenement in the High Street at £3 a year rent which incurred a 12s 0d poor rate.

They soon had a baby daughter.

William's entire income went on maintaining the family.

He coped by careful use of every penny but when the vestry set a second 4s 0d rate in November he could not find the money.

His rate remained unpaid.

Several other people were in the same predicament.

Assistant overseer Godman carried out his duty and reported the matter.

The non payers were taken before the justices at the Petty Sessions.

William Vinall stated his circumstances explaining with all honesty how his entire earnings were spent. He did not have any money left to pay the extra rate.

The justices had no sympathy. The man had been rated by the parish vestry and must find the money. They issued a Distress Warrant ordering assistant overseer Godman to seize enough goods and chattels to cover the rate plus all extra costs incurred. [2]

Godman turned up at William Vinall's house and presented the warrant.

He went in and commandeered as much property as he calculated would be required to raise the money.

William and his wife had to stand by and watch helplessly as the pile grew.

He had five days to produce the money or lose the lot.

William swallowed hard and paid.

There was cheerful news for copyhold tenants when the Government implemented their Parliamentary Reform Act giving the vote to copyholders with property valued at £10 a year.

It was up to the people concerned to register for the vote.

The list of those who did so was published.

Any name on it could be objected to. Decisions would be made at the Petty Sessions.

Three objections were made; to Richard Pattenden because he had a vote for the borough, Thomas Muzzall for informality in the description of his qualification and newcomer George Hall because a necessary deed was missing.

The objections were considered at the next court sitting.

They were upheld. All three names were struck off the list.

Newcomer George Hall had moved into a new house with his wife, his son Cornelius, just five years old, and their middle aged housekeeper, Sarah.

Behind their house was another building, much larger, constructed for use as a Congregational Church – and frowned upon by some devout members of St. Peter's.

George Hall was the Minister.

He proved a sincere man of many words; words of encouragement and duty, particularly for the working man.

Gradually people were drawn to the new church.

Three families chose it for the baptism of their babies. The Nep Town carpenter Charles Martin and his wife Caroline were the first with baby Sarah.

Charles and Caroline had a comfortable home far better furnished than most of their neighbours could achieve coping on a day labourer's income.

Another Nep Town couple, John and Elizabeth Peters, from up near the workhouse chose for their baby girl to be baptised, Elizabeth.

John was a day labourer. For him, household furniture was minimal; he had enough on his hands to provide food and clothing for his family.

George Hall's other baptisms were for James Patching and his wife, Elizabeth, from the 'Bee Hive' Brewery at Golden Square. They took their son John Theophilus to the chapel.

In due course they had a daughter – yet another Elizabeth. She too was baptised at the chapel.

A month later, grief hit the Patchings when their son died. The curate conducted the burial service. Little John Theophilus was laid to rest in the churchyard.

By that time the chapel was also registered for marriages. George Hall had certainly brought a new dimension to worship in Henfield.

A new dimension was brought to family life in Henfield by Mary, the wife of farmer William Trower, down at Harwoods near the New Inn. They were the proud parents of two year old Mercy.

Mary was in child again.

When her time came, she gave birth to a very little girl – followed by another, and yet another. Triplets in Henfield.

Soon everyone knew the news; what an event!

Although so small, the babies proved healthy and a month later were baptised at St. Peter's Church.

The curate had the pleasure of officiating and recording their names in the register; Faith, Hope and Charity.

Such was the occasion, he felt compelled to add the remark; 'born on 15th. Sep: at one confinement'.

There was no pleasure for anybody when a Brighton overseer turned up at the workhouse with a family and an official Quarter Sessions document stating Jonathan Franks, his wife Matilda, seven year old Hannah and five year old Jonathan were to be removed 'Home' to Henfield.

William Godman signed for the safe arrival of the family and found space for them in the workhouse.

He also reported their arrival to the vestry.

The news caused concern because the name Franks was not a familiar one in the parish. A true Henfield settlement did not seem certain.

The vestry decided the removal had all the hallmarks of a miscarriage of justice. They would question its validity.

Local solicitor Thomas Coppard was consulted.

He first held a long interview with Franks at the workhouse. The man explained who he had been working for in Brighton and how he had lost his job. Nothing he said supported him having a valid Henfield settlement.

The vestry were delighted at the news and determined there was only one course open; to appeal at the next Lewes Quarter Sessions for the Removal Order to be quashed.

Mr. Coppard agreed to represent Henfield.

His first objective would be to ascertain the parish where the couple's marriage had taken place.

He rode down to Brighton and interviewed Franks' last employer. The pauper seemed to have been telling the truth apart from the possibility he was not a Franks at all but a Shallcross.

Written evidence was needed. This necessitated another workhouse visit. Franks maintained he had been baptised at Worth where his father had been married.

Solicitor Coppard rode the 12 miles to Worth and searched the parish registers.

The search revealed the baptism of a Jonathan Shallcross. There was no trace of the father's marriage but another source of information was suggested, the inmates of Worth Workhouse.

Several Worth inmates were determined the answer lay at Bolney. Alternatively there was a Franks uncle living in Turners Hill.

Mr. Coppard decided to contact the uncle by letter. It proved an expensive one – ten shillings for horse hire and messenger although the price did include a reply, hardly helpful; "Probably Bolney."

Mr. Coppard returned home to Henfield. It was time the vestry did some searching. He instructed their clerk Henry Martin accordingly.

Next day Henry Martin rode to Brighton Workhouse where there were another two Franks brothers – hopefully not destined for Henfield.

They had nothing useful to offer.

His next trip was longer; right up to London for a sight of Jonathan Franks' marriage certificate at Somerset House.

The search revealed the marriage not to have taken place in Worth at all but miles further east at Wadhurst. Henry Martin returned home in high spirits.

Mr. Coppard sent his clerk over to Wadhurst. Two days later, the clerk came home bringing good news; the marriage details were clearly recorded in the Wadhurst marriage register – the family did not have a Henfield Settlement.

There was just one day to finish preparations for the court appearance. Henry Martin took the family over to Lewes. Mr. Coppard would speak for Henfield, his clerk would be a witness.

They were three days at court before the case came up. The justices listened to evidence from both sides, considered the matter and quashed the Removal Order. Victory for Henfield.

Brighton had to take the Franks family back to their workhouse. Furthermore they had to pay Henfield £7 16s to cover the costs of the family during their stay at Henfield.

The vestry could congratulate themselves. True they had to pay Henry Martin's costs in London but Franks had been sent packing and would not after all be a burden on the parish poor rate.

Parish of Henfield to Henry Martin

Expenses in going to Brighton to see the 2 brothers of Jon Franks and thence to London after the marriage certificate and then to Horsham to Mr Coppard

Expenses and hire at the Quarter Sessions at Lewes	*£3 1s 0d*
conveying the pauper Franks and his expenses	*19s 0d*
This Bill is correct Thomas Coppard	*£4 0s 0d.*

The final score became apparent when the solicitor's bill arrived; another nasty surprise. Mr. Coppard had meticulously itemised everything down to the last detail, two shillings postage for the final letters. The case would cost Henfield a grand total of £44 18s 4d; well over a year's workhouse keep for the family. The vestry could only lick their wounds. [3]

Chapter 8

New Poor Law – A workhouse mill – Pauper confrontation

In 1835, Henfield became part of Steyning Union with 13 other parishes. The Government had passed a New Poor Law to put an end to perceived bad practices seen as placing too heavy a financial burden on ratepayers and as encouraging labourers to depend on aid instead of determining to be self-reliant.

Under the new law anyone could still apply for relief but it would be by residence in a union workhouse.

Each parish had to appoint guardians. William Borrer Esquire, the acclaimed 'Friend of the Village', and Stephen Faulconer of Henfield Place agreed to be Henfield's.

Workhouses were placed under the jurisdiction of Poor Law officials. Steyning Union and neighbouring Cuckfield Union became the responsibility of Assistant Commissioner Hawley, a very conscientious man determined to uphold the Poor Law in all its intricate detail. He quickly earned a reputation as a man whose visits nearly always brought trouble.

When Workhouse Governor William Godman was informed that Assistant Commissioner Hawley intended to visit Henfield, he determined to have everything ready in advance; spotless workhouse, spotless inmates and account books to hand.

In the event, the visit was sprung on him without a single day's notice when Doctor Charles Morgan arrived with a stranger.

William Godman immediately realised who the stranger was.

The inspection of the workhouse took place there and then – no chance to prepare – followed by instructions to be ready with all relevant parish books at the George Inn the next day at twelve noon.

As soon as the visitors went, William was able to begin preparations.

Able-bodied paupers were sent to inform vestry members of the next day's visit. That done he checked his bookkeeping was in order. Thankfully all proved correct.

The next day he made sure he was in good time for the meeting. Others had done likewise.

Well before noon they were all seated at the table, the parish books spread out.

The landlord had dinner and drinks prepared.

Nervous exchanges were made as the final minutes passed.

The clock chimed noon.

Mr. Hawley's arrival was obviously delayed.

More minutes dragged by.

Minutes dragged into hours, three of them, and still the officers sat at the table; the drinks untouched, the dinner waiting on the range. Nobody was going to offend a man like Mr. Hawley.

At four o'clock the men's resolve was broken. Something must have happened. Mr. Hawley would surely not be arriving that day.

Hunger and thirst were assuaged. The officers left.

William Godman gathered his books and returned to the workhouse, still bewildered.

No explanation was made for the failure of the Assistant Commissioner to arrive until a brief report appeared in the next week's Sussex Advertiser explaining that the obsequious Governor of Henfield Workhouse had fallen for a practical joke played on him by a Gentleman of the village and his friend from another parish.

The following week's Advertiser published a retaliatory letter from William Godman disclosing that the 'Gentleman of Henfield' alluded to was none other than the parish surgeon Dr. Charles Morgan. Readers would doubtless concur in reprobating such conduct in a person deriving his subsistence from those he endeavoured to render ridiculous.

Doctor Morgan felt bound to reply with just indignation. He had made ample apologies for his accepted indiscretion. He disclaimed any knowledge of the author of the original report and would treat any further letter from Godman with perfect contempt. As a Most Obedient Humble Servant, he concluded his letter. [1]

Apart from the men concerned, nobody was too particularly interested except for slight amusement or distaste. Life continued undisturbed.

On the 28th of July the Board of Guardians held their first meeting, at Steyning. There, Mr. Faulconer seconded the proposal that the new Union

Workhouse should be built at New Shoreham. Until then the old workhouses at New Shoreham, Steyning and Henfield would continue. Henfield vestry would receive an annual rent of £35 for their house.

An advert was sent to the newspapers for medical men to serve the Union's three districts. The meeting ended; all others would be at New Shoreham where people seeking relief would have to apply.

The medical advert caught the eye of Dr. Morgan whose practice now had the services of his two sons, Nelson and Frederick.

His skill had become widely known even outside Henfield following the successful amputation of the cancerous lower limb of a 67 year old lady; a procedure reported in the pages of the Brighton papers. He felt confident of being appointed regardless of his rather indiscreet practical joke.

It was with considerable professional concern that he learnt of an application from Henfield's other doctor, Adolphus Caudle, a newly qualified practitioner with a young family who had been in the village only a few years.

Dr. Morgan decided on the one action open to safeguard the well-being of the district's poor, a suitable letter to the Union Guardians explaining Caudle's lack of important qualifications.

The letter was sent, read and acted on.

Dr. Morgan was appointed Union Doctor for Number 3 District comprising Henfield and surrounding parishes.

District 3's final need was a Relieving Officer.

The Steyning guardians promoted their own Relieving Officer, James Puttock, a man who had always proved diligent and dependable. Any possible slight weakness in his efficiency would be more than compensated for by his loyalty. The committee were happy to appoint him.

With the officers in position, the guardians could concentrate on the problem of the New Poor Law Commissioners objecting to the continuation of out relief.

The commissioners solved the dilemma by revising all entitlements and requiring each parish to determine a venue for payments to their paupers – but strictly not a Public House. At least the expense was being curtailed.

At the guardians' first meeting in Shoreham they decided Henfield Workhouse should be equipped with a corn-mill. It was a seemly decision because the influential Duke of Richmond, Lord Lieutenant of Sussex, had purchased one for the workhouse at Yapton near his Goodwood Estate.

Mr. Borrer and Mr. Faulconer gave their support; the Steyning Union would purchase 'A Mill and Dressing Machine precisely upon the same principles in all respects as the one at Yapton for the sum of £40'. [2]

Brickmaker Joseph Shepherd was instructed to install it by the end of September. Times were certainly changing.

News of the mill became speculative gossip round the village. It would surely be a windmill because the only water power at the workhouse was the well in the yard. Yet there were already two windmills. What need was there for another?

When the paupers realised what the source of power was to be, there was dismay; it was them – just like the prisoners on Lewes Prison treadmill. Mr. Borrer 'Friend of the Village' was being shown in another light.

The New Poor Law stipulated that all paupers should be classified with each category being accommodated separately:- aged or infirm men from aged or infirm women – able-bodied men and boys over 13 from women and girls over 16 – youths and boys 7 to 13 from girls under 16 – children under 7. Children aged below three would remain with their mother.

The inference of the system invoked heated conversation.

How could justice tolerate the separation of parents and children; the end of family life?

Feelings ran deep among rate-payers and paupers alike.

The guardians could have no qualms; the new law had to be adhered to, classification had to be implemented.

Until the new workhouse was built, Henfield would have the able-bodied inmates, Steyning the children and Shoreham the old or infirm.

An advert was put in the Brighton and Lewes papers: –

> A Man and his Wife as Governor and Matron for the Workhouse at Henfield, to take the management of able-bodied paupers. The Governor's salary to be at the rate of £45 per annum, the Matron's at £15: board and lodging included.

And also:

> A Man and his Wife for the workhouse at Steyning, which is intended for children. The Governor to undertake the management and instruction of the boys. The Matron ... of the girls. The system of education to be the national. The positions to commence the 1st of September. [3]

Knowledge of the advertisement's implications soon spread. The New Poor Law was forcing parents in one direction, their children in another. Uncertain rumour was now plain truth; families forced apart like farm stock herded to separate pens.

Willam Ede jokingly reckoned he might throw in a tender for the Henfield position. He was working for Joseph Shepherd preparing the corn-mill. Joseph Shepherd knew what the outcome would be; William Ede's character was too well known, he was a bitter man.

The guardians appointed John Henry Seaborne and wife, Mary Anne, to Henfield confident the workhouse would be in safe hands.

Classification was the main topic of the guardians' next meeting on the 2nd September at the Star Inn just off Shoreham High Street.

Union Clerk Mr. Tribe prepared the list of necessary transfers. 29 forms were completed stating which workhouse each pauper was to go to.

The next day the paupers were informed they had to move.

At Henfield, Governor Seaborne coped easily; eight children to Steyning and seven old and infirm to Shoreham along with simpleton Jane Golds and her son Henry, now 12 years old and proving as simple as his mother.

At Steyning, Relieving Officer Putttock produced the orders. All went well with those destined for Shoreham, three old men and two young women nursing baby daughters. Five single men going to Henfield were also submissive but two married men, Hayler and Moon, refused point blank. They were convinced their children were being kept at Steyning. Nobody was going to trick them into having their families split apart from each other. They had no intention of moving. Anybody trying to force them would find out.

The pair were young, muscular and determined. Other inmates openly supported them.

They pointedly accused Puttock of participation in making the orders. He promptly denied any involvement and cleared off, leaving the workhouse governor to his own devices.

The men turned on him and threatened a beating. The governor backed off seeking refuge in his room.

The next day, he organised the removal of the other paupers but Hayler and Moon remained

Two days later the families were still in Steyning Workhouse. [4]

When Mr. Borrer and Mr. Faulconer were informed of the situation in Steyning they were affronted. Their authority as Henfield Guardians was being undermined by incompetence in another parish. An immediate response was imperative. They decided an extraordinary meeting of the Union Guardians should be held to address the failure.

The same day, Mr. Borrer had to deal equitably with two Henfield paupers seeking out-relief, Thomas Walker and William Ede. For them, it was perhaps an unfortunate time to appear. Mr. Borrer felt able to give Walker relief but was adamant he must enquire further into William Ede's character before allowing him anything.

William was bitterly disappointed. He had explained how his work with Joseph Shepherd had finished the previous week. There was no harvest work to turn to. His six year old eldest child had recently died and his wife was in low spirits dependant on him; all that, yet Mr. Borrer was again preventing him looking after his family. Angered and dispirited he made his way home past the workhouse and down the lane by the windmill to his cottage at the edge of the brooks. Mr. Borrer, "Friend of the Village"? Never.

Chapter 9

Workhouse riot – Midnight fire – Tempting reward

On the Monday evening Mr. Borrer chaired the extraordinary meeting at Henfield Workhouse. Just three guardians were present; the two Henfield men and one from Shoreham. Mr. Borrer was elected to take the chair.

There were two items for discussion; the refusal of the Steyning men to quit the workhouse and the refusal of some of the Steyning parish officers to lend their assistance in the matter.

The facts were clear, detailed discussion was unnecessary. They resolved that Steyning parish officers should ensure the workhouse governor removed the recalcitrant paupers immediately. Orders were prepared and the meeting concluded. Their action would be explained at the Wednesday meeting in Shoreham.

On the Wednesday, it was not only guardians making their way to Shoreham. Paupers, too, were arriving to ask for out-relief. Seven walked from Henfield; William Ede and his wife, the parish beadle Charles Legg and his wife, Thomas Waller, John Jupp's wife and Louisa Holden. They called at the Red Lion in Old Shoreham for a refreshing pot of fourpenny beer. It set Ede off about Mr. Borrer again. Waller checked him; Ede needed to be careful – idle talk did nobody any good. Ede shut up.

By the time they reached the Star the meeting had already begun. People waiting outside seemed unusually restless.

The new arrivals soon found out why. The guardians had announced that no relief would be considered at the meeting. Applicants would have to come back the following Wednesday.

People were confused and annoyed. Relieving Officer Puttock had said they must apply at Shoreham. Now the guardians were saying they could not have any for another week. Why were they being refused? They had come from home in good faith; they would wait until relief was given them.

The guardians could hardly ignore the growing numbers. Eventually one suggested that because Puttock had made an error, some relief should be distributed. There was grudging agreement.

Nine paupers were called inside and given money.

The chosen few set off home. The others became increasingly frustrated.

Frustration became resentment. Voices were raised, threats made – nobody would be let out of the Star until relief was given.

The guardians ignored the clamour and completed the business of the day. It was time to return home.

They stepped outside into a volley of abuse closely followed by a shower of stones. Not until each guardian had been accosted and harangued did the crowd begin to disperse taking their discontent with them.

The Henfield group made another call at the Red Lion. William Ede's beer again loosened his tongue. He tried explaining his plight to the landlord;

"I asked the guardians for work but they wouldn't give me any and they wouldn't allow me any money. They're all a pack of rascals and Mr. Borrer's a shameful rascal and a rogue; from being a friend to the village he's now a blackguard and it's no matter what becomes of him. If he burnt in his bed it would be no matter."

That was more than enough for the landlord; he knew the one weapon when liquor took control of tongues. He refused Ede any more beer and turned him out. The others joined him and they walked back to Henfield with empty pockets and intense frustration at being pushed around yet again by the Board of Guardians. [1]

Unknown to William Ede, the Board's decisions at the Wednesday meeting included ordering him and his family into the workhouse.

He was informed on the Friday. The news reduced his wife to tears. William's anger overflowed. He and his family were not animals to be herded at a guardian's command. Nobody was going to throw his family into the workhouse.

Early that evening he and his wife were walking home through Nep Town, his wife again in tears. People around noticed her state. Ann Legg, the beadle's wife, and Elizabeth Parsons commiserated with her.

William told them the reason for her upset and what he thought of it;

"I'll be damned if I'll go in. It's all Borrer's doing. If his house was on fire and he in the middle of it I'll be damned if I'd pull him out."

Ann Legg remonstrated;

"That's a hard thing to wish any person."

William, too angry to hear, was aware of only one thing – there was no way Borrer would be putting them in a workhouse. He would move into Brighton and find work there.

With that, they parted. William and his wife continued down the hill to their house beside the brooks.

Richard Whiteman on Oreham Common had also received orders to go in the workhouse with his wife and family. He was out of work having just returned from a month's imprisonment at Petworth House of Correction for what he described as a difference with his employer Mr. Hall over some wood.

Richard did not enjoy the prospect of life in the workhouse but Friday was the day some of the guardians could well be there granting relief money. He went early hoping they would allow him a bit. He was lucky and gained several shillings; enough for him to go round to Thomas Browning at strangely named Oyster Cottage in the next lane.

Thomas Browning kept a donkey and cart for hire; the cart in the shed by his cottage and the donkey left to graze on the meadow he rented, Burning Mountain, at the top of the lane.

Richard Whiteman now had enough to hire them. He would try round Steyning, Shoreham and Brighton to see what the prospects were there.

Progress was not all it should have been.

At Steyning a noisy commotion was going on in front of the workhouse. A crowd of people blocked the road.

News had spread of officials arriving early morning to remove Hayler and Moon but failing because other paupers had helped the pair resist.

Relieving Officer Puttock had ridden for help to Storrington and come back with the Shoreham Member of Parliament H.D. Goring and half a dozen helpers including Sergeant Lee of the Yeomanry Cavalry.

Mr. Goring stated who he was and commanded Hayler and Moon to cooperate.

It became a scuffle.

Goring and Major Sandham J.P. collared Moon and dragged him into the workhouse. Puttock and Sergeant Lee went for Hayler but the two wives threw themselves into the fray.

Moon managed to break free and ran to help his mate.

The protesters felt the confidence of crowd power. They were not going to stand by and let officials cart people off as if they were market animals.

People clambered up the wall into the workhouse garden. Others followed.

Moon and Hayler leapt down the wall and escaped into the crowd.

Stones were hurled at Goring and his men. They looked to their own escape. He, Puttock and Sergeant Lee ran for the shelter of the workhouse.

A stone thudded against Goring's hat; Sergeant Lee was hit on the head. Blood streamed down his face but he kept moving.

They wrenched open the door, staggered through and locked themselves in.

It was the beginning of a long afternoon.

Outside, the crowd grew denser. Threats increased, stones hit the workhouse.

The hours passed with the noise becoming more intense.

The crowd bayed for Relieving Officer Puttock. They were going to have him. They were ready to get him.

More stones thudded against the house; windows shattered.

Those inside feared for their lives.

The rest of the officials were safely beyond the crowd but helpless to assist. The day had become serious riot. Aid was essential. It had to be found.

Unnoticed, Union Clerk Mr. Tribe mounted his horse and rode away.

He reached Shoreham, requested the coastguards to be ready to accompany him on his return and continued to Brighton.

His ride ended at the barracks of the Royal Irish Dragoons. He was ushered inside where he quickly explained his mission.

Within a quarter of an hour sixty dragoons were mounted and on the road. An hour later they and the coastguards were approaching Steyning.

The crowd round the workhouse had maintained their vigil in the fading light of evening completely unaware of Mr. Tribe's ride.

Suddenly they were conscious of a new noise; trotting horses, far too many for chance arrivals.

Protest stopped abruptly. People melted into the dusk hurriedly heading for the safety of home.

60 Royal Irish Dragoons and the Shoreham Coastguards halted before a quiet workhouse. Just a litter of stones and shattered glass belied the peace.

The coastguards and twenty dragoons stayed to keep watch. The rest rode off again.[2]

The trapped officials were safe – with the features of several protestors sharp in their minds. Justice would have the final say. Benjamin Hayler and Thomas Moon, the two recalcitrant fathers, would pay for their disobedience.

It was late, very late, that night when Richard Whiteman returned the donkey and cart to Thomas Browning; later still by the time he had walked the two miles to his shared house on Oreham Common. His neighbour heard the return, almost 11.30, yet a normal body was almost abed by eight.

About 2.00 a.m. that same night up at Nep Town, James Randall's little daughter Nancy fell out of bed. The noise woke her parents.

James got up to see to her. As he did so he became aware of a red glow through the window. He looked out. Far across the fields something was alight, a building or haystack. He put little Nancy back to bed and raised the alarm among his neighbours.

Half a dozen of them responded. The glow was across the brooks, seemingly closer than Buckwish Farm at the far side. It had to be either the barn or the cattle hovel in Browns Land.

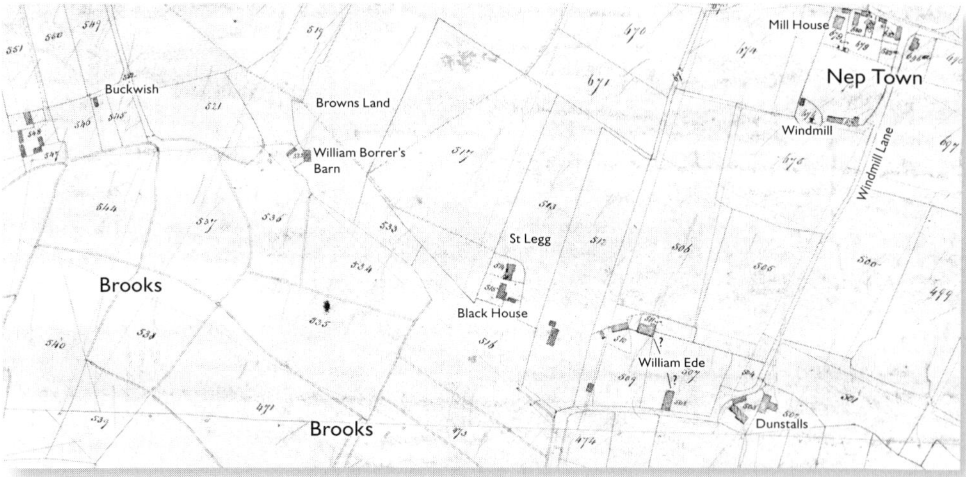

1845 Tithe map; Mr. Borrer's barn, William Ede's house and Windmill Lane

They hurried across the fields and arrived far too late. It was Mr. Borrer's barn, well ablaze, flames fanned by the wind – thatched roof and wooden walls a sheet of fire, some of the rafters already fallen.

Wooden fencing threatened to spread the fire to the nearby hovel. Men hurriedly tore the fence down and moved the wood clear. More of the barn rafters fell, the building collapsed. There was nothing more anybody could do.

People returned to their beds for a little sleep before work. Masters did not accept late starts.

James Randall would need to be halfway back down the lane almost before he was home. He was a journeyman miller at the Nep Town Windmill. The wind was favourable. His master would want the sails turning; there was wheat to grind.

William Borrer Esquire slept undisturbed, completely unaware that he no longer had a barn with 25 bushels of barley. How fortunate that only the previous day he had fully insured his complete property against fire.

In the morning, John Faulconer was one of the first on the scene a bit before 5.00. He had come down the lane and round past William Ede's house about a quarter of a mile from the barn. Ede's front door was wide open, yet there was no sign of him at the fire.

Thomas Piper got there about 7.00 and soon afterwards William did arrive with a mate, Samuel Woolgar. Thomas went over to him;

"Hey! Hey! Will, how is it you were not here before?"

"Pon my soul, I am only just up, and have only just heard of it."

Conversation moved on. There was nothing to see; no barn, just the glowing embers. People lingered, mused, exchanged opinions and set off home.

William's wife was ready for him. They were going to Brighton to find a situation but not for them a donkey and cart. They would walk.

Their route took them past Oreham Common. Richard Whiteman was loading a cart there, horse drawn this time courtesy of his old employer Mr. Hall.

William called across to him;

"Holloa, Dick, how come you set Mr. Borrer's barn alight last night?"

Richard ignored the jibe;

"Yes, I have heard of that just now of Master Scott up at New Hall drying hops."

William and his wife moved on.

By about 10.00 they were in Fulking at the Shepherd and Dog. William regaled them with the story of the fire; Mr. Borrer's barn burnt down with the roof falling in about 3.00 a.m.

By the time they reached Brighton that afternoon William was content to explain how he had been completely unaware of any fire until the next morning because he had not been out of bed all night. His concern now was to find employment

Back at Henfield, Mr. Borrer had been told the grim news. He knew it must be arson; no doubt at all. He prepared an advertisement and sent it off to the Brighton Gazette;

INCENDIARY FIRE

Whereas, the Barn on the Browns Land in Henfield, the property of William Borrer Esq., was last night destroyed with its contents by Fire. A Reward of ONE HUNDRED POUNDS is hereby offered by the said William Borrer, to be paid on conviction. Henfield, September 12th 1835.[3]

There was no immediate response but at the end of the following March the authorities at Lewes were suddenly given the name of a suspect. The informant was Willam Ede. He named Charles Legg, the Henfield beadle, a man respected for moving beggars out of the village and for ensuring attentive devotions during Sunday service.

Charles Legg was apprehended and examined.

It was quickly obvious he had no involvement which in turn threw suspicion onto William himself.

He was arrested in Brighton, his wife again reduced to tears.

An examination was arranged at the White Horse in Steyning. Sir Charles Goring chaired the magistrates. Three hours of probing examination took place as witness after witness told their tale of William Ede's ill wishes towards Mr. Borrer. At the end William could do no more than protest his innocence.

The magistrates ignored him; the evidence was more than sufficient to commit him to stand trial at the ensuing Lewes Assizes.

Mr. Borrer encouraged everyone by again inserting his advertisement in the Brighton Gazette – now £200, sweetened with the prospect of a free pardon for any confessing accomplice.

At the trial, witnesses again gave their evidence and declared they expected no part of the reward.

Nothing seemed more intimidating than Ede's talk of fire until Richard Whiteman took the stand.

He declared there was evidence he had previously not been going to reveal. When he heard of Charles Legg being detained for something he had not done he changed his mind feeling obliged to explain what he had seen on the night of the fire.

His was telling evidence;

"I was at Brighton the day before and had Thomas Browning's donkey and cart. It was late when I got back. I took the donkey and cart back about nine to Browning's cottage near the mill. I continued to Mrs. West's over the brooks near Buckwish nearly a mile from Browning's to pay her for a duck and I also owed for a pig trough. Borrer's barn is midway. I did not get in at Mrs. West's. I tried and then sat down on the bridge which goes up to the house out of the lane nearly an hour and started home. I went by the pond just past Mr. Borrer's barn and I thought I heard as if somebody was striking a light. I stopped to listen and heard it again. I went a little further and turned to the right, heard it again, saw the man and who it was. He was close to the barn and I saw him down on one knee. He lighted a match and put it in a crack of the boards of the barn. I was as near the man as six or seven yards. William Ede was the man. I could see him plain when the match burnt up. He had a dark lead coloured round frock on. I went away directly as fast as I could being struck with horror at what I saw. I don't think he could see me, it was so dark."

The defence cross-examined him and the judge asked why he had not told of it before. Richard explained that he was afraid of seeming to be involved in the affair.

William Ede had little defence to offer except to maintain he had nothing to do with it.

A friend did his bit by telling how he had stayed with William on September 11th, the night of the fire. Just William, his wife and their two children were in the house. They had gone to bed between eight and nine o'clock but he did not sleep well that night. He could hear William snoring and would have noticed if he had left his bed. He himself got up about 5.00 and left to go to his work 7 miles away at Withdean.

Under cross examination he explained he could not say if the house was in a field or a garden because he had never been there before and it was dark when he got there and when he left. He had pulled the door to as he thought and he never saw any sign of fire. How he knew it was the 11th was that he went to church the next Sunday and heard them say it was the 13th.

The judge summed up. Richard Whiteman's evidence was the crucial factor. The rest amounted only to the prisoner making wicked expressions and threats. If the jury were not satisfied with Whiteman's evidence there was nothing to support the indictment. The witness had stated he stood in the position of an honest man who had detected crime. Why, then, had he not disclosed the facts at the time?

The jury listened attentively to the judge's comments and quickly agreed their verdict; not guilty. Mr. Borrer's £200 remained intact.

Chapter 10

Corn-mill strike – Union Workhouse – Cricket Club

Mr. Borrer had far more money set aside for the seating improvements he wished to make in the church.

Even with the galleries inserted above the pews, there were insufficient places.

Very few of the seats could be used free of charge. Most were apportioned to people who paid a rent for reserving them. Higher society families included enough for the entire household.

The benches inserted along the nave for the schoolchildren were a great nuisance to worshippers. The brass memorials on the floor were being damaged with scratch marks made by the children scuffing their nailed boots.

Mr. Borrer envisaged overcoming the problems by an extension to the south side of the nave with places for 120 boys plus free family pews. In a gallery above it, reached by an external stairway to ensure propriety, would be places for 80 girls, a pew for reeve Percy Gregory and more free seats to be allocated at Mr. Borrer's discretion.

The vicar was informed and gave his full agreement although his commitments at West Stoke precluded him from attending the necessary vestry meeting to approve the idea. Mr. Borrer quite understood. Travel of 30 miles from beyond Chichester was too much to expect of their vicar.

The vestry meeting was called, the curate again representing Rev. Guy. 17 parishioners (male) attended; a broad cross section of the village lacking only agricultural labourers. All five occupants of the new houses on the Hay Croft were there. As rate payers they could now have their say in deciding parish matters and sign their attendance in the minutes book.

Mr. Borrer explained his plans and gave assurance that he alone would be responsible for financing the work. Agreement was unanimous.

The Bishop of Chichester's permission was gained on the understanding that the materials used would blend with the stonework of the church and would not impinge on the chancel which was in the gift of the Rt Hon. Lord de la Zouche at Parham House. [1]

Building contracts again went to village men. They worked hard, completed the extension and moved on to their next assignment.

Mr. Borrer's church extension for the schoolchildren

When the new building was consecrated, the school children prayed and praised under the watchful eyes of their teachers. The congregation worshipped without the litter of benches in the aisle.

One group of pews did have more space that summer. The number of Henfield Workhouse inmates fell and their pews just inside the west door were not quite so crowded.

The respite was short lived. As autumn progressed, farmers dismissed surplus labourers. More fit and able people were forced to seek relief.

The number of inmates rose to 58. The workhouse's 20 iron double-bedsteads provided adequate sleeping space.

An advert in the Brighton papers invited tenders for food.

The meals would be served as breakfast gruel, meticulously portioned rations of midday meat, suet pudding or soup, and evening cheese.

At the Union's Shoreham meeting they decided the workhouse diet should be the same as that in use at St. George's, Hanover Square in London.

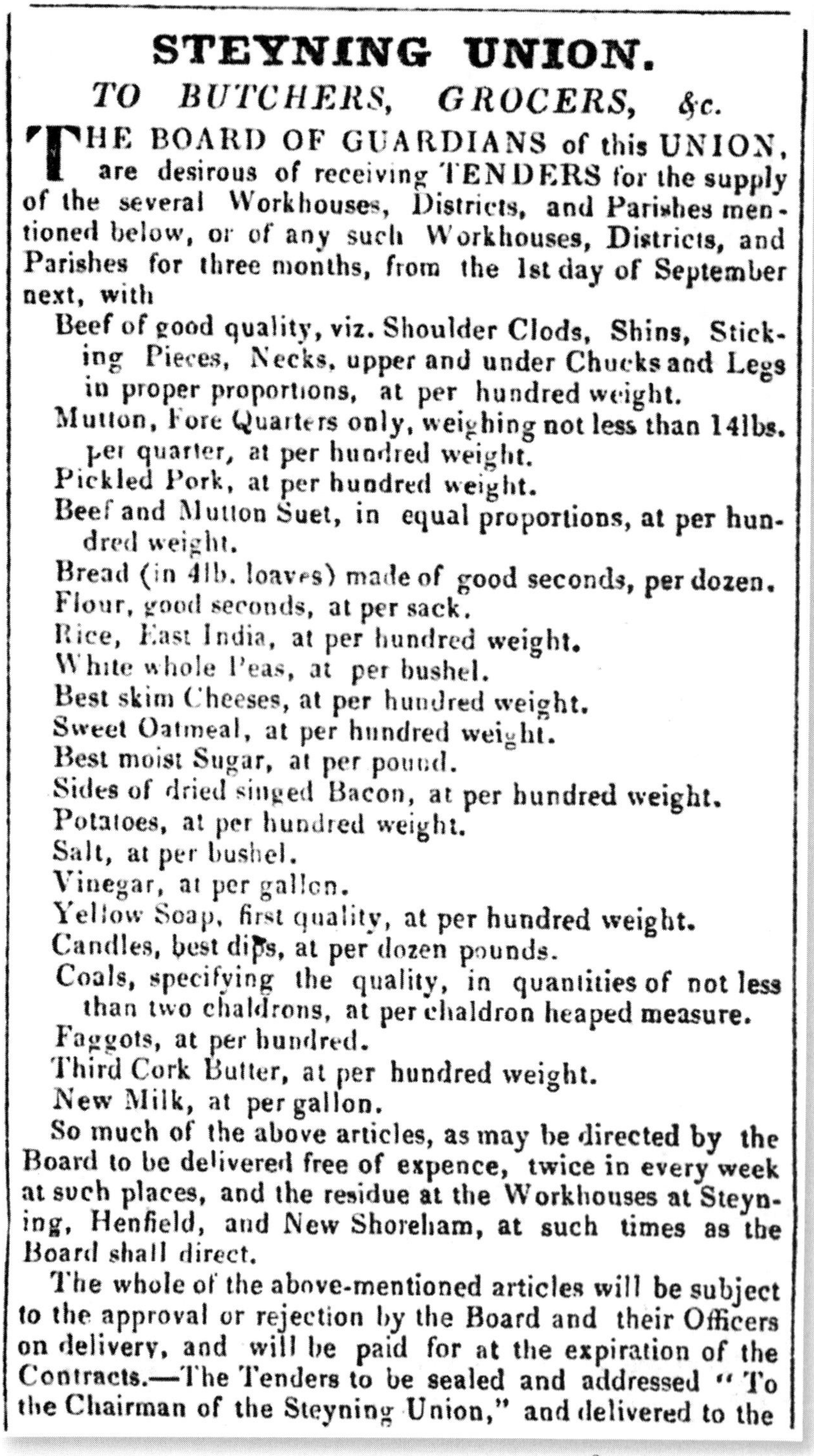

STEYNING UNION.

TO BUTCHERS, GROCERS, &c.

THE BOARD OF GUARDIANS of this UNION, are desirous of receiving TENDERS for the supply of the several Workhouses, Districts, and Parishes mentioned below, or of any such Workhouses, Districts, and Parishes for three months, from the 1st day of September next, with

Beef of good quality, viz. Shoulder Clods, Shins, Sticking Pieces, Necks, upper and under Chucks and Legs in proper proportions, at per hundred weight.
Mutton, Fore Quarters only, weighing not less than 14lbs. per quarter, at per hundred weight.
Pickled Pork, at per hundred weight.
Beef and Mutton Suet, in equal proportions, at per hundred weight.
Bread (in 4lb. loaves) made of good seconds, per dozen.
Flour, good seconds, at per sack.
Rice, East India, at per hundred weight.
White whole Peas, at per bushel.
Best skim Cheeses, at per hundred weight.
Sweet Oatmeal, at per hundred weight.
Best moist Sugar, at per pound.
Sides of dried singed Bacon, at per hundred weight.
Potatoes, at per hundred weight.
Salt, at per bushel.
Vinegar, at per gallon.
Yellow Soap, first quality, at per hundred weight.
Candles, best dips, at per dozen pounds.
Coals, specifying the quality, in quantities of not less than two chaldrons, at per chaldron heaped measure.
Faggots, at per hundred.
Third Cork Butter, at per hundred weight.
New Milk, at per gallon.

So much of the above articles, as may be directed by the Board to be delivered free of expence, twice in every week at such places, and the residue at the Workhouses at Steyning, Henfield, and New Shoreham, at such times as the Board shall direct.

The whole of the above-mentioned articles will be subject to the approval or rejection by the Board and their Officers on delivery, and will be paid for at the expiration of the Contracts.—The Tenders to be sealed and addressed "To the Chairman of the Steyning Union," and delivered to the

Workhouse Food Tender advertisement [2]

It took less than a month to prove inadequate. Mr. Borrer explained how the Provisions Committee had monitored the new dietary and found it did not meet the needs of the able-bodied at Henfield or the children at Steyning.

An amended dietary was accepted.

For the able-bodied, men's breakfast would be 5 ounces of bread with 2 pints of gruel; women's, 4 ounces of bread and 1½ pints of gruel.

Dinner was to vary: –

Sunday, Tuesday and Thursday: 6 ounces bread (women 4 ounces) 5 ounces cooked meat 8 ounces potatoes or other vegetables.	*Monday:* 4 ounces potatoes 16 ounces suet pudding (women 12 ounces).
Wednesday and Friday: 6 ounces bread, 4 ounces potatoes or other vegetables. 2 pints soup (women 1½ pints).	*Saturday:* 6 ounces bread 2 ounces cheese.

Supper was constant; 5 ounces of bread with 1½ ounces of cheese and a pint of small beer (but no beer on Fridays).

The old and infirm had lesser portions but could choose gruel or a pint of tea at breakfast and had another pint of tea as their supper drink.

Children from 9 to 14 had women's rations. Younger ones ate what the matron decided as appropriate.[3]

Poor Law Assistant Commissioner Hawley (rigid stickler for rules, arch-critic of workhouse administration) directed the guardians to cease providing beer in the workhouse.

The guardians knew full well that the beer was the one highlight of a pauper's day. They resolved to hold out against Hawley and refuse to desist. As a safety precaution they asked for the Workhouse Regulations to be sent them.

Supper's pint of beer continued.

The improved rations kept the paupers going through the summer without too much open grumbling until October.

It was in October that Joseph Sayers fitted the corn-mill and received his £40.

Governor Seaborne introduced his paupers to their new task; providing the muscle power to activate the mill.

William Ede's brother, Henry, was there with his wife and two year old son. Thomas 'Quality' Shoulders and his wife had their two year old daughter. The children were being weaned off mother's milk onto Union diet. Both men were part of the gang keeping the corn-mill in full production – satisfying for Governor Seaborne, hard and humiliating for ill nourished paupers.

With Christmas just a week away, Governor Seaborne was suddenly taken aback. The corn-mill gang were refusing to work. Nothing would shake their resolve; reading rules, reciting the consequences or calling in the overseer and guardians. The men would not return to the mill.

On the 19th, Governor Seaborne attended the Board meeting at Shoreham and reported how all his able-bodied paupers had defied his authority. The guardians listened to his account. He named two of the main culprits, Shoulders and Caplin.

The Beeding Guardian proposed summary legal proceedings against them, William Borrer Esquire seconded him and the Board gave unanimous approval. It was imperative that pauper disturbances should have clear, unequivocal consequences.

On the 21st, Thomas 'Quality' Shoulders and John Caplin stood before Justices of the Peace at Steyning Petty Sessions. They were found guilty of refusing to obey the orders of Governor Seaborne and were sentenced to three weeks hard labour at Petworth House of Correction. Theirs would be a very different Christmas.

The two men became numbers printed indelibly on their prison clothing. Only as those numbers were they ordered or berated whether in their cell, at the exercise yard or attending Sunday divine service.

Petworth hard labour did not grind corn but raised water 150 feet to a newly installed water tower above the building.

Water was to play an increasingly important part in improving the hygiene and welfare of the prisoners. It was raised by a pump worked through a series of cranks rotated by prisoners, each man completing 32 turns per minute for a daily total of 13440 revolutions.

Petworth food barely provided sufficient nourishment for such labour.

Short term prisoners had 8 ounces of bread with a pint of gruel for breakfast and for supper. Dinner was just the bread.

They did not discuss food, living conditions, the weather or anything – not even in the exercise yard. There they walked the circuit, a strict three paces apart, eyes ahead, with each number thinking his thoughts to himself. Silence was the watchword. If a prisoner dared turn his head, the charge was 'attempting to converse with another prisoner', and the probable result, loss of supper with its essential eight ounce ration of bread and pint of gruel. Supper and silence were golden.

The Henfield men began their very silent "Twenty-one days of Christmas".

'Quality' Shoulders proved the more adaptable.

For John Caplin life was extremely difficult. He had found the Henfield corn-mill labour enough; Petworth was almost unendurable. The first nine days were a struggle; poor health, poor food and 13440 crank revolutions per day. Caplin did his utmost but the unremitting effort was telling on him.

On the tenth morning a warder discovered him dead in his cell.

The surgeon held a post-mortem and presented his findings at the inquest. The body showed sufficient disease in the head to cause death but the immediate cause was water about the heart and in a cavity of the chest. The jury returned their verdict; "Natural death from the effect of water on the chest." [4]

'Quality' Shoulders carried on, unaware his mate was dead, until release day dawned and he returned home to his family and the workhouse corn-mill.

The next month, in the cold of mid February, while he and Henry Ede worked their daily stint at the mill their two children lay ill in their workhouse bed – Ellen, daughter of Thomas and Amelia Shoulders, 2 years 8 months; George, son of Henry and Martha Ede, 2 years 6 months. Workhouse food, workhouse clothing and workhouse warmth did nothing to promote health. On the 22nd both children died. On the 23rd they were buried in a pauper grave. No memorial would record their short lives.

Workhouse life continued uneventfully for the other inmates through summer into autumn but all of them knew that unless they could regain independence their Henfield days were numbered. The new workhouse at Shoreham was nearly ready.

In November, moving arrangements were finalised, rules and regulations posted. The guardians met to appoint a governor and matron. They were unanimous in their choice, John and Mary Seaborne of Henfield Workhouse – the Union paupers could not be in better hands.

Just one factor caused concern. The man employed by Mr. John Shepherd to move the corn-mill had failed to reassemble it properly. The guardians warned Shepherd what would happen if the work was not done in a proper manner forthwith. The mill was soon ready.

Early in December, Henfield's Union paupers were moved to Shoreham; the Nep Town workhouse stood empty and silent.

Properly classified, the paupers occupied their pristine new quarters ready to continue a daily life as daunting as ever.

They were far from Henfield but all had the chance of a link with home by visits from friends any Tuesday or Friday between 10.00 a.m. and 4.00 p.m. – at the Governor's discretion.

There was one relaxation planned for them all. On Christmas Day the inmates would sit down to a dinner of roast beef and plum pudding provided by the generosity of their Union Guardians.

That Christmas certainly proved special. Snow began to fall Christmas Eve, soft and silent at first but late in the day increasing to a violent blizzard. Roads were completely blocked. In places the snow drifted fifteen feet deep. Stagecoaches halted at coaching inns, the White Hart happy to accommodate the "Royal Clarence"; driver, guard and passengers glad to have warmth and shelter. A flock of sheep at Betley Farm were buried deep and perhaps sheltered from the worst of the cold. All but one were later dug out alive. [5]

Amidst it all, the Union paupers settled to enjoy their roast beef and plum pudding. The pleasure would have to last a full year.

For the ordinary people of Henfield, Steyning and Bramber the year finished with a flurry of newspaper announcements promising astonishing speed in travel; the formation of a London to Brighton Railway 'Without a Tunnel' via the Adur Valley and Shoreham. Such were the claimed advantages of easier gradients and curves than on other proposed routes that it simply needed Parliamentary approval for the line to become reality. The New Year would tell.

The year began with a specially convened meeting of the parish vestry agreeing to sell the workhouse along with its stable, garden and orchard plus the adjacent three cottages and a plot of building land. The resulting money would be earmarked as part of Henfield's portion of costs for the new Union Workhouse.

The potential purchaser was George Vinall who had helped build the headmaster's house on the common. He saw it as an investment provided he could negotiate a favourable price.

Early in February the vestry met again and agreed that the buildings were actually in a very dilapidated state requiring a considerable amount to repair. Everything considered, they estimated the value at £835.

George Vinall was satisfied. The sale went ahead.

Through the months he converted the workhouse itself to a small terrace of tenements which he auctioned;

> A Freehold Property, 48 feet by 200 feet, of four tenements known as the Old Workhouse with a well of excellent water and an attached garden large enough for building houses – much wanted at Henfield. [6]

He sold the garden and plot of building ground as a separate lot.

William Borrer saw it all as another good investment and outbid other contenders. He decided to build a new school for the girls. They deserved modern, up to date facilities. The old converted cottage near the church did not provide them.

There was no joyful outcome for investors hoping to profit from the London to Brighton Railway 'Without a Tunnel'. Their hopes were dashed when M.P.s in Parliament decided to reject the idea.

In Henfield the stagecoach could rule supreme.

A group of Henfield enthusiasts more inspired by bat and ball than by speculative money ventures decided the cricket club should be reorganised.

Few now were the exploits famed on Henfield Common since the 1720's. It was high time to revive old challenges and contact new clubs.

The game had progressed over the years. No longer was the bowler content with an under arm delivery, accurate as the efficient proponent may be. There was a new style, round arm, legitimate as long as the arm was not raised above shoulder height. Speed could be astounding; skill in directing the ball not so easily achieved.

In May the men met and drew up rules for membership of Henfield Cricket Club: -

> A five shilling subscription due each 1st of May.
> Wednesday 5.00 p.m. practice games with forfeits, one penny, for anyone missing a fair catch or failing to score 5 in each innings.
> Failure to appear three Wednesdays, a sixpenny fine.
> A friend from out of the village may be invited if there are not sufficient numbers present to form the game.
> Any member degrading himself and party by getting in liquor before the match is played out, forfeit 2s 6d. [7]

With the rules agreed, they had just six weeks practice to prepare for their first fixture across at Hurstpierpoint's new Home Field ground.

The great day came and the match began, Henfield batting first with Songhurst and Fillery against the round arm might of Hurst.

What a start they made; both back for nought. Woolven went in, hit the ball, scampered and was run out, 0. Next in, secretary/treasurer Bignell; bowled, 0. Herrington; bowled 0. Blaker; hit 2 and run out. Williams; bowled 0.

Six wickets down for two runs!

In came Vallence. He hit and he banged and Hurst just could not dislodge him.

The tail wagged well 6 - 9 - 10 and 3 leaving hero of the team Vallence carrying his bat for 33 in a total of 68.

Hurst, far more used to the pronounced slope of their pitch, made 118 although none of them achieved a personal 33.

Henfield did well in their second innings. Nobody was out for 0 and Songhurst out hit everyone with 39. The side made 89 leaving Hurst 40 to make, a difficult task in the evening light. Henfield's confidence was high but evening light rapidly became failing light and the match ended with both teams certain they were denied victory.

The next season's Town Field match with Brighton proved a nail biter.

The first innings score would be crucial because it was to decide the result if the second innings could not be completed.

Brighton batted and fared none too well. The team's 65 run total was mainly thanks to wild deliveries by the Henfield bowlers – 21 wide balls.

In went Henfield. The opening pair were soon back; 6 for 2.

Batsmen were having great difficulty in coping with under arm bowler, Batchelor. His deliveries were consistently accurate. Runs came slowly.

At last the bowling change came and Henfield got into their stride. The new bowlers helped with 9 wides as the runs began to flow.

Eventually Henfield gained a commanding position, two to make with two wickets left; Lanaway unbeaten on 19 and keen to regain the strike, Fillery facing on 2.

The Brighton captain tried the only thing he could, give the ball to Batchelor. There would certainly be no more wides.

Batchelor bowled as straight as ever. His second delivery dismissed Fillery, his third did for last man Knight giving Brighton the vital first innings lead of just one run.

Their second innings closed at 88. 25 wides this time by Henfield's fast and furious bowlers.

Henfield went in again but at 29 for 3 there was no light left. Bowler Batchelor had gained the victory for Brighton.

Henfield could have pondered; their 46 wides against Batchelor's zero. Batchelor, the staunch proponent of under arm bowling – a sobering lesson. Henfield bowlers dismissed the incident; it was the sort of thing that happened in cricket.

One thing needed to happen for certain, having the common as the venue for matches. The Town Field was fine with the George so close for socialising but the true home of Henfield cricket was the common.

Members knew there were difficulties to overcome. Copyholders valued their Commoners Rights. For a man to stop grazing his animals just to accommodate cricket was asking a lot – but it would have to be asked.

Sheep on Henfield Common Cricket Pitch

An event that could go ahead on the common without infringing anybody's rights was a pigeon shoot. The prize was a new gun presented by Henfield gunsmith Peter Ward.

There were seven participants. Among them were the cricketing brothers Alfred and Arthur Smith, Henry Hughes (now owner of his late father's brewery and coal business at Mockbridge) and Peter Ward himself.

They would shoot from 21 yards at five birds each, with the charge of shot limited to two ounces.

The man who began missed his first and hit the rest. The next man missed his second and third so was out. The rest downed all five birds.

They had another three pigeons to shoot. Four men again scored 100%. The gun was now contested by placing two birds in the trap and shooting with a double-barrelled gun.

Alfred Smith shot first, downing both birds with each of his first two shots and missing one bird with his last. His brother missed one on his second shot and the chance came for Mr. Hughes. He fired; three double barrels, six birds.

It was now up to Mr. Ward to win his own gun. The trap opened. Out flew the birds. Bang, bang went the gun and only one pigeon fell. [8]

Henfield Common grew quiet again.

Henry Hughes set off home through the village, up Crouch Hill to the toll-gate and round to Mockbridge, happy owner of a new gun.

Chapter 11

Horse thieves – High Street oil lamps – Threatening drunks

Crouch Hill was a junction where a branch toll-road ran east to Ditchling across the main Brighton to London Turnpike.

It formed a useful alternative route to London with travellers able to join one of the fast five-hour coaches at the first staging inn out of Brighton, the Royal Oak near Hickstead.

The development of toll-roads had opened up the kingdom. Country hamlets, county towns and cities were now connected by a myriad turnpike companies.

In late July down the far end of West End Lane, William Keywood provided a horse and John Muzzall a spring-cart that would travel the toll-roads quite extensively. The eventual mileage would surprise them both.

The horse was in good condition; a strongly made, light chestnut seven year old with a small white streak down the forehead, light mane and tail, clean legged with a small scar on the knee. The cart, being well sprung, was a sound vehicle for travel; noticeable too in green paint with JOHN MUZZALL scribed clearly on the name board.

A Muzzall wagon at the carpenter's shop

The men's initial surprise was in discovering their property had been stolen.

John Muzzall's name board was soon recovered from Henfield Common but that was of little solace. Nor was the later news that a horse and cart answering the descriptions passed through the Hickstead Gate on the London Road between three and four o'clock.

It proved part of a spate of thefts in the area from Cowfold and Twineham right down to the coast at Portslade where a Mr. Cordy had his horse stolen; the ease of turnpike travel making life simple for thieves.

There was little the Henfield constable could do. William Keywood and John Muzzall had to accept their loss and carry on farming.

Down at Portslade, Mr. Cordy was riled and made no secret of it. He kept on about the theft, never let it out of his mind and spent an inordinate amount of time searching for his horse.

He made numerous enquiries, listened for leads and travelled the roads to London and beyond.

In late September word came of shady horse dealings going on in the Suffolk village of Ixworth beyond Bury St. Edmunds. Mr. Cordy decided to investigate.

He set off on the long journey. When he arrived at Ixworth he was shown an impounded horse and cart. The prospective vendors were under arrest. The horse was his. His determination had borne fruit.

Word was sent to William Keywood and John Muzzall. They, too, made the long journey and so had their second surprise; being reunited with the horse and cart.

Comfortably ensconced in the cart they made their way home at the steady pace set by the chestnut mare. Gates were reached and tolls paid until at last they passed through Cowfold and paid their final toll at Crouch Hill. The journey had been long but at last they were safely home.

The Cowfold and Henfield Road ended at 'the old maypole' which once stood in the meadow beside the 'Bee Hive' Brewery at Golden Square. There it became the Henfield and Brighton Road making its sharp turn onto the common. Although the roads were maintained by different trusts there was no toll house where they met, the next payment not being due until Terry's Cross a mile towards Brighton.

The two trusts favoured different materials to surface their roads. The 'Cowfold' used gravel from Shoreham brought by barge to a private wharf at Mock Bridge. The 'Brighton' kept to traditional flint off the Downs, 60 loads each of 60 bushels heaped, delivered as the turnpike trust decreed and chipped to size by the road gang.

At Terry's Cross the traveller could go from the sublime to the ridiculous; off the flint of the toll road onto a parish road to its abrupt end at the edge of Oreham Common. At the far side could be seen more parish road to Woodsmill but in between lay the 'ridiculous', the common itself, patterned in summer by wheel ruts and hoof dents, in winter by impassable mud holes.

It was Nathaniel Borrer of Hurstpierpoint who decided enough was enough. He was paying a highway rate to Henfield vestry at sixpence in the £1, the approach road ran beside his land and he was not going to ignore the issue. He had begun a case against the parish the previous summer but fine weather had set in before court proceedings could be carried out and the common had become dry and hard.

Now February mud lay thick. He determined to reopen proceedings.

He instructed his bailiff to lay a complaint at the Petty Sessions against Messrs Wisden and Sharp, waywardens of Henfield, for neglecting to repair a highway called Horn Lane, leading from Woods Mill, over Oreham Common to a highway called Bramlands.

At court the vestry's responsibility for roads was outlined. Although Horn Lane each side of Oreham Common was a Parish Road, the condition of the common itself was not a vestry matter.

The magistrates seemed unimpressed.

Mr. Kinchin, a respected Sussex road surveyor, deposed that he had inspected the road and about half a mile of it was out of repair being impassable for carriages and horses. The court instructed a Horsham surveyor to prepare a detailed report ready for the next special session for highways.

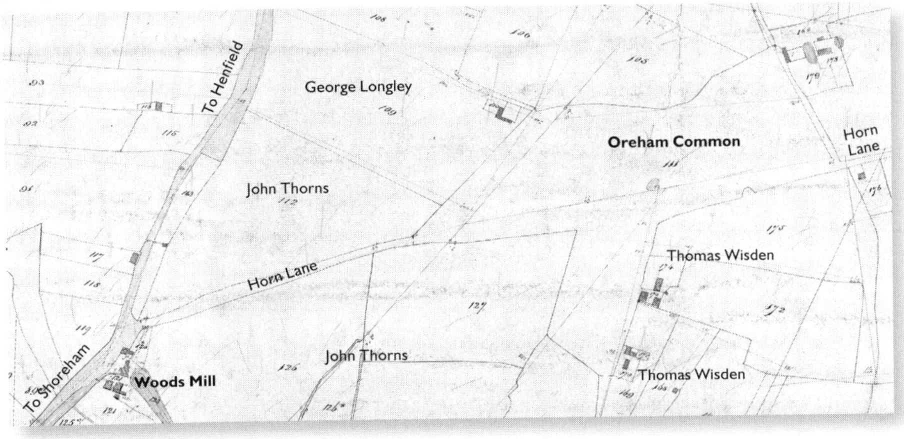

1845 Tithe Map; Horn Lane and Oreham Common with landowners

The Horsham man found all was as had been described. He estimated a considerable sum of money would be needed to put the road into proper repair. The magistrates ordered the work to be done by Michaelmas and imposed a small fine plus costs on the waywardens.

The vestry paid both fines and costs. Henfield rate payers dug deep for finance and the road gang had seven months work making an acceptable surface across Oreham Common.

Nathaniel Borrer could feel satisfied that his coachman would now be able to negotiate the way in complete safety.

Safety precautions proved a deciding factor one day for John Piper out at Pokerlee Farm.

As an agricultural labourer, John had chosen The Plough Club as the safety net for his wife and five children should his employment fail. Normally there was no danger. Through spring and summer there was continual work progressing from seed time to haymaking and harvest. In winter they cleared ditches, laid hedges and coppiced, pollarded or felled trees.

One day, John and two mates were set to fell a pollarded oak. It was run of the mill work; tie a rope a fair way up the tree, cut partly through the trunk, drive wedges in and finally heave on the rope to bring the tree down.

This time the men dispensed with the rope. They made the cuts, drove the wedges in and put their shoulder to the trunk; John between his mates.

They were tough men. The tree toppled.

John's mates ran – the tree was doing the impossible, falling their way! John, trapped in the middle, could not get out quickly enough and was crushed to death.

At the inquest, the coroner's verdict was; "Accidentally killed". That afternoon, The Plough Club members, with black gloves and hat bands in accordance with Club rules, attended John's funeral.

His widow would be unable to bring her children up on Club payments. Work or another marriage were her alternatives to the family being taken into the Union Workhouse.

'Lossam' and Mahala Ward also suffered bereavement.

Their older son Samuel, at 21 beginning his manhood, developed a cough that worsened and gradually sucked away his vitality until he was obliged to take to his bed.

'Lossam' and Mahala knew he had consumption, the disease that seemed to strike at random and carry off so many.

Through the months, they gave Samuel as much devoted attention as they could but no matter what they tried he became weaker and during the summer he died.

The curate conducted the burial service and Samuel was laid to rest.

Their grief was overwhelming.

They somehow found money for a proper headstone and had it engraved;

"Himself took our infirmities and bare our sickness" Mat 8, 17. [2]

Mahala bore her grief. 'Lossam' became more aggressive.

The question of the ministration of the church during the vicar's continual absence at West Stoke was a matter of great concern weighing on William Borrer's mind. Sunday worship at St. Peter's would remain as a single service unless the means were found to improve the stipend of their curate. Either the parish found the money or the present situation continued until Rev. Guy passed on to the greater life.

Mr. Borrer quietly sounded out parishioners willing to give sufficient financial backing.

He found a like mind in Lucretia Wood who still championed the village and its people although she had moved away to Brighton.

Together they provided £2000 for trustees to finance future curates who would hold two services each Sunday and celebrate Holy Communion at least once each month.

A conscientious young curate, Charles Dunlop, was appointed.

St. Peter's again held two Sunday services, parish events were supported and people knew they had a man who cared.

Both Lucretia Wood and William Borrer were delighted that their endeavours were having such effect.

William Borrer had the added delight that the new curate was the fiancé of his lovely daughter, Fanny.

They were married the next year and William Borrer acted towards them the very way his own father had to him. He had an elegant house built, Red Oaks; a spacious mansion set back at the end of Cagefoot Lane.

People, if they chose, could suggest Rev. Dunlop's appointment was manipulated but all would agree he was a sincere man willing to accept all duties incumbent upon him and more beside.

Indifferent health was Rev. Dunlop's handicap, something to which he would never readily succumb.

Sunday church continued an occasion of strict decorum, a time of quiet worship with a stirring sermon.

On occasions a visiting clergyman took part leading the prayers at morning service.

Rev. Wallinger did so coming all the way from Hastings for the occasion. Charles Dunlop preached; his chosen text, Job, chapter 14, verses one and two: "Man born of woman is short-lived and full of disquiet. He blossoms like a flower and then he withers."

The curate, warming to his theme, was delivering an impressive sermon – apt comment, anecdotal tale and telling testament which reached a sudden climax in an enormous crash as Rev. Wallinger fell senseless at the reading desk. The congregation were stunned; such disquiet, such withering – the foreboding of Job.

The correct people reacted the correct way and soon there was solemn rejoicing as Reverend Wallinger stirred to life again. He had merely fainted. [3]

On the Tuesday, Rev. Dunlop hosted the Sunday School children and teachers in a spacious marquee on the lawn in front of Red Oaks. Great was the pleasure of the curate, of Mrs. Dunlop and of William Borrer Esq. with several resident gentry as some 300 children enjoyed their bountiful tea. The gleeful festivities lasted into the evening only to be brought to an early end by the onset of heavy rain.

The day had also been important for those who chose to worship at the Congregational Church; the 12th Anniversary of its institution in the High Street close to but entirely apart from The Plough Inn. A visiting preacher from Arundel gave an excellent sermon in the morning choosing a New Testament text from St Paul's 2nd Letter to the Corinthians; "I believed and therefore I spoke out." The congregation sat listening for well over an hour – how vast were the depths and length of their preacher's belief.

In the afternoon they held a public meeting to encourage people to great efforts for benevolent purposes in general.

That evening they listened intently to the Rev. Ashton. He had travelled down from Putney especially to deliver an important lecture on the extensive range of parental responsibility.

Rev. Ashton was a very thorough man. Parents could but wonder at the extent of their responsibilities as he continued unabated, raindrops rattling on the roof. In the shelter of the chapel, inclement weather would not cause a premature end to the Anniversary Celebrations lecture.

Finally Rev. Ashton finished. The congregation left the shelter of the building and stepped out into the High Street.

Although wet and puddled, it was a High Street they were now able to negotiate with greater ease. The vestry had undertaken to make the pavements safer by the installation of oil lamps strategically placed to brighten the way. The lamps were now working.

Lamplighter, Jonathan Sayers, ensured there was always sufficient oil and kept the wicks neatly trimmed. He took a pride in his work serving his public well by ensuring the lamps were lit and extinguished at the correct hours.

To cover expenses, a lighting rate was set at 3d in the £1. For some rateable families just above the poverty line it proved too much and the vestry exempted them; a decision authorised at the April Petty Sessions when the waywardens presented their account books.

The police accounts for the year were audited at a meeting of the principal inhabitants and rate payers chaired by Rev. Charles Dunlop at the White Hart. A new rate was set for the coming year. [4]

The organisation of policing in West Sussex lagged behind neighbouring authorities. East Sussex and Brighton already had efficient police similar to Robert Peel's Metropolitan Police but the Western Quarter Sessions had not instituted Parliament's advisory legislation for establishing their own force. Instead, they continued with annual parish constables and made piecemeal alterations to the ancient Night Watch.

Two improvements were made by the Government. The parish was able to appoint a constable with authority over three parochial constables. Staves had to be issued to them for protection and assistance in making arrests. [5]

Henfield appointed William Short. The parish men would continue normal life and be called upon only when needed. An allowance was set for each task they undertook. Night watching to prevent felony was 3s 0d, pursuing offenders 2s 6d and apprehending a vagrant 1s 0d.

Constable Short was a dependable man but not a native of the village; in some ways an advantage, in others not. He and his wife lived in one of the tenements converted from the Old Workhouse by builder George Vinall.

Much of the constable's time was spent maintaining the peace in the evening well after most people's working day had finished.

Saturdays were busiest, particularly around the Plough on a summer evening. There, the wide forecourt with its two shady elm trees was the venue for regular bare-knuckle contests for any man from around the area to prove his prowess. A show of blood spattering fights was an almost guaranteed accompaniment to the evening's beer.

The landlord's profits were assured. The constable's handcuffs were ready.

Late December was another prime time.

Constable Short was standing quietly alert in shadow between the High Street oil lamps at 11.30 p.m. with the New Year just half an hour away. Down the road, the Plough door opened and noise erupted. A group of men emerged, loud-voiced from drink.

Constable Short moved forward. Holding his lanthorn aloft he commanded them to calm down and go home quietly.

His words were answered by a volley of abuse and the promise that his lanthorn was about to be smashed.

Five drunken men in threatening mood; confrontation would be risky. He stepped back out of trouble and advised them to disperse quietly. He could make out the features of three of them but the other two were indistinct.

They disappeared into the night; ribald comment tracking their way.

Constable Short finished his duty and returned home.

He accepted that the less responsible type of men became drunk wherever they lived and would continue to do so. He was also determined that belligerent drunkenness would have but one outcome, appearance before the Justices of the Peace at the Steyning Petty Sessions. The Plough mobsters, those of them that he could identify, would rue their behaviour.

Summonses were issued.

The three identified men duly stood before the justices.

The charges were read out. Constable Short gave his evidence. He was questioned;

"Did the men raise any stick or strike you?"

"No," he replied and explained how he had felt very apprehensive for his safety; one man against five threatening drunkards. Furthermore, he had a witness.

The witness affirmed the account. The accused men expressed sorrow that the constable had been caused any alarm.

It was judgement time; "Guilty". Each defendant would enter into his own recognisance of 10s 0d to keep the peace for a year and pay 18s 0d costs.

The men walked back to Henfield in sober mood. A week's wages for back chatting a constable, plus the chance of losing their ten shillings if they dare get a bit merry again during the next twelve months – must life be all drudgery?

Constable Short was more at ease. With the support of the Justices he could have greater confidence in dealing with future incidents.

That April he was again appointed police officer.

The White Hart

During November, members of the White Hart Benefit Club held their quarterly meeting; two hours of convivial camaraderie, drink, chatter and song. At its close they stepped outside into the night air and began exchanging unacceptably noisy Good Byes.

Constable Short noticed river men among them, hardened bargees. He would not risk kindly words of advice this time. He stepped forward and swung his truncheon. Richard West felt a fierce blow across his head. He staggered an instant and grabbed at his assailant. Next moment a blow across the nose left him gushing blood. He let go; the pain too intense.

So severe was the bleeding that friends took him up the street to Dr. Caudle. The doctor dressed the wound and sent West on his way – more than a mile's walk to his house out by the Adur near the New Inn.

Life as a bargeman had taught Richard West never to be put upon.

He had been severely assaulted. He would make his assailant pay for the insult.

Charges were made. This time it was the constable who appeared before the justices. Richard West described the attack. William Short explained how the bargeman had insulted him thereby causing the fracas.

The justices were well aware of drunken behaviour. After listening attentively to both men they consulted for several minutes and announced their decision. Constable Short was guilty of assault; he must pay a fine of £5. [6]

Richard West returned to his barge, a happy man.

Constable Short was able to regain something of his lost esteem by helping one of the day labourers, William Knight, who had gone out at 4.30 a.m. to go to work leaving his wife and little daughter alone in the house. He had not locked the door; he never did when going to work.

That morning when he returned a little after six he walked in and discovered a strange pair of shoes on the floor. He called up to his wife. She was still in bed and replied that she had not heard anyone about.

When she came downstairs they noticed a coat was missing. They then realised more clothes had gone – a pair of trousers, two shirts, a pair of half-boots, socks and two handkerchiefs.

The old shoes left in the kitchen suggested the thieves were vagrants. If so they must be on the road to somewhere.

William Knight guessed Brighton; their route probably the coach road over the hills behind Poynings. He set off.

Just beyond Poynings he saw a man and boy tramping the hill by Saddlescombe Farm. The man's boots were William's boots. On the man's back was William's coat.

William accosted the boy. He ran off crying, sobbing that he was frightened.

There was good reason. He had one of the shirts and a handkerchief.

The man insisted they had found the clothes and William should take them back if they were his.

William did, and being both strong and angry he took the two thieves as well.

It was when they reached Henfield that Constable Short was able to help. He took the pair into custody and prepared charges against them.

The case was heard at the Steyning Petty Sessions. 20 year old George Sebur maintaining the clothing had been found. His 10 year old young brother, another William, remaining silent.

The justices passed sentence: - George Sebur; four calendar months imprisonment, the first and last fortnight in solitary confinement. William Sebur; one week solitary confinement and to be once privately whipped.

Young William would surely break his silence.

15 year old Thomas Saunders, oldest child of sheep stealer Samuel and second wife Harriet, could have found himself in similar circumstances.

Their home was still the isolated farmhouse on Rye Island; coldly damp in winter and comfortless in summer.

It was a crowded house with eight children plus 80 year grandfather John Saunders. Samuel's weekly money hardly provided for daily needs.

When the younger children, from 12 year old Samuel to the year old twins, Abram and Isaac, went down with summer sickness, Mrs. Saunders sent Thomas up to the village for medicine from Dr. Morgan.

Whilst the doctor was out of the room preparing it, Thomas had time to look around. Fascinatingly near was something seemingly nothing to do with medicine or doctors, a small bottle with a strong smell of peppermint exceedingly attractive to a boy brought up on minimal food. Thomas was intrigued.

At last the doctor returned with the medicine and Thomas was able to set off on his mile walk home; medicine for sick children in his pocket along with a little something for himself.

Dr. Morgan discovered he was missing his bottle of essence of peppermint. There could be little doubt about who now had it.

Constable Short was called in. Enquiries were made at Rye.

Thomas next found himself in front of Steyning magistrates. Doctor Morgan declared he did not wish to press charges as the boy's master gave him an excellent reference. The magistrates confined themselves to giving him a severe reprimand leaving him in no doubt whatsoever of where he would be housed if he transgressed again. Thomas could consider himself exceedingly fortunate.

He returned to his comfortless home glad to be sharing the food his mother managed to provide without recourse to peppermint essence.

Chapter 12

Emigration – Midnight mutton – Transportation

Emigration was the extreme measure to escape life's privations. Henry Hoadley and his wife decided they could have a better future in Australia.

The next Christmas Day, Henry wrote home.

Adelaide 25th December 1840

Dear Cousin and friends,

We left the Thames on the 21st of April in the ship Lalla Rooki. We arrived in Adelaide on the 13th August, thus making the voyage, 16000 miles, in sixteen weeks .... There is one stage-coach that runs from the port to town and back every day. This is the only conveyance that looks at all English like. It was dusk when we arrived in Emigration Square, which consists of about forty low-built houses or huts of wood without chimnies. The country at first sight appeared something like a gentleman's park in England nicely studded with trees, which, all evergreen, instead of shedding their leaves shed their bark or rind yearly. The wood is very hard and much heavier than the timber in England. The stringy bark is most useful and is used here for roofing houses. Of birds, the parrot species is very numerous. There is also a bird, from its peculiar note called the "laughing jack-ass". It is about the size of a crow, of a black and white colour. The kangaroos are various; the emu, the black turkey and the opossum are all good for food. We have a good stream about half a mile from the town; it is called the River Torrens and supplies nearly the whole town. Many people get their living by fetching water. It is supplied at about 2s 6d a week. The town is already laid out, planned and mapped and the various streets named; but there are only three or four of any note yet .... There is a post office about half the size of one of your bathing machines .... We have as yet no coals here; we all burn wood and it is brought into the town on bullock drays and sells for 10s and 12s a load. Rent is very dear; the smallest cottage, if cottage it may be called, with only two rooms fetches 10s a week and so on up to £1; neither yard or garden, wood nor water, included. Carpenters, masons, sawyers, brick-makers and smiths get 14s a day. Other workers from 6s to 12s a day. Provisions are getting much cheaper than they were when we landed .... Almost everything else you may buy as in England except fruit; we can not get that at any price yet for there is none in the colony, except what is sent out from England such as preserved fruits. The natives are blacks, very harmless and very amusing. It is very hot now. The thermometer today stood at 112½ degrees. We have had no rain since September; the plains as far as the eye can see seem literally parched up, not a blade of grass to be seen for miles. The river runs no larger than the neck of a glass bottle but the water remains very good, yet the cattle seem to do well. We have very often heavy thunder and lightning, and whirlwinds innumerable, sometimes as many as a dozen in a day. We are troubled with hot winds from the north. The mosquitoes and the flies are a great nuisance; but speaking truly, with all these annoyances a persevering man may do better here than in England .... About 2000 acres of corn were grown this year in the colony; and the owners seem pretty well satisfied with their crops. I suppose the corn must be sent to a neighbouring colony to be ground; for we have no mills or barns. We very often see fires in the country. I suppose the blacks set the long grass on fire, to burn out the kangaroos. There are no fences or hedges for thousands of miles so that the fires often spread far. I have told you all I know; and it is the truth. I don't regret coming here. I am doing very comfortable. I shall not yet persuade my friends to come out that have a home in England for here are a great many men out of work. We continue to have fresh arrivals of emigrants. HENRY HOADLEY. [1]

Henry's Henfield friends and relations were pleased to receive the news of their safe arrival. For themselves they would stick to England's ice-cold north winds.

One of Henfield's single girls, Jane Shoulders, tried for a better life by journeying five miles away to Hurstpierpoint. Life was soon much brighter there because she was courted by William Peters, a tailor almost twice her age, who had journeyed a much greater distance himself having made his way from Cambridge.

They married at Hurst but moved down to Brighton finding lodgings with a labourer in Preece's Buildings off Regent Street; a passage way cul-de-sac of drab flint-faced houses with a door's width exit at the far end into neighbouring Church Street – shared water, shared toilet and shared knowledge of what everybody was doing.

The next year Jane gave birth to a son. William decided its name,

Hericlythus; perhaps involving confused echoes of Cambridge days. Two years later, Jane had a second son, Olinthus.

The children had fine names but there the finery ended. Life gave no favours, nothing to nourish infant bodies properly.

Another two years passed and Jane gave birth again, a daughter; no romantic naming this time, plain Sarah.

The arrival of little Sarah marked a change in family life. Within a few months, William walked out on his family.

There was no way Jane could find money for rent, clothes, fuel or even food. She had only one course open to her, ask aid from the Brighton Vestry.

The vestry responded. The family could have temporary shelter in the workhouse as soon as entry formalities were completed.

That done, the taking-in process began with a visit to the probationary ward for thorough cleansing and an inspection by the medical officer. They were then issued with Brighton Workhouse purple dress. Their own would be stored until they became independent again. Next they were shown the day room and sleeping areas. The stay would be as permanent as need be provided Jane's correct settlement parish was Brighton.

The guardians took her before the magistrates for her examination to ensure she really did belong to Brighton.

She explained how her grandfather and her father were both Henfield people but that she was lawfully married to William Peters by whom she had her three children.

The magistrates accepted her statement and explained that her husband's desertion meant she now reverted to her maiden settlement which, as she had told them, was Henfield. She and her children would be removed 'Home'.

Brighton promptly provided transport and an escort.

Dressed in their own clothes again, they arrived in Henfield, Jane grateful to be back in familiar surroundings.

The Henfield overseer was confident room would be found in the Union Workhouse and took them off to Shoreham. Jane would not be in familiar surroundings after all.

Once more entry formalities were carried out. This time the workhouse dress code was steel grey.

Jane had to undergo more questioning which threw doubt on the validity of the Removal Order. It seemed the man Peters was possibly a bigamist. Steyning Union commanded Henfield to lodge an appeal.

It was heard at the Lewes Quarter Sessions. Solicitors argued and magistrates listened. There was no easy answer. The magistrates favoured confirming the removal but accepted the case should be decided at a higher court, The Queen's Bench in Westminster Hall.

At the High Court, Henfield's case was upheld. Jane Peters should be moved back from Shoreham Workhouse to Brighton's – dressed in permanent purple.[2]

That autumn 7 year old Hericlythus died. Within two years brother Olinthus was also dead; he, too, was 7. Each was given space in pauper graves to lie unmarked and quickly forgotten. Jane and Sarah disappeared within the folds of Brighton pauperism.

The Henfield Peters, John and Elizabeth, in their tenement up the alley near the workhouse had been through the sadness of losing their first daughter – Elizabeth, baptised by Rev. George Hall in his early days at the Congregational Church. They now had the blessings of four children; Harriet, Caroline, John and Mary Anne.

John led the normal labouring man's life; six days a week hard work throughout the year with precious little to show for it.

Just before Christmas, life fell apart for him at the death of his wife. Without her, normality ceased.

Although devastated, John determined to keep doing his best. He hired a young housekeeper to look after the children whilst he made sure he supplied them as well as he could. This had never been easy and now, without a wife to organise the day, he had to be more inventive.

The provision of meat caused most difficulty but he did manage to provide regular mutton, something he had previously considered beyond his means. Had the neighbours known he was giving his children such food there may have been raised eyebrows. John wisely did not discuss such things.

Late on an April evening when most households were already settled for the night, John set out for his next mutton. He made his way down by the Tanyard, past the church, along the Parsonage Farm lane and across two meadows into Farmer Stapley's turnip field. There, wattle fencing separated 45 fat wethers ready for market from a larger group of store animals still to be brought up to condition.

John leaned over the wattles, seized a sheep, pulled it out and set to work. He cut its throat and let the blood flow before beginning the heavy task of carrying the carcass back to Nep Town.

It was uphill much of the way home. The weight of the sheep on his shoulders made it a slow walk.

When John reached the the bridleway beside the Town Field he stopped. He lowered the sheep onto the path and made a quick diversion into gardener Gander's Potwell Field of vegetables. There he picked a good supply of broccoli.

His foraging complete, he took up his sheep again, carried on to the Nep Town road, crossed it and quietly went up the alley to his house.

By dawn next morning Farmer Stapley's shepherd was back at his Turnip Field flock doing the morning numbers check. 169 store sheep all correct but only 44 fat; one missing. The shepherd knew at once – sheep stealing again; a third theft in three months. He walked round the wattles and found blood. Leading from it were foot prints neatly paced amongst the turnips.

The trail continued across fields, along the lane and right up to the Nep Town Road. There they ceased, lost among the mud and wheel tracks.

The shepherd told Mr. Stapley. He informed parochial constable, John Burtenshaw.

John Burtenshaw reported the matter to his superior, Constable Short at his Workhouse Cottage.

Together they went to the scene of the crime and from there traced the footmarks again across the fields, up the lane and almost back to the cottage.

All the evidence indicated a Nep Town crime. It would mean a systematic search being made house by house beginning at the tenements in the first alley.

There they came to John Peters' home.

The housekeeper answered their knock and showed them into the kitchen.

On the fire was an iron pot; in the air an appetising aroma, a meaty aroma.

Constable Short lifted the lid – a sheep's head simmering. They would have to investigate further.

In a cupboard were three sacks; two empty, the third containing the skin of a sheep. Beside the sacks lay an axe – a new axe in Constable Short's opinion.

Burtenshaw was instructed to find Peters. Short continued his search.

Upstairs in a side cupboard was more mutton; two shoulders, two legs and two pieces of neck.

Back downstairs he found yet more boiled neck and a crock full of boiled fat. The evidence was overwhelming. This was no longer investigation, it was confirmation. Could there be more pieces outside?

He took a spade and dug at the soft area where the water ran from the house – he unearthed sheep entrails.

There was still the garden – entrails of a second sheep.

Constable Burtenshaw returned with Peters. He was marched down to the police station, made to take off his half-boots and was secured in the lock-up.

The next morning the constables set off with the half-boots to match them with the footprint trail.

At Parsonage Farm the shepherd was waiting. Together they fitted the boots into eight of the muddied footprints; the perfect match.

There was another line to follow, the axe line. Carpenter John Martin had reported one missing.

He was shown the axe and declared it was his. Blacksmith John Hider recognised it as the one he had recently made for a client. His journeyman blacksmith, Richard Holcombe, further along Nep Town, recalled having been given it to regrind and sharpen.

Constable Short now had to use his organisational skills to ensure everyone attended the magistrate for the prisoner's examination.

The following day they were assembled ready for magistrate Mr. Hugh Ingram. Each gave his evidence, scribed by the clerk and signed by the witness.

Constable Short signed his with a flourish; he was accustomed to such procedures. Richard Holcombe managed a very misshapen X – his skill was with hot iron. John Peters put a respectable X at the end of his deposition explaining how he had been offered the axe by a man on Barrow Hill who asked three shillings but had been given only two.

Most then returned home. The constable continued to Petworth with his prisoner who would spend the next eight days in the House of Correction. At the end of that time he would be called to answer two charges of theft at the Quarter Sessions.

John Peters spent a lonely week meditating. How long before he was with his children again? He had been trying to look after them, to give them food like other families. They had lost their mother. They needed their father.

Quarter Sessions day began. The mutton case came on. Yet another case of sheep stealing, this time with a second offence as well, theft of an axe.

The prisoner was offering no acceptable defence. The case was clear, as was the nature of the sentence that law decreed the court should impose.

The judge had no hesitation. Ten years transportation. Next case. [3]

John Peters was stunned, bewildered.

He did not have long to wait. A fortnight later he was beside the River Thames in a cell of Millbank, the holding prison for those sentenced to transportation. He kept himself to himself as all the men did. It was solitary confinement; wooden stool, wooden wash tub, hammock, bedding and bible with a small window overlooking the exercise yard.

His prison report stated him deeply affected by his situation; no previous conviction, behaviour in prison good, destination Van Diemen's Land.

On the 5th of May he sailed, still penned behind bars, on the ship *BARROSA* bound for the opposite side of the world. He would never see his children again.

Their welfare was in the hands of the Union Guardians.

Harriet and Caroline were old enough to enter into service as kitchen maids. Places were found for them.

The younger two, John and Mary Anne, still needed a secure home.

The guardians decided it would be the Union Workhouse.

The task of carrying out the decision fell to Relieving Officer, James Puttock.

Puttock took John and Mary Anne down to Shoreham and left them there.

Although he and his wife were childless, he had no wish to condemn any person's children to the workhouse. At such times, a Relieving Officer's duties seemed not so much relieving as sentencing; a disturbing feature of life.

Chapter 13

A gunshot - Workhouse life - A mother seeks justice

The Union Guardians held their weekly meetings Wednesday evenings. James Puttock's custom was to drive his chaise to the Bridge Inn at Shoreham, partake of his chosen refreshment and leave for the meeting soon after five o'clock.

One April evening, about an hour after he had taken his leave of the landlord and gone out, another Relieving Officer entered the inn asking after him.

The landlord was able to put him at ease; Puttock had already left and was on his way.

Later that evening, the landlord's young daughter went across the yard to the privy. The door was locked.

When her mother went across a few minutes later it was still locked. She spoke to her husband and he too tried the door.

He decided to force an entry. It was difficult, an obstruction of some sort.

In the end he broke the door down.

The obstruction was revealed; James Puttock in a puddle of blood – a pistol in his hand, a hole through his head.

Next day, the inquest jury ascertained the time of death as about 7 o'clock when the landlord's son had heard a gunshot. Suicide they agreed but not whether the man was sane at the time. [1]

The Union Guardians kept to essentials and advertised for another Relieving Officer explaining that provided the essential qualifications of good handwriting and accounting ability were met, preference would be given to a married person.

A Storrington man, William Stent Challen, fulfilled all the criteria.

He was given the position and moved to Henfield, a house right on the Common Corner at Golden Square – the house vacated by Widow Puttock.

William Challen's wife had recently given birth to her first child. Their future was secure.

One of his first tasks was to deal with the family of Thomas 'Quality'

Shoulders who belied his nickname and went off leaving them chargeable to Henfield vestry.

The case was a simple introduction. Quality's wife and children would follow John and Mary Anne Peters into the workhouse.

Once there, they were thoroughly cleansed and inspected by the medical officer.

That done, they received their regulation clothing in the Union's distinct style and colour. For Mrs. Shoulders it was the steel-grey dress, a bonnet, purple hose and leather boots. Her girls were mini editions with the inclusion of a close fitting white woollen jersey. The older boys mirrored the men; corduroy trousers, fustian waistcoat and steel-grey jacket but with a cap instead of a felt hat. The boys younger than nine wore a simple 'dress' with their jacket and trousers. The final item for men and boys alike was the round frock worn to protect their other clothes.

Tailors tendered for the supply of jackets, coats and trousers; shoemakers for boots and shoes.

Female inmates made most other clothing, cutting and sewing their way through bulk orders of cloth; Welsh Flannel, Brown Holland and Check Linen.

Any finished garments surplus to workhouse needs were sold to local retailers; important income for the Union.

The seamstresses took great care over their work. Any error could be construed as a 'Wilful Mistake' under the wide umbrella of 'shall be deemed disorderly'. For any such offender there was distinguishing dress, special accommodation and reduced food as the Board of Guardians considered appropriate.

Men were more likely to offend through 'neglecting to work'.

Their contributions to the Union purse came through the sale of offal from the corn-mill, potatoes, coffins and coffin boards.

The final money maker, oakum, came via the sore fingers of both men and women unravelling and separating tightly bound old rope. It was a tedious task, the aspect of workhouse life causing most resentment.

The authorities were confident four hours work picking a minimum two pounds of oakum was fair return for food and lodging. Any recalcitrant pauper would face Petty Sessions justice.

The Union's 'disorderly' umbrella also covered obscene or profane language, noise when silence was ordered, insulting another pauper, failing in personal cleanliness, pretending illness, wilfully damaging property and disobeying authority. [2]

Apart from those things, the inmates could concentrate on living by the bell – the six o'clock rising bell signalling time to prepare for the morning roll call and inspection, the breakfast bell, work bell and dinner bell through to the 8.00 p.m. bed bell.

Children had their own tasks; cleaning their living and sleeping areas and mending their clothing. If they needed help they could apply for it.

Their education was of great concern to the authorities. Each day except the Sabbath had to include at least three hours schooling – reading, writing and the principles of Christian religion – by a school master and mistress having good references and appointed after interview by the guardians.

Despite references and interviews, the guardians had difficulty retaining their schoolmasters. Several resigned and moved on. One who did seem content to stay had a penchant for drink and became intoxicated once too often which, added to other deeds of disobedience towards the guardians, caused his dismissal. [3]

A new schoolmaster was appointed at a £15 salary. He was young, not yet 20, and came from a London workhouse with good references concerning his ability and his attention to worship. He was doing well until he, too, fell from favour with the board. He was called before them to explain himself. His explanation was not entirely satisfactory and he was told to await their decision.

He knew his good standing with the board was over and he pre-empted them by resigning. They paid his outstanding salary, £3 3s 6d.

When the Poor Law Commissioners enquired the reason for his resignation, the Board gave a guarded reply; he had caused disruptive trouble on more than one occasion.

Such sudden resignation made it difficult for the schoolmaster to apply for another position and he wandered the roads through to Hertfordshire where he was detained and imprisoned as a vagrant.

During his weeks of wandering, the Poor Law Commissioners enquired more closely into his resignation and required the Union Guardians to be explicit in their answer.

That explicit answer in turn required the involvement of the police. Their information network became operative and as the schoolmaster stepped free from prison in Hertford he was arrested on a charge of perpetrating abominable crimes with the boys under his care.

He was conveyed to Petworth and put on trial at the following assizes. There he was found guilty of having committed a criminal assault on a ten year old boy. He was sentenced to two years' imprisonment with hard labour. The guardians could express considerable satisfaction that the man had been brought to justice.

School education was supplemented by training in habits of usefulness, industry and virtue.

Opportunities were there for every child reaching employable age. Shoreham shipping masters offered apprenticeships to 16 year old boys, a secure future and adventure at sea. Henry Martin jumped at the chance to sail with Capt. Cheesman on the brig "Sussex". Documents were completed and passed to the Comptroller of Customs for registration. He refused the registration. Henry's hopes were dashed.

The Guardians sought a Poor Law ruling. Assistant Commissioner Hawley redeemed himself a little by castigating the official. Henry could sail aboard the "Sussex" suitably clothed at Union expense as soon as Captain Cheesman had completed another voyage to the north of England where seamen's outfits could be bought at a cheaper price.

The girls had to be content with going into service at a wage of one shilling a week, with clothing provided by the Union.

Matron Mary Seaborne was responsible for ensuring the girls' necessary training in habits of obedience and good manners.

Occasionally a child stepped out of line. Harriett Sayers did so and had to be summarily corrected.

When Harriett's parents heard of the incident they took exception. Medical officer Mr. Martin (no relation of sailor apprentice Henry) became involved and supported their concerns. He wrote a strongly worded letter to the guardians.

The incident was considered at the next Board Meeting attended by Mr. Martin, the child with her parents, the governor and the matron. It was decided the matter should be investigated further. Letters were sent calling all guardians to attend the following week.

At that meeting, both sides stated the facts as they saw them. The governor and matron were closely questioned about the girl's complaint. The guardians were determined not to condone any untoward disciplinary retribution on the children. They considered the facts in detail.

Finally they announced their unanimous opinion that Harriet Sayers had not been hit in the eye by the matron with her clenched fist.

Members were equally of the opinion that although the matron was being acquitted of the more serious part of the charge, enough had been admitted to call forth the guardians' strong disapproval of the initial concealment of the affair.

The Chairman admonished both the governor and his wife. In future they would limit the use of the cane to the palm of the hand.

Harriet Sayers had unwittingly done her part for the well being of the children but Mr. Martin was not really satisfied with the findings.

He wrote again requesting to be informed whether the board declared the case of Harriet Sayers so trumpery that it ought never to have been brought before them and also what the opinion of the board was regarding his conduct therein.

The board informed him of their approval of his calling their attention to the event but they disapproved of his stance over it.

That done, they referred to the final part of his letter calling attention to the case of Mary Shoulders who had complained of a severe beating and kicking.

Mr. Martin attended the next Guardian's meeting and provided particulars saying the assault had taken place about five months previously and that Miss Deane the late schoolmistress and Mr. White, the schoolmaster knew something.

The board proceeded to investigate the case but decided the girl appeared well enough and there was insufficient evidence to support any assault.

Mr. Martin made no more complaints but he was able to feel partial satisfaction when the guardians decided that the well behaved female paupers should be separated from 'those of an opposite character'. Plans were drawn up and the buildings were adapted. The good girls could keep good.

By her fifteenth birthday Mary Shoulders had a place as servant with a Henfield family. Workhouse days were past.

The failure of the girls to receive any compensation for ill treatment was reflected when a young workhouse mother, Ann Hunter, appeared in neat workhouse dress seeking justice at the Petty Sessions for her baby's upkeep.

She had moved to the workhouse from the Bull Inn where she had been living as a servant. She was confident her removal from there had been instigated by a Henfield tailor, Alfred Cain. He denied any involvement in the matter but she stood by her word; he was her little baby's father.

The judges explained that without corroborative evidence no order could be made. Ann flared inwardly. Corroborative evidence! What did their lordships think life was?

Ann and her baby returned to the workhouse where the facts of life were stark: nothing to do with love – just the provision of work in exchange for the provision of succour.

The cost of providing such succour was of constant concern to the Guardians. It was imperative to keep the poor rate minimal.

When some of the grandchildren of James and Sarah Hoadley became chargeable to the Union, the Guardians decided that the pair were perfectly able to provide maintenance and should be doing so.

The Henfield Overseers were told to begin summary proceedings.

James Hoadley farmed Eastout – appropriately named being out in the east of the parish – a small farm but productive enough to support them all. He and Sarah were happy to look after their grandchildren.

Union proceedings proved unnecessary.

For the children it was a completely new experience.

They slept in beds with feather mattresses. On the fiercest winter evenings a warming pan could be slipped in for a few minutes on its way to their grandparents' big four poster bed. A commode allowed night comfort.

They washed at a basin in a special stand and ensured neat appearance by using a swing mirror, something outside their old life.

Oak and deal chests held freshly laundered linen.

Downstairs was different, too. Their grandmother had a thick carpet in her parlour with another thin cover on top to keep it clean. The table was polished. There were two tall clocks she wound up, one each day.

The children had tasks to carry out; eggs to collect, hens to feed and swill to go in the pig troughs.

In autumn there were apples to gather and pile in the cider press.

Discipline was strict. There were places to keep clear of; the big box churn turning cream to butter, the press for the farm's distinctive cheese and most particularly their grandfather brewing beer, sufficient for his thirsty farm labourers.

Long experience had taught James Hoadley how to run his farm efficiently; how many times to plough each field, how many times they needed to be harrowed before rolling, his best crop rotation, the meadows to set aside for grass and clover hay, when cattle should be in the fatting barn and the day to day tasks that should never be overlooked. [4]

The children shared the rewards. Thanks to the tireless efforts of their grandparents, their future was as secure as that of the majority of village children.

Chapter 14

Village farms – Ploughman's whip – Haymaking frolics

There were more than 20 farms in Henfield. Even the biggest was small – certainly so compared with the 11500 acres of the Duke of Richmond's Goodwood Estate where large scale farming improvements could be developed. Henfield had mimicked the duke over the workhouse corn-mill but farming was incomparable.

Most of the smaller farms were leased to tenant farmers.

Stephen Tugwell worked his way up to become foreman and then tenant at Rye and neighbouring Brookside farms.

Ancient droveways linked them with Pokerlee towards the old manor house at Streatham and with Bineham Bridge over the Adur giving access to Ashurst and the market at Steyning.

He built up a herd of ten cows, all in calf, 14 steers and heifers and 11 calves just weaned.

The brooks were excellent summer grazing for the cattle and provided hay for winter feed. He had stacked about 40 tons of meadow hay and 7 tons of clover.

When his harvest was complete and ready for the threshers there were10 loads of wheat in the straw, 60 of oats and 50 of barley.

He cropped 10 loads of peas and 20 of beans. An acre of rich arable land had been planted with potatoes soon to be dug up.

Stephen had every reason to feel satisfied with his harvest but before he could set his men to threshing he received a communication from the Sheriff of Sussex. Creditors had taken action to recover unpaid debts.

Everything was subject to auction on the 18th October at 11 o'clock precisely; his stock, crops and implements.

He lost the lot, slid back down the social ladder and became a labourer.

Brookside's owner, Dr. Weekes of Hurstpierpoint, advertised for a new tenant describing his farm as 105 acres in a high state of production with arable, meadow and woodland abounding with game. The farmhouse, which was in some need of repair, and two barns were on good land near one of the streams intersecting the brooks.

The successful applicant was Stephen Stammer who farmed in Rustington. He refused to inhabit the farmhouse, locked the door and waited at Rustington while a new house was built on the higher ground above Dagbrook Lane, the occupational road from Broadmare Common.

William Keywood farmed Rye along with his adjacent land at New Inn. The inn, although small, had good custom from the surrounding farms and the barges working along the river. It supplemented income when farm returns were poor.

With New Inn and Rye having some of the lowest lying fields, William kept three rowing boats – a necessity for winter floods, the downside of brookland farming.

At William's death, the farms' livestock, carts, ploughs and implements were put up for sale. The advertisement was inclusive enough to attract the attention of farmers throughout the area.

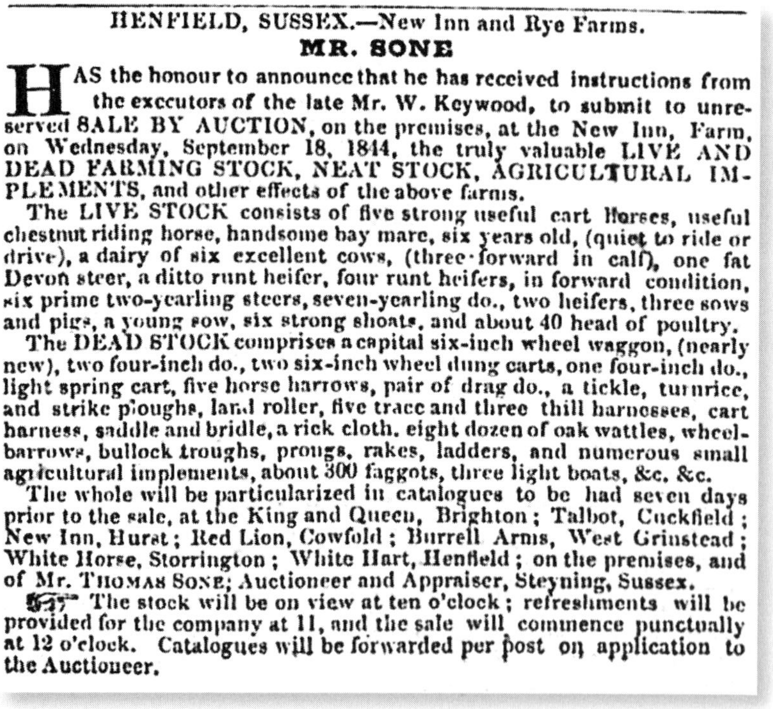

HENFIELD, SUSSEX.—New Inn and Rye Farms.

MR. SONE

HAS the honour to announce that he has received instructions from the executors of the late Mr. W. Keywood, to submit to unreserved SALE BY AUCTION, on the premises, at the New Inn, Farm, on Wednesday, September 18, 1844, the truly valuable LIVE AND DEAD FARMING STOCK, NEAT STOCK, AGRICULTURAL IMPLEMENTS, and other effects of the above farms.

The LIVE STOCK consists of five strong useful cart Horses, useful chestnut riding horse, handsome bay mare, six years old, (quiet to ride or drive), a dairy of six excellent cows, (three forward in calf), one fat Devon steer, a ditto runt heifer, four runt heifers, in forward condition, six prime two-yearling steers, seven-yearling do., two heifers, three sows and pigs, a young sow, six strong shoats, and about 40 head of poultry.

The DEAD STOCK comprises a capital six-inch wheel waggon, (nearly new), two four-inch do., two six-inch wheel dung carts, one four-inch do., light spring cart, five horse harrows, pair of drag do., a tickle, turnrice, and strike ploughs, land roller, five trace and three thill harnesses, cart harness, saddle and bridle, a rick cloth, eight dozen of oak wattles, wheelbarrows, bullock troughs, prongs, rakes, ladders, and numerous small agricultural implements, about 300 faggots, three light boats, &c. &c.

The whole will be particularized in catalogues to be had seven days prior to the sale, at the King and Queen, Brighton; Talbot, Cuckfield; New Inn, Hurst; Red Lion, Cowfold; Burrell Arms, West Grinstead; White Horse, Storrington; White Hart, Henfield; on the premises, and of Mr. THOMAS SONE, Auctioneer and Appraiser, Steyning, Sussex.

☞ The stock will be on view at ten o'clock; refreshments will be provided for the company at 11, and the sale will commence punctually at 12 o'clock. Catalogues will be forwarded per post on application to the Auctioneer.

New Inn and Rye Farms for Sale

John Burtenshaw, a keen cricketer, farmed Rye including Mr. Borrer's rebuilt barn that had been burnt down the night of the Steyning riot.

William Keywood's son took over as landlord at the New Inn.

Six or so dairy cows were the norm for Henfield's smaller farms; hardly a herd but sufficient to supply the household and customers in the vicinity.

At Barrow Hill farm, Richard and James Martin had small Alderneys, docile and famed for their rich, creamy milk. They also fattened Sussex steers and Herefords for beef.

Steyning market was an important, but not guaranteed, sales outlet for beef cattle attracting butchers from a wide area.

A spring market could have over a hundred cattle and a thousand sheep along with a far smaller number of calves, lambs and pigs.

A day of too many animals favoured the butcher. Farmers had to reduce their asking price even for good class beasts. Days of small supply commanded higher prices.

Market days were busy days for Steyning High Street with farmers, butchers and drovers on social or shopping missions in town.

Very occasionally an incident upset the rhythm of the day.

Baker's assistant Mrs. Standing sparked one when a drover came in for a twopenny loaf of bread. The drover was hardly out of the shop when Mrs. Standing noticed a money bag on the counter. She quickly went to the door and called after the drover. He fortunately heard her and she was able to hand the bag to him, thankful to have served her customer well.

Business continued smoothly until a worried looking Thomas Muzzall came in. He had just realised he was minus his money bag and guessed at once that he must have left it on her counter. Was he right?

Mrs. Standing knew he was right; had known the end of the tale before he reached it. She did her best to explain. Thomas Muzzall blanched.

He had left his West End Farm early morning, concluded his market business and grown six sovereigns richer. Was he to go home empty handed?

He searched Steyning but found nothing. Somewhere a happy drover was on his way home at far greater speed than he achieved with animals. [2]

Richard Martin also had a story. He had ridden to market from Barrow Hill early in the morning but the day did not prove propitious; two gold sovereigns and a few copper pence were the extent of his dealings.

Not being one to bemoan his lot, he set off home.

As he rode through the narrow valley just past Beeding, four men jumped him, dragged him off his horse, held him fast and rifled his pockets. His takings fell to zero; his buck's horn hunting knife and silver watch went too.

The robbers had no use for the horse.

Richard rode home subdued but determined.

He reported his loss to P.C. Short.

The constable passed the watch details on; a watch without a maker's name but numbered 2189 and having a ring attached with a black ribbon on which was suspended a seal without an engraving.

The information appeared in the next edition of the Police Gazette with a reward of £3 for the arrest and conviction of the offenders.

Efficient as the Police Gazette was in promoting the arrest of criminals, Richard Martin eventually had to accept that his loss was permanent.

The agricultural labourers, too, could have trying days.

On Lucretia Wood's Wantley Estate, farmed by Alfred Smith, ploughman John Brownings had an annoyingly mouthy ploughboy, 15 year old Isaac Piper.

Ploughing a straight furrow needed skill and concentration unhindered by idle prattle and backchat. One day the boy overstepped the mark. His cheek was more than any man could stomach.

John snapped, reacted spontaneously and turned his whip on Isaac giving him a good thrashing – a lesson to be remembered. Isaac, too, reacted spontaneously yelling loud and long but no one heard; the pair were on their own, way out among the furrows.

When they returned to the farm it was Brownings' turn to wince. His actions could not be hidden. Raw, red whip marks stood out on the boy's back.

Alfred Smith was a man of esteem in the village particularly in the field of sport – hunting, shooting and cricket. To him, whipping was foul play whatever the circumstances. Action had to be taken.

A court case followed. John Brownings did not deny the whipping but he explained how the father had given permission for the boy to be flogged if he; "Runs any way mouthy."

Mr. Piper refuted the claim. He had given no such permission.

The magistrates had heard enough. They passed sentence: - nothing would justify the treatment of the boy in such a cruel manner; fine five shillings and 16 shillings costs (the equivalent of a gold sovereign). The alternative was 14 days imprisonment. [3]

John Brownings promptly produced the money; the best part of two weeks wages for checking a ploughboy's constant prattle – it hurt.

Alfred Smith's gamekeeper had to be physical in a controlled manner when he confronted two trespassing youths damaging the estate woodland. He managed to grab one but the other made off.

The keeper frogmarched his captive to the farmhouse and explained how the two had been damaging oak trees by breaking off a number of branches.

Wantley land belonged to Lucretia Wood. Alfred Smith had no hesitation in deciding on her behalf that prosecution was necessary.

The case was heard at the Petty Sessions. The magistrates accepted the keeper's clear account of events. Thomas Stillaway, 16 years old, of Nep Town, Henfield, in company with labourer Thomas Wilson, who had absconded, did wilfully and maliciously break some oak trees, the property of Lucretia Wood of Chestham.

Thomas Stillaway had no adequate answer.

A ten shillings fine was imposed plus a shilling payment for the damage to the tree and ten shillings costs or in default of payment commitment to the House of Correction for a month. Thomas did not have a shilling to his name, let alone a sovereign. He faced a long month at Petworth.

Thomas Wilson was soon caught and took his turn at the sessions.

Alfred Smith attended as a possible witness.

Thomas made no attempt to deny the charge explaining that he committed the offence in order to get something to eat.

Nobody in the court could really doubt him. The state of his clothing told its own woeful tale.

He had more to relate. He had been apprenticed to a London chimney sweep. His mother had deserted him. He had come into Henfield with nothing. He still had nothing. He was utterly destitute.

Thomas finished his tale and stood waiting.

Court officials consulted an army sergeant seated at the back of the court on the look out for any likely recruit. They would turn Wilson over to him.

The sergeant refused. The prisoner was far too unkempt for acceptance.

Up spoke Alfred Smith offering to purchase clothing for Wilson decent enough to enable him to enlist in the army.

The sergeant was pleased to agree; it meant another recruit to his name.

The magistrates gave the choice; Petworth Prison or army barracks.

Thomas chose the army.[4]

Decently dressed, he accepted the Queen's Shilling ready to be arrayed in army red.

Dr. Weekes of Hurstpierpoint had little reputation as a public spirited man. His heart lay more in making as much profit as possible from his property.

The woods of his Brookside Farm were well studded with oak and elm. Dr. Weekes decided many of them should be converted to money.

He detailed Stephen Stammer to have his men mark the trees with paint and to conduct interested buyers wishing to appraise the timber.

A detailed advertisement listed the trees;

HENFIELD, SUSSEX. – OAK, ELM AND ASH TIMBER
TO BE SOLD BY AUCTION, BY KENSETT & SON

On Friday, the 17th day of April, 1846, at the White Hart Inn, Henfield, In five lots, at three o'clock in the afternoon, by order of the proprietor.

LOT 1. – Comprises 75 Elm Trees, standing in Brookside Farm, Henfield, marked with white paint.

LOT 2. – 37 Elm Trees and 32 Ash Trees, also marked with white paint standing on the same farm.

LOT 3. – 232 Oak Trees and 84 Oak Tellows, standing on the same farm marked with blue paint.

LOT 4. – 163 Oak Trees, numbered with white paint, standing on the west side of the same farm.

LOT 5. – 295 Oak Trees, numbered with white paint, standing on the east side of the same farm.

The tenant, Mr. STAMMER, will show the lots;
for further particulars, apply to KENSETT & SON, Auctioneers, Ditchling.[5]

The timber was auctioned and Dr. Weekes became sovereigns richer.

For the labourers felling Dr. Weekes' trees, sovereigns were seldom on offer. The shilling with its twelve pence was their general currency. They had a struggle to stretch their money to embrace everyday needs. Even a wife's income at haying and harvest was needed if enough was to be put aside for rent, clothing and probable doctor's fees.

Mrs. Sarah Tidey and Priscilla Hoadley were glad to make a few extra shillings by haymaking for John Muzzall down West End Lane. It was hot, sweaty work but they put in as much effort as the men, differing perhaps in managing with less farm issue beer. The men, Philip Cutress and Henry Woolgar were glad of company.

One day, well refreshed by their afternoon beer, the men joked and chortled as they decided an amusing leg pull.

When they settled to work again, they laughingly rolled the ladies in the hay. The day had its funny side.

The women took the joke resignedly; stupid men acting like children. When the rolling became pushing into the hedge, Mrs. Tidey walked off. Priscilla stuck it a while more but the men seemed unable to understand that enough was enough and she, too, got out.

Both women told the farmer the reason for them quitting. Both had bruised arms. They wanted justice.

Cutress and Woolgar had to explain themselves at the Petty Sessions. Supportive friends attended at court keen to be witnesses for the defence.

The magistrates listened to the case; women associating with men in a hay field and then complaining about inappropriate behaviour. It was such a trivial affair the two parties should consult and come to an agreement over paying the costs of the case.

The aggrieved ladies saw no justice in sharing costs and would not be persuaded.

The magistrates reconsidered their findings and decided a shilling fine should be imposed on the men plus the full costs of 15s 6d. The alternative would be 14 days at Petworth.

The men had insufficient money.

For a few minutes the affair became anything but trivial. Prison seemed a horrible reality until the friends pooled their resources and produced enough money for the justices' clerk.[6]

Two relieved haymakers accompanied their supporters back to Henfield. The ladies kept aloof.

No sooner was hay safely home and stacked than the August corn harvest began.

Down at Lipride beyond Broadmare Common, Farmer Baines had his wheat cut on his South Worms field and the sheaves put ready in stooks for carting the next day. Provided there was morning sun to dry the dew, carting home would begin.

The sun rose clear, the men assembled on the field and Farmer Baines checked the crop. It was ready.

The first cart was filled, sheaves stacked high and dry. The carter set off.

Farm beer was drunk and work continued until a man shouted from a stook saying it had gone.

His mates looked across wondering what he was on about; the sheaves were there plain as could be.

The man walked across to his master and explained; the stalks were stacked neat enough but not a blade of wheat, it was all gone.

Farmer Baines went over; that stook, the next and the next – 27 sheaves of wheatless stalks. [7]

They finished carting the rest home. A reward was offered but nothing resulted.

Somewhere, somebody was busy grinding ill-gotten grain.

Chapter 15

High Street traders – Gamekeepers – Poachers

Percy Gregory's decrepit cottages opposite Broadmare Common were up for sale.

Each was still home to a married couple and their children. Day labourer Peter Cragg lived in one. Next door was chair-maker James Newland, an irascible "Man of Kent" from Chatham. At the far end was his eldest son, also James, a basket maker of far quieter temperament whose own son was another James. Village sweep James Humphrey with his wife, daughter and deaf son, again James, had the final house and lodged his 14 year old sweep's assistant.

The complete row was bought for £900 by William Borrer who demolished the lot and replaced them with homes designed to provide decent accommodation.

Of the unhoused occupants, just Peter Cragg moved into one of the new homes.

Sweep James Humphrey and old James Newland found neighbouring tenements up at Nep Town. James Newland junior moved into half of tiny Dogham Place, just 12 yards long and home for two families, at the back of Henfield Common. There he earned his living as a tin worker.

William 'Sunny' Woolgar, a skilled basket maker, moved in from Oreham Common.

The final house went to a journeyman basket maker from Lewes with his wife and two young daughters which left enough room to lodge 'Sunny' Woolgar's oldest boy,15 year old Henry – basket maker.

'Sunny' Woolgar proved a competent business man. He persuaded Peter Cragg to take up the craft and before long had set up a little empire as master basket maker employing three men. He worked hard and kept his men up to the mark. Basket making led to ready sales but returns were low.

Up in Nep Town, James Humphrey and the irascible James Newland found themselves surrounded by neighbours, six of the 18 houses being let as tenements to 17 families.

Almost hidden was a parish owned cottage and garden occupied by one of the essentially Nep Town families, Harry Dale with his wife and six children down to baby Abraham just 10 months old. Harry's brother William lived next door with his six finishing at two month old Orpah – (widowed descendent of Abraham's nephew Lot). Both babies also had a 'Biblical' cousin in 10 year olds Moses and Joseph to go with worldly Kitty, Maria, Barbara and Robert.

The Poor Law Commissioners had their eye on Harry Dale's cottage.

They issued an order for the vestry to convene a meeting of rate payers and property owners to agree the sale of two parish owned houses. The proceeds would be offset against Henfield's portion of the Union loan taken out for building the Shoreham Workhouse.

The meeting went ahead and the houses were advertised; Harry Dale's copyhold cottage and the freehold Hope Cottage occupied by 'Lossam' Ward on the south of the common by the track up to the windmill. Both men were instructed to open their house to prospective buyers. [1]

The vestry officials were confident Harry Dale would be compliant but 'Lossam', muscular and outspoken with his reputation as a stubborn reprobate, might prove troublesome.

All went smoothly. Hopeful buyers inspected the properties and the sale took place at the White Hart. Dr. Morgan bought the Nep Town cottage. A Brighton man bought Hope Cottage.

Harry Dale and 'Lossam' continued their occupation undisturbed.

Most craftsmen were able to continue their trading undisturbed but a few were struggling in times that were proving very difficult.

Down at the bottom of the High Street, Stephen Yeates was kept busy making and repairing boots and shoes, Peter Ward had sufficient gentlemanly customers for his guns and Richard Lashmar was fully employed making clocks as well as watches.

Henfield's other watchmaker, James Bailey, in his Hay Croft shop had even more custom. Some were children with a penny to drop into the slot that started James' ingenious model church bells ringing. His masterpiece was the large clock on his shop giving Henfield time for all who passed. James Bailey had such a name in the village he would never lack work.

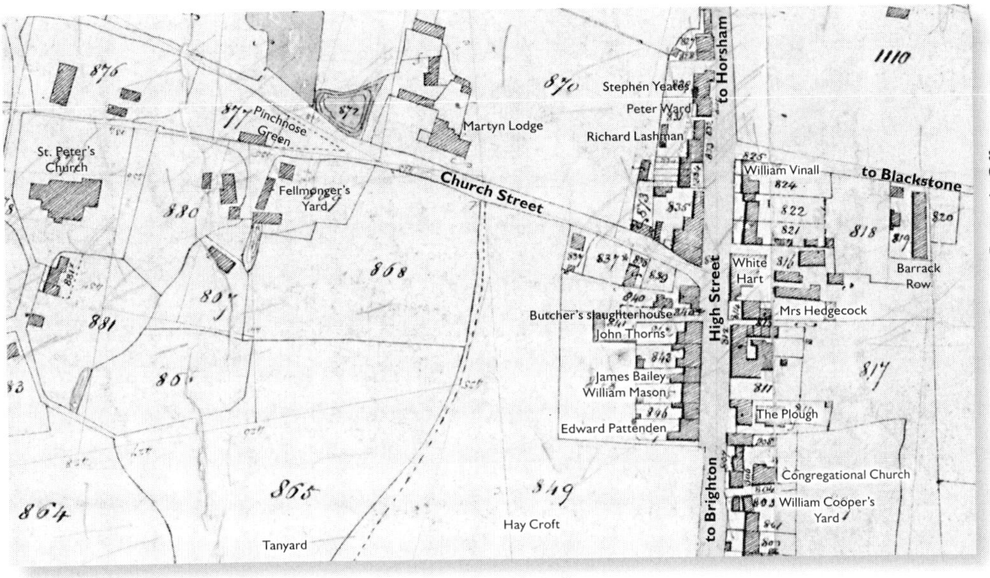

North end of High Street

His neighbour, plumber and glazier William Mason, was another respected High Street trader noted in all the County Directories. He was a family man sometimes seen driving through the village, his spring-cart laden – he, his wife and their eight children from 14 year old Rosina down to little Fanny Weaklin, just a year old, who nobody thought would survive the first days of her life.

William ensured his house and garden were well kept and as up to date as anyone's. His forthcoming task was to glaze the new greenhouse frame he had just made. He had more than enough glass in his workshop store.

His stock there provided for all aspects of trade; linseed oil, glue, copper shoots, sheets of tin, patent lead piping, window lead, lead sash weights, brass taps, bells and bell wires, casks of different coloured paint – and a display of 150 paper hangings in various designs.

William's central High Street position had helped him build up his business but the last few years had been hard. Trade slumped to become worryingly slack. Insufficient orders were coming in. The stock stayed put.

The purchase of such a good range of stock had incurred heavy bills. Not all had been met. He found himself sliding into debts deeper than he could manage.

Two of his Brighton suppliers became difficult demanding money he could not provide. William asked for understanding and patience. The creditors were determined business men.

The end was inevitable. Bankruptcy proceedings took William's entire

stock in trade, his tools and implements, his benches and fixtures.
Along with them went his furniture, his garden tools and his family's personal items apart from one stated omission; "the necessary wearing apparel of the said William Mason and of his family only excepted." [2]

Everything else was sold. At the creditors' discretion, he could receive an amount not exceeding £20 from the proceeds.

Mr. Lawrence Smith who had not been repaid the £200 loan on William's house became owner by default of a good High Street property.

When the census was taken in Henfield the following year the Masons did not figure. Somewhere, the family was clinging on to life.

The Plough Inn also changed hands. Brighton brewers William and George Wigney bought the lease which included the stable, outbuildings, garden and orchard. Ex landlord Henry Martin moved down to the White Hart leaving the brewers to install their own man.

The Plough was just another inn to the Wigneys. Their real interest in the village was the family mansion. In Henfield terms it certainly did reach the status of mansion; two stair cases leading to the first floor's large drawing room and three principle bedrooms with a further five on the second floor. Through the entrance hall on the ground floor were two parlours, the kitchen and the pantry.

Only invited guests would know of the expensive furnishings and enjoy the fruit and vegetables of the walled garden that trapped the sun's warmth so effectively for the fine orange tree and extensive greenhouse grapery.

The Wigneys' mansion was every inch a gentleman's residence.

Their brother, Isaac, had become chairman of the Brightelmstone Bank started by their late father. Isaac had also been elected one of Brighton's first M.P.s at the 1832 Reform Election and again in 1841 just before the opening of the long awaited London to Brighton Railway that was rapidly transforming travel.

Four jolting hours by stage-coach had become two clackerty-clack hours by train whether in low cost open wagon or in covered compartment.

As a successful banker, Isaac Wigney had no trouble finding money for travel up to town in one of the railway's new 1st Class luxury carriages.

Until, that was, the March morning when Brighton businessmen were taken aback by a notice on the door of their Brightelmstone Bank stating Wigney & Co's deep regret at the painful necessity of suspending payments.

Brightelmstone Bank had gone bust.

Isaac Wigney was ruined. He resigned from Parliament. There would be no more championing Brighton at Westminster; no more luxury 1st Class express train travel up and down the busy main line.

The family mansion went on the market, its furnishings described for all to wonder at. Everything would be sold to support a bankrupt M.P. ruined in reputation and health.

The hustle and bustle of the Brighton Line as yet had little effect on village life. Henfield's link to the new trains was with the Great Western Railway by The Hero coach heading for Oxford. The Hero now left Brighton at 8.00 a.m. stopping for fresh horses as usual at the White Hart and at other stages as far as Reading. There the horses were unhitched ready for the coach to be positioned aboard a train. It continued by steam engine power to Steventon, as near Oxford as the Great Western went, where horses took over again for the last 10 miles.

In due course the Brighton Line did effect a marked advance in village life – new postal arrangements with mail from London being carried by railway as far as Hassocks Gate where a covered mail cart collected bags for Henfield and Steyning.

It was welcome progress; letters delivered earlier each day and posting-times being later.

For the business and commercial people of Henfield, postal times were important. For men struggling against poverty they were nothing.

Time for them concerned work; when to start and when to stop.

For a few of the more daring spirits, the time of day marked the gulf between providing meat for the family by taking game (daylight) or by poaching (night) with its latent risk of transportation.

The skilful man with a working knowledge of the land could obtain meat readily enough provided he was careful. Snares cunningly positioned could provide hare or rabbit. Pheasants were available for the man with a gun but needed the cover of darkness to minimise detection.

Ranged against them were the gamekeepers.

Edward Bushby looked after Lawrence Smith's land and some of William Borrer's.

Bushby was young, well built, athletic and very determined. He had an excellent knowledge of his master's woodlands, the intricate lay out of land boundaries and the most likely fields for taking game – essential for an efficient gamekeeper.

To satisfy interfering keepers, a sportsman needed an annual game certificate and the landowner's permission to be there hunting.

Thomas Marchant had a game certificate and was welcome to take as many hares and rabbits as he trapped on his friend Mr. Weston's land.

He spent a spring evening setting snares. Totally relaxed, he reached the end of the field, stepped across the ditch and placed his next wire in the hedge.

It had almost immediate effect; a big gamekeeper barring the way.

Thomas Marchant explained how he was allowed all the hares and rabbits he caught on Mr. Weston's land.

Edward Bushby replied that he had no objection but the hedge where they were standing was on William Borrer Esquire's land and any trespassing intruder setting wires always had to face charges at the Petty Sessions.

The court case took place.

The magistrates ignored Thomas' claim that his error was due to lack of local knowledge. They imposed a fine of forty shillings plus costs, making it an expensive day's sport.

Pheasants were reared on several estates. John Wade Dennett had fine 'pheasant' woodland spreading from Henfield into Woodmancote. He was a dedicated breeder, selective and sensitive in whom he invited to shoot on his land. His gamekeeper was Michael Harmes, another determined man.

Michael Harmes had an unexpected midnight assignment just a couple of days before New Year when gunshots were heard in his master's game preserve – poachers, surely more than one. He needed help.

He called on the Silverson brothers, John and James, both in Mr. Dennett's employ.

They made their way to the Alder Wood. As they reached it more shots rang out.

The gamekeeper's own movements would also be heard once the trees were reached. There was no chance of a quiet pursuit.

"Come on, my lads, stick close to me," said Harmes and in they went.

Very soon there was confrontation – three law keepers against four armed and alarmed intruders.

"Halloa," yelled a poacher and struck at Harmes with his gun. Harmes knocked it to the side, grabbed the man and hung on grimly as they fell to the ground.

While they struggled, the man shouted for help, "He won't let go. Joe. Pull into him."

A friend rushed across. "I'll break your bloody arms," he swore thumping the butt end of his gun into Harmes' head and back.

It was Harmes' turn to cry for help. None came. One of the Silverson brothers had been felled with a heavy stick and lay stunned on the ground. The other was still grappling with the fourth man.

Harmes had no choice. He let go.

It was the end of the affray. The man scrambled to his feet and all four intruders made off, the call of the gamekeeper ringing in their ears;

"Damn your eyes. You came here tonight to do as you liked but you are taken in for I know you."

Harmes and James Silverson were in a poor way, both bleeding copiously. They struggled back to Mr. Dennett's house and John Silverson went straight off to fetch Doctor Morgan.

He arrived within an hour and dressed the wounds; a five inch gash on Harmes' face and extensive bruising on the back of the head. James Silverson had a badly cut face and a small wound on the back of the head but more seriously he showed symptoms of concussion of the brain. His life could be in danger.

In the morning the police constable was alerted. The wood was searched; a gun stock in two bits, part of a ramrod, a hedge stake stained with blood, two dead pheasants, three pools of blood and a poacher's hat.

Michael Harmes' pronouncement about the men's identity proved only half true; two he knew, two he did not.

The known pair, carpenter John Pierce, 21, and labourer Henry Sayers, 33, were arrested. They were remanded for trial at the Lewes Assizes.

There, the prosecution recounted the events of the night. Michael Harmes swore to the prisoners' involvement.

Both men had cast iron defence – witnesses who were able to state with full cognisance on their solemn oath that the prisoners had been elsewhere the night in question.

The judge listened diligently and determined which account was true. He instructed the jury. Their verdict was unanimous; Guilty. The judge solemnly passed sentence; ten years transportation beyond the seas. [3]

Two anonymous poachers kept discreet and distant silence.

Pierce and Sayers joined other convicts on the hulks awaiting their turn to board a convict ship bound for Australia.

Chapter 16

A warm rabbit – Pigeon egg hailstones – Mustard poultices

One bright moonlit night, 'Lossam' Ward went out shooting at the far end of Henfield Common where Percy Gregory's Middle Field met Mr. Dennett's Furze Field.

Henfield's new constable, P.C. Buckwell, was out on the common that night as well with the two Harding brothers on a quiet anti-poaching mission. Their quarry was 'Lossam'; notorious as a poacher, slippery as an eel but not infallible.

Just after midnight there was a gun shot. In Buckwell's estimation it came from somewhere on Mr. Dennett's property. He sent one of the Harding brothers up to the turnpike road while he and the other lay out of sight close by the gate in the Furze Field hedge.

Their wait was rewarded when a startled bird flew squawking from the Middle Field hedge. Moments later a man pushed through into the field. Clear in the moonlight, he walked down to the gate and opened it.

Buckwell leapt to his feet and confronted him;

"Ward, is that you?"

"Yes,"

"What are you doing out with a gun past midnight?"

"That ain't none of your business."

Buckwell did not waste further time on words. He took 'Lossam' into custody, handed the gun to Harding and searched his prisoner; a warm rabbit in the coat pocket.

'Lossam' declared he had shot it on Mr. Gregory's land. Buckwell ignored him. He had his man and the case would go to court.

At the Petty Sessions they went through everything. Buckwell maintained Mr. Dennett had intimated he gave Ward no permission for shooting. 'Lossam' refuted the idea. He told them how he had worked over 40 years for Mr. Dennett shooting rabbits and foxes – once even managing to shoot eleven foxes for him in 16 days!

He then confounded everybody by producing a letter stating he had permission to shoot rabbits on Mr. Gregory's land.

The magistrates consulted and gave their ruling. Because the prisoner had emerged from Mr. Gregory's hedge no one could determine where the rabbit had been shot. Case dismissed. 'Lossam' had slipped the law yet again. [1]

'Lossam's' hunting ground was where cricket had been played for countless years before the Town Field with its nearby George Inn became popular.

The Town Field had been the scene of some great games of cricket but the many club members hankering after a return to the common were coming near to achieving it. With enough impassioned men of influence in the team, a permanent move seemed feasible.

The difficulty would be keeping animals off the pitch.

It would need the cooperation of every Streatham Manor copyholder who held rights on the common. That was a tall order because some were absentee tenants and few were interested in cricket.

Secretary/treasurer Bignell contacted all those concerned and explained the club's position. The outcome was encouraging.

A meeting was held and they agreed a document setting out safeguards for both interests: –

> We the undersigned copy holders of the Manor of Streatham do hereby agree not to pare dig burn or carry away any of that part of Henfield Common called the cricket ground. But that we do hereby agree to do everything that lay in our power to prevent any intrusion on that particular part of the common.
>
> And that we do further agree that such particular piece of ground shall be set apart entirely for the use of the members of the Henfield Cricket Club. Provided it is made use of for that particular purpose and at the same time reserving to the said copy holders the full enjoyment of their rights of pasturing. [2]

Thirteen copyholders appended their signatures, both Mr. Dennett and Percy Gregory among them. Henfield cricket's home on the common was secure.

Work began on preparing the ground for the season's matches.

Before then, a day of uncommonly hot and sultry weather at the end of May ended with a thunderstorm. It came north over the hills. The Brighton

Gazette described its violence in town;

> Towards evening dark and murky clouds rose in the south and south-east and soon extended over the heavens. About eight o'clock the storm burst in violence over the town. For about an hour and a half vivid flashes of lightning came with such rapidity as to cause an almost incessant blaze of light with thunder of appalling force. The rain fell in torrents.

In Henfield it was worse; incessant lightning, deafening thunder and horrifying hailstones smashing glass to smithereens.

At Barrow Hill House next morning, the gardener cautiously picked up congealed hailstones the size of pigeon eggs. Amongst them were shards of glass. He was standing in all that remained of his master's two wonderful greenhouses, one of them 18 yards long, the other 21 yards.

The damage to them alone was estimated at £500. Mr. Borrer would have to accept having no greenhouses or stomach the cost of replacing them along with the other damage his house had suffered. [3]

Across the back of the common at Dogham Place, James Newland and his neighbour came through the storm unscathed. Dogham Place's 12 yards of shared living space with its minute windows tucked beneath the eaves had proved perfect defence against monster hailstones.

'Lossam', too, had suffered little damage at Hope Cottage. His trouble came on a sunny day in June.

'Lossam's' son, Alfred, weak from a long eighteen months of illness, was out on the common in the warm sunshine when two men confronted him completely unaware that the house close by was his home.

First they jibed him over his sickly appearance and the annoying cough he kept doing.

Gaining little satisfaction, one of them knocked his hat off and punched him on the nose.

Alfred fell to the ground unconscious.

'Lossam' saw and erupted. He had lost one son to consumption. No one would strike Alfred.

The air was heavy with oaths as he leapt from his garden and collared the assailant.

The man's mate rushed in, threatened to peg two stones into 'Lossam's' head, grabbed a prong and swore to run it through his body.

'Lossam' wisely let go and the assailants made off but his anger was deep and emotional. He was determined that he would bear Alfred's infirmities all he could. He knew the attackers and they were going to suffer.

Alfred was able to get to his feet again still bleeding from his nose and mouth. He went indoors.

'Lossam' made his way into the village and reported the assault to P.C. Buckwell.

Buckwell set out immediately and accosted the pair, Christopher Taylor and Thomas Murphy. Both were drunk.

They were handcuffed together and taken into custody.

When the case came to court each pleaded guilty and apologised. They explained how they were totally unaware of the assault because they had been blind drunk. They asked that the regrettable fact could be taken into consideration by the magistrates.

First, P.C. Buckwell had evidence to give. He explained how during the men's time in custody they had caused an amount of damage, had broken the handcuffs and behaved very badly.

The bench of magistrates consulted together briefly and declared the defendants deserving of great reprobation. Their drunkenness was an aggravation of the offence. Taylor, as major aggressor, should pay £6, Murphy £4 and in case of failure to pay they should forfeit 6 weeks and 4 weeks freedom at the Petworth House of Correction.

No money was forthcoming. The aggressors were conveyed to Petworth. 'Lossam' walked home to Henfield satisfied he had protected his son and gained justice. [4]

In August, cricket on the common at last began with a two day match against Chalvington.

Gamekeeper Bushby left his pheasants to fend for themselves, wicket keeper Songhurst made his usual journey from across Rudgwick way and all rounder Hammond came over from Storrington.

The game excited plenty of interest. Both teams included talented men with Chalvington having slightly more which determined the betting odds for the match at 6 to 4 in their favour.

The early play proved the odds. Chalvington made 60 in their first innings to which Henfield could only muster 49.

With Chalvington knocking up a second innings of 65 Henfield had a lot to do. Four wickets went cheaply. The odds were proving right.

Hammond came in. He had bowled well, eight victims plus a catch but he had made a duck in his first innings. Back at the wicket again he whacked his way through the Chalvington bowling to a bold 29. Things were looking brighter. Gamekeeper Bushby replaced him and was still there for the final match-clinching run. Henfield's victory – but perhaps it was Hammond's game; Hammond, the Storrington man.

They played the return match at the end of the month. Hammond claimed another six victims, managed to avoid a first innings duck and again was top second innings scorer with 26. The rest were woeful. Bushby was second highest just 25 behind along with Alfred Smith Esquire which left the other seven batsmen red faced with ducks. A drumming for Henfield; delight for Chalvington.

Summer gave way to autumn and the damp coldness of November.

Boys tramped through mist across the common to spend their day at a school partially warmed by a single stove fired by an occasional shovelful of coal. For the scholars giving silent attention to the lessons and for teacher William Godley providing them it was equally chilling.

William Godley became ill and took to his bed in his house beside the school.

Nourishing broth provided no benefit; his illness persisted. The doctor was called.

He prescribed mustard poultices and bleeding. They proved ineffective. Medicine gave little relief. William's condition deteriorated.

Within a few weeks he died.

People knew they had lost a worthy man, a much respected servant of the community who had devoted his time to the education of the village boys.

A special space was chosen for his grave beside the church extension where the school children sat for their Sunday worship.

Curate Rev. Charles Dunlop entered a comment in the burial register;

> For a period of nearly 27 years the master of the National School (the duties of which situation he discharged most faithfully).

As a mark of respect, the school committee financed a fitting memorial stone which also included his wife and baby;

To the memory of William Godley, the zealous and
conscientious master during a period of 27 years
of the Henfield National School, who died November 9 1843:
Aged 56 years.
Also Sarah Godley his wife, who died July 18th 1826
Aged 34 years.
And of Henry their son, who died March 14th 1825
Aged 9 months.
This stone was erected as a mark of respect for the above
named William Godley by the Committee of the School. [5]

Just a month later 'Lossam' and Mahala Ward had the intense sadness of losing Alfred. He had lost his fight.

They gave him a quiet funeral; Samuel's epitaph was true for both sons.

Chapter 17

Corn Law opinions – A new map – A skeletal beggar

By the next summer Mr. Borrer's new school for girls in Nep Town was complete and a simple panel had been inserted, INFANT SCHOOL 1844.

Mr. Borrer had decided to follow the modern approach and provide a school specifically for infant children. The girls would remain in their old cottage school near the church.

It was exactly 20 years since William Wilberforce and others had formed the Infant School Society to give a safe environment for such young children to receive education by trained infant teachers. Mr. Borrer could feel personal satisfaction in providing such an establishment.

At the Boys' School, the teacher vacancy was filled by the appointment of Mr. Obadiah Hall.

He soon discovered that the school was not only an educational establishment but also the largest location for village events.

It was there on a dark winter Wednesday evening that the Henfield branch of the Church Missionary Society held their sixth anniversary.

A lot of work had gone into organising this important meeting.

At Sunday church, Rev. Charles Dunlop had preached preparatory sermons. With his remarkable fervour he outlined the noble and glorious work of the society whose missions had begun in the vast country of India where the misguided natives followed Muslim and Hindu heresies. Work to return those misguided natives to the fold was being repeated in other pagan parts of the world. Henfield should show its true Christian support.

Persuasive as the sermons were, the collection was less than the previous year's; a shortfall accredited to the unavoidable absence of several influential supporters.

At the anniversary, the visiting speaker told of the society's wonderful achievements in West Africa and New Zealand since 1814.

He explained how the truly awful deeds of blood and war once so prevalent in those heathen lands had, by the influence of indefatigable missionaries, been transformed to times of peace where charity abounded. No more did the natives worship idols of their own invention.

The meeting closed with prayer after which people made their way home convinced it must have been the inclement November weather that evening which had caused the disappointingly sparse attendance.

The curate had another mission entirely within the parish; to urge his congregation to come forward and be prepared for confirmation. The last such opportunity had been well before his time.

Almost 300 responded, among them some of the oldest residents. The curate felt humbled. [1]

Through the long months of winter and into spring, the necessary tuition took place to ensure candidates knew the answers to set questions on the Catechism and could recite the Lord's Prayer, the Creed and the Ten Commandments.

At last all were ready for the Bishop of Chichester's visit on the first Monday morning in May.

The church filled with contemplative candidates and their supportive parishioners. It was a solemn occasion.

The service over, the bishop had lunch with Rev. Dunlop at Red Oaks before proceeding to his next engagement, another service of confirmation at Steyning.

Later in summer a meeting was sprung on the village with such brief notice that no preparatory instruction could be arranged.

The subject was the Corn Laws which were splitting the country into two camps; farming south and industrial north.

Farming landowners in general favoured the Corn Laws, industrialists opposed them.

The unexpected visitor was Mr. Buckmaster, a member of the Anti-Corn Law League. Word of the imminent meeting spread quickly and he had a 200 strong audience of tradesmen, their employees, farm labourers and even some of the tenant farmers.

Mr. Buckmaster weighed straight in; the Corn Laws not only prevented the free importation of corn but also the free export of manufactured goods. The law designed to protect the price of wheat for the agriculturist was wicked. The result was the working man paying artificially high prices and, much worse, unemployment for thousands in the industrial north who otherwise would be gaining an honest living to support their families.

His audience listened attentively. They knew just what he was talking about; low wages, low living standards and low hopes of change unless the Corn Laws were repealed. [2]

With Henfield in the heart of a county littered with titled landowners, there was little prospect of real Anti-Corn Law activity.

Other local farmers and traders anxious to demonstrate their support for 'protection' were bestirring themselves in order to be present at the great meeting scheduled to take place at Steyning. This would be a thoroughly organised meeting guaranteed to demonstrate overwhelming support for the Government to keep their promise of continuing the Corn Laws.

The day came.

The Henfield contingent was led by William Borrer along with Alfred Smith of Wantley and Mr. Dennett from Woodmancote.

They were small fry, mere listeners, as lordly landowners clarified the debts to agriculture accrued during Napoleon's time, the despicable actions of the Anti-Corn Law League, the needs of the Empire and how the labourer depended for his well-being on the success of his farming master.

Mr. Ellman, the famous Southdown Sheep breeder, supplied figures: - Great Britain's population of 10 million in 1801 almost doubling to 18 million in 1841; the import of foreign wheat falling in the 1830's with the price decreasing until the infamous 'Manchester League' of northern industrialists began agitating.

Everyone agreed a counter movement should be established, 'The Sussex Society for the Protection of Agriculture.'

Who should be its figureheads? Indubitably, the Duke of Richmond as president with vice-presidents the Duke of Norfolk, the Earl of Egremont, the Earl of Sheffield and Viscount Gage.

The Henfield men joined in three hearty cheers for the Duke of Richmond and returned home pleased to have done their part for Country, Empire and the Sussex Farmer.

Back in the village they had to concentrate on the practicalities of daily life and the more pressing topic of Government legislation over church tithes. In future all tithes were to be a money payment.

Official cartographers were mapping each parish to enable new valuations to be calculated for each property. Every landholding was being plotted and recorded; name, acreage, use, owner and occupier.

The first step for Henfield was a Sussex Express newspaper notice;

> We the Undersigned being landowners whose interest is not less than one-fourth part of the whole value of lands subject to tithes in the said parish call a meeting to be held at the George Inn on the 15th June next at 3.00 p.m. to make an agreement for the General Commutation of Tithes. [3]

The four 'Undersigned' included Rev. Dunlop, supportive father-in-law William Borrer and Thomas Beckett, church-warden.

The clarity of the notice could not be faulted.

It prompted a letter of 1300 words to the Brighton Guardian from 'AN OBSERVER', Henfield, explaining that to impose Church Rates on men of every faith for the benefit of only the Church of England was very wicked; "Our legislators have modelled a hateful image, a frightful creature – O, that this point were rightly known by British hearts. O, that it were rightly felt by Christian minds! Then would they no longer disgrace their name, their bible and their God. O, then, is it not a piteous sight to see a professed follower of the gracious Saviour forging chains, and for what? Even to bind his fellow, his friend and his Christian brother. The chariot of truth is running on and travelling with a railroad speed; and soon must the error of compulsory support, in all religious matters, be crushed beneath its mighty wheels. Religion, if there be any, must be voluntary; it knows nothing of compulsion." [4]

Henfield readers mused. Could Rev. George Hall at the Congregational Church of less than 10 years standing be jousting with the might of St. Peter's? Who else would pen such comments?

The Steyning Union concentrated on organising procedures.

They advertised for tenders to survey the land in readiness for the valuation.

More parochial meetings were held urging the matter forward.

Cartographers Hitchins were engaged to make the survey.

Somehow they took longer than expected, demanded ten pence per acre as their rate, declined the guardians' offer of eight pence and were told where to go.

The Union found a better man in Mr. Mitchell. The map was completed with the land assessments compiled in detail. It was displayed at the White Hart for public perusal and comment. [5]

People were keen to find fault. They complained that the cartographer had failed to distinguish the quantity of less valuable 'rough' ground from the 'smooth', consequently no valuation could be made.

Mr. Mitchell reassessed the land which increased the total cost of the survey to £200, far more than the parish could find. A benefactor was needed willing to loan the amount at acceptable interest.

William Borrer, ever "Friend of the Village", stepped forward with the money. He would be repaid in five annual instalments of £46, a modest profit at 15%.

The completed map was put on show again for people to scrutinise for any remaining points of discord. That done, it became operative.

The 'Great Tithes' were held by the Hon. Robert Curzon, Lord de la Zouche, responsible for the upkeep of the chancel. He would accrue the benefits at an annual tithes feast. The vicar's portion was the small tithes.

Not all property incurred a tithes payment but the new assessment also increased the valuation which determined the Poor Rate – bad news for almost everyone.

An increasing number of families exempt from tithes but liable for Poor Rate were having difficulty finding the extra money. A person's failure to pay caused more work for overseer Morley in issuing non-payment summonses answerable at the Petty Sessions.

Philip Alfrey had to justify why he should not be rated.

He explained how he was an agricultural labourer and that he, his wife and their young daughter lived in just two rooms of the Mill House up at Nep Town. The owner let them have it free without any rent payment because they were looking after the house and its garden, protecting both.

The magistrates considered the matter several minutes and informed him that as occupier he was liable for Poor Rate charges. He must pay the full rate of £1 2s 2½d plus the costs of bringing the proceedings to court.

Philip Alfrey promptly did so – a very rapid increase.

William 'Sunny' Woolgar, the Broadmare Common basket maker, told the magistrates his case had previously been referred back to the vestry who took into consideration his low income and allowed him a 'pay one, miss one' system. Now they were demanding every rate.

Overseer Morley explained how the rate reassessment meant the vestry had to collect every payment.

'Sunny' retorted that his rent was £9 a year for a house without a garden. He lived a long way from any turnpike road so being rated at 6s. 3d. was unfair compared with the similarly rated house of butcher

Cutress in Church Street close by the turnpike road.

He had brought a disinterested witness to court. The witness corroborated the claim and the magistrates conferred.

They decided the case should be referred back to Henfield Vestry for them to adjust the matter. 'Sunny' Woolgar felt satisfied.

George Ward complained he was assessed too high and did not earn enough to enable him to pay. The magistrates told him the appeals procedure. He replied that he should be excused payment entirely. Overseer Morley stated that the case had been taken before the Henfield Vestry and they had instructed him to recover the money.

That satisfied the magistrates. George was given a fortnight to raise enough and pay his rate.

The final appellant was William Vinall, the tailor who had once been threatened with having his possessions sold to fund the 12 shillings Poor Rate he owed.

He was now a family man with two children. He and his wife, Sarah, had found each other rather late in life. They were content to be a small family.

William rented a double-fronted house plenty big enough for them; two sitting rooms, a kitchen and three bedrooms.

There was still the difficulty of providing enough to give the children a decent chance in life. To supplement his money from tailoring, William had opened business as a hairdresser.

He now had a scheme to guarantee income; use the shed in his garden to brew beer and open a beerhouse in one of the sitting rooms. Although his house was close to the White Hart, it was in a good position at the corner of the old road that led right through to Blackstone.

William's appeal at court ran counter to the other men's. He felt that being rated so low reduced his chance of a successful application for his beerhouse. Could the justices kindly reconsider his case?

The magistrates promptly accepted his request and increased his rateable value.

William was satisfied. With another two guineas to the excise office he would soon be brewing and selling his own beer – and reaping good profits.

William Vinall's reliance on his own endeavours was one of the ideals of the benefit society that Mr. Challen and others were promoting in the village, the Manchester Unity of Odd Fellows. Henfield was a small branch of the Loyal Myrtle Lodge.

A number of traders and farmers had already joined.

Sydney Street of Kidders Farm up by Mock Bridge was secretary. He and Henry Longley were encouraging others by stressing that as a brother in the Odd Fellows a man could obtain help no matter where he went.

Sydney Street was determined Henfield's branch would flourish.

Village ratepayers were generally more intent on grumbling about the affect on their pockets of the increase in Poor Rate payments. Not that they wished ill on the parish poor; poverty could creep silently upon a man and enshroud him within a clinging web from which it was hard to escape.

Poverty exhibited by intruding vagrants was different; an ever increasing problem.

P.C. Buckwell moved any tramping person out of the parish without recourse to law whenever possible. Sometimes he had little alternative to apprehending one.

The day John James begged his way along the High Street no one could fail to notice how pathetically thin and destitute he was.

His behaviour, however, was gross – constantly bewailing his lack of even a shirt, opening his coat wide and exhibiting a skeletal body. Passers by shuddered; in all decency, such behaviour was unacceptable.

Constable Buckwell stopped the display by arresting him. No stave was needed; the man was beyond resisting authority.

The next day, John James appeared before the magistrates. They admonished him for his gross behaviour and issued a 14 days hard labour sentence at Petworth. There he would perform his daily thousands of crank revolutions raising water and be fortified by prison meals; the bread and gruel of breakfast and supper plus the plain bread dinner. It would hardly put the flesh back on him. [6]

Constable Buckwell had a lot more trouble with Henfield's exhibitionist John Seymour.

Whatever the subject of any public meeting, John Seymour would be there dressed as ever in his sailor's uniform noisily recounting his days at sea fighting fierce battles under the leadership of the immortal Lord Nelson. At Henfield's meetings he was accepted by most as part of the fittings. He was accepted, too, as part of the High Street scene selling ballads.

The crunch came the afternoon he wobbled down the street to the Brighton coach, its horses being changed at the White Hart, and began conversing with the inside passengers.

Constable Buckwell was on hand. He had been watching Seymour's erratic progress. The man was openly begging. It was the final straw.

Buckwell ordered him off the coach.

Sailor Seymour refused with noisy gesticulations.

Buckwell seized him. Seymour pleaded; he was only selling his ballad sheets.

It became a battle of wills gradually won by the constable as he conducted his man down the road to the lock-up.

The next day they both recounted their recollection of events in front of a Petty Sessions magistrate.

Constable Buckwell outlined the incident.

John Seymour, complete with sailor's uniform, denied he was begging and insisted he was only selling his ballads. His drunkenness he accepted;

"I acknowledge my fault, your worship. I like a drop of liquor, your worship, but nothing more."

The magistrate imposed a five shilling fine.

Seymour had neither the money nor the opportunity to earn it selling more ballads because there was an immediate alternative – three hours in Henfield stocks.

There he was free to recount his navy days if he wished.

Harriett Dale, one time servant in the White Hart, had business at the Petty Sessions; a heartfelt complaint about a fellow servant and an application for an order in bastardy against him as the father of her child, now two months old.

Harriet explained how she had lived-in as a maid for over two years, hard working and obedient. All that time she had been faithful to James Parsons. He had promised her marriage. She had carried his baby and because of it lost her position. As a result she no longer earned any money so had to apply to the vestry for help.

Because she applied for help, she was put in the workhouse where she gave birth to her baby girl.

As soon as they were strong enough they were moved back to Henfield. She took her baby to church to be baptised Harriet.

When she asked James Parsons what he meant to do for her baby's upkeep, he said he did not really object to paying for a little while, but if he did so she would always expect money.

Harriet finished her evidence and stood down.

Any defence hopes James Parsons may have had were shattered when a witness confirmed the conversation about the baby's upkeep.

The magistrates ordered him to pay a weekly 1s 6d child maintenance.

It was some compensation for Harriett, but fell well short of marriage. [7]

Blighted romance also affected servant John Stillaway, rejected suitor of one of the maidservants at their master's house. A passionate dispute between them had almost disastrous results. John resorted to swallowing poison.

Commotion arose. A servant ran for Dr. Morgan.

The doctor arrived armed with a stomach pump.

Efficient Dr. Morgan, another life saved. John Stillaway was back at work in the morning.

The Union had awarded Dr. Morgan the contract for carrying out smallpox vaccinations in the parish. They paid him 1s 6d per success for pauper children.

People were slow to bring their children forward.

The Poor Law Commissioners drew the Union's attention to the paucity of vaccinations being carried out in Henfield.

The guardians required Dr. Morgan to give his reasons.

He wrote back that the prejudices of the poor against vaccination were in numerous instances insurmountable during the absence of smallpox in the area hence the apparent failure to discharge his duties. He was not yet prepared to suggest a better system.

By the end of the year 25 children had been vaccinated before their first birthday and 172 later. All were successful.

Chapter 18

Hungry visitors – A bargee's booty – The Sparrows Club

Steyning Union's great concern was the expense of flour and potatoes; staple foods for the poor. Prices had risen so high that more and more families were seeking help through outdoor relief.

The Guardians wrote to the Poor Law Commissioners asking them to relax restrictions. Assistant Commissioner Hawley refused.

The hungry man, when starving hungry, found it difficult to be sensitive to the niceties of the Poor Law – or law and order in general. Empty stomachs prompted remedial action, particularly by passing visitors.

Down at West End, Thomas Warden farmed Lashmars, almost alongside the river. Thomas was a family man; him, his wife Mary and three young children. A servant girl dealt with housework, Mary with constant cooking for the large household – three lusty farm labourers lived-in at the house.

One Sunday morning, visitors called.

The family and the servant were at church, the labourers away enjoying their day off. No one was home to hear the knock at the door of somebody seeking a little money or bite of food.

There being no answer, a small pane of glass was broken and the inside bolt withdrawn. The door opened.

It was not robbery, just a breakfast call; seven loaves of bread, three apple pies and a roasted spare-rib. The visitors pocketed their food and left.

They would eat at leisure elsewhere.

When the family returned they discovered their loss and the means of entry but there was never a clue as to who or how many visitors had been.

Another three ill nourished travellers in Henfield sought sustenance down West End around the New Inn.

Harwoods, the home of William and Mary Trower, was just a field or so the village side of the inn. William and Mary were the parents of triplets, Faith, Hope and Charity. The girls were all out at service. Just their 15 year old brother, William Luther, remained at home, a labourer on his father's farm.

The Trowers' closest neighbours the other side were at Frogs Hole, home of Stephen Woolgar, ex bargeman now agricultural labourer, with five toughened teenage sons. Almost as near was Leeches, home of Thomas Payne, bargeman, and his bargeman lodger, Thomas Lelliott.

At some time past a moonless midnight, the three travellers assembled outside Harwoods – masked, cudgels in hand and with material wrapped firmly round their hob-nailed boots. It was a carefully chosen rendezvous; Frogs Hole and Leeches contained too many muscular occupants.

While the Trowers slept upstairs, a man took out the casement of the kitchen window, climbed in and opened the door for his friends.

They lit candles and began gathering; two bottles of home made wine, four loaves of bread, a ham, home made cheeses, a caraway seed cake and a pound of moist sugar. That done, they mounted the stairs very quietly.

They burst into the bedroom, flourished their weapons, shouted dire threats and demanded money. William handed over his money bag.

The men grabbed his cotton shirt, a black silk handkerchief, an orange one, two dark coloured round frocks and a razor with its case. With those and a couple of blankets they made their way back to the kitchen satisfied their victims would not retaliate. They put the food and wine in a large basket, tied the other stuff in a table cloth, went out by the door and disappeared, monetarily richer by sevenpence halfpenny.

When all was silent again, William went down and closed the door. He and his wife assessed their losses and waited for dawn.

At daylight, William reported the theft. The police took active measures but those of the thieves proved too many; the men were safely away.

Further up West End Lane towards the village was a shared tenement right opposite Stonepit Lane, the narrow way which led round to Lashmars and to Great Betley Farm where Thomas Muzzall worked.

Thomas had one end of the tenement with his wife Hariett and their two young daughters, 7 year old Bengemina and Sarah, 4. Hariett managed to find time to grow garden flowers and had a rose bush right outside their kitchen window.

At 2 o'clock on the last Friday afternoon of September, Hariett locked both doors, put the key in its hiding place and took the girls up to the village.

Thomas had been threshing at Betley. They finished their last load for the day and he returned home.

When he came through his gate he noticed the rose torn down, some of the flowers as well. He made no effort to straighten them; Hariett did the flowers, she would deal with it. He fetched the key, let himself in and concentrated on finding something to eat.

Hariett herself noticed the broken rose when she returned with the girls at 6 o'clock. As she walked into the kitchen she also noticed the door to the stairs wide open.

Thomas was about to go up the village; Friday night was drinks night. Hariett asked him if he had been upstairs. He assured her he had not.

Hariett felt distinctly uneasy. She went up to their bedroom.

A small wooden box should have been there securely nailed down to the table. It was missing. Also gone were the children's two earthenware money jars, Bengemina's red one and Sarah's yellow. 11½d in copper was also missing.

She came back downstairs to tell Thomas but he had already left. She would have to carry on investigations herself.

Hariett next discovered she was short of two loaves of bread. She then noticed a patch of water on the floor. She put her finger in, tasted the water and realised it was brine. She immediately went to the pork tub. Just one small piece was left; three complete pieces had gone.

Clothing, too, was missing; three shirts, a pair of stockings, her husband's brown round frock – his best despite the torn sleeves – along with sheets and a tablecloth.

She could do little but wait for Thomas.

Thomas returned about half past nine. Hariett told him the news and he went straight back out for Constable Buckwell at his cottage beside the church.

Next day the news travelled the village and Constable Buckwell began his enquiries.

A possible witness came forward, Mark Dowell. He had been working down West End Lane towards the river that Friday afternoon when one of the Beeding bargemen, George Sharpe, walked by with a bundle under each arm, one bundle a dark colour, the other light.

Buckwell made his way to Beeding. Only Sharpe's wife was at home.

He searched the place. In the pantry he found a brown round frock with torn sleeves. Upstairs in the back bedroom was a crock full of pork pieces.

Mrs. Sharpe said her husband was away at work in Beeding Chalk Pit.

Constable Buckwell next went to Steyning to consult Constable Poiney, the constable in charge of the district. Together they went to Beeding Pit and found Sharpe loading chalk onto a barge.

Buckwell apprehended him. Poiney searched the barge.

Stowed in the cabin were three shirts, a table cloth, sheets, linen and a wooden box.

Sharpe was taken into custody.

When the case came to court, he explained how he had found the things.

The jury took full note and decided he was guilty. [1]

The judge passed sentence taking into account the court records showing the prisoner to have a previous conviction of four months hard labour for stealing timber from a barge-load of planks being conveyed between Mock Bridge and Shoreham.

George Sharpe heard his new sentence and shuddered – ten years transportation.

There was more trouble across the parish at Oreham Place where farmer John Thorns had special nest sites for his hens. In summer there were eggs a plenty but when a carpenter was called in to do some repairs the hens seemed to become distracted. Few eggs were being laid.

John Thorns sent for the constable who suggested that any eggs the hens did lay should be marked by pencil. One of the men did so.

The next day, the carpenter carried out more repairs which had an even greater effect on the eggs. When the farmhand counted them at noon they had decreased by six. At the end of the day they were down another five.

Close by the farm, the constable was keeping secret watch.

The carpenter finished work, packed up and with basket in hand set off towards Steyning. The constable, too, headed that way.

At Steyning the carpenter went into a shop. The constable increased his step and arrived just in time to see things being placed in the shop keeper's egg basket. He opened the shop door, stepped inside and announced himself.

He inspected the basket. At the top were 11 eggs with pencil marks. He instructed the shopkeeper to mark the eggs again. That done, he gathered them up, charged the carpenter and took him into custody.

It was all explained at the Petty Sessions where the case was referred to the next Quarter Sessions.

There, the carpenter made no defence and awaited sentence. It came; two months hard labour at Petworth – eight weeks of silence cranking water punctuated by two weekly spells of solitary confinement.

For Thomas Wisden, who farmed 150 acres in various parts of the parish, potatoes were the problem. 15 of his fields, each named, were arable. Every year he could select different ones for potatoes; Carrot Field, Shady Field, Browns Wood, Earth Plot. They could be relied on to crop well; a reliable source of income, especially with Brighton providing such a ready market.

Among Thomas Wisden's older employees was John Thomsitt. John and his wife, Mary, lived in West Mill Cottage, lonely among the fields opposite Woods Mill.

John was able to supply Mary with potatoes. More were in store and would be available when she needed them.

The supply failed when his master accused him of theft.

Thomas Wisden was not a vindictive man but what was his was his; any employee thinking otherwise would be brought to task. He began court proceedings.

At the appointed time John made his way to Steyning Petty Sessions. His plea of guilty was accepted and he was given two months hard labour at Petworth; an indigestible way to stomach so small a quantity of potatoes, one basketful out of thousands.

Potatoes hit the 1846 headlines when crops in Ireland failed for the second year running, the staple food of millions rotting in the ground.

Newspaper reports detailed the suffering.

Gradually the extent of the horror sunk in. Too many families were in dire distress.

In February 1847, Curate Dunlop called upon his congregation at St. Peter's to contribute to the fund to assist the distressed in Ireland. They responded with £113 to show their concern for the suffering people.[2]

Curate Dunlop was well aware that there were also tough times for people in Henfield itself with the winter price of flour almost beyond the reach of labouring families.

He initiated a local fund to help them and called upon his worthy parishioners to subscribe. They again responded with more than £30 to enable flour to be supplied more cheaply for the necessitous poor. The impoverished housewife would still be able to bake bread.

Some of the farmers had been doing their best to ensure the corn harvest went to those it was produced for. They were the members of the Sparrows Club undertaking to rid the farms of as many grain eating birds as possible.

How the cull was made did not matter but the favourite means was by shooting.

The season's tally was complete. Beaks and broken eggs had been counted and taken to the club's White Hart headquarters to be recorded.

It was the day of the annual dinner. With food eaten and toasts drunk, chairman Sydney Street rose to his feet. 5451 sparrows and 701 other small birds had been killed with 1017 sparrow eggs destroyed. The three leading marksmen had been very closely grouped, a difference of just five sparrows between first and second.

Sydney Street sat down.

A colleague rose to announce the top men; Sydney Street, 505, Arthur Smith, 500 and John Muzzall, 411. Polite clapping was followed by an evening of song to round off the Annual Dinner. [3]

Members returned home determined to ensure as little as possible of the next harvest's grain went to sparrows and the like.

Chapter 19

Starving immigrants – Cholera – Round frock missionaries

The next October there was a General Thanksgiving by Royal Command to mark the abundance of the new harvest just gathered in England.

Rev. Hall set aside a Monday evening for the event. His thanksgiving would include as many of the Henfield farmers and general inhabitants as he could persuade to subscribe to his fund to give the labouring class real cause to be thankful for such an excellent harvest.

The response was so good that he was able to entertain his congregation with tea in the church followed by a half hour of their pastor's most ardent thanksgiving and praise. The rest of the evening was spent in serious conversation and speeches from the friends connected with the church until about half past nine when the meeting broke up. Rev. Hall felt a sense of warm satisfaction.

In Ireland the story was different. The previous year's crop failure had meant less seed potato to plant. New crops were insufficient. Intense poverty and eviction by landlords was rife. Starvation, disease and death spiralled.

Many people deprived of home and livelihood emigrated. Some wandered their way from English ports down into Sussex.

The Union Workhouse suddenly found itself confronted by thirty Irish people seeking admission. One of the Board of Guardians was so taken aback by what he could only describe as "their disgusting state – people who disregard common decency as well as common cleanliness" that he felt obliged to suspend his functions as a visiting guardian. [1]

Governor Seaborne expressed no opinion. Admission had been granted. Entrance procedures began.

The applicants gave up their clothing willingly and subjected themselves to the cold bath and medical inspection qualifying them for workhouse clothing, food and a bed. That done, they became their ordinary selves again; poverty-stricken to the extreme but cheerfully sociable with a lilting cadence in their speech. Other inmates were happy to accept them.

The next summer, crops in England were poor by contrast to the previous abundance.

Only carrots and turnips seemed to thrive. Wheat and oats were thin, peas spotted and decayed as if they had been eaten by insects, beans had not fruited properly, mangel-worzels were diseased, apples few on the trees.

One crop failed completely and the smell from rotted plants drifted through the air – potato blight itself had arrived in Henfield. For farmers and gardeners alike there were more hard times ahead.

The extent of farmers' difficulties was highlighted by a totally unexpected announcement at the George Hotel during the December tithe audit of Baroness de la Zouche of Parham Park. The steward caused great surprise among the assembled tenants by announcing that with the consent and approbation of Baroness de la Zouche's husband, the Hon. Robert Curzon, a 10% reduction was being made that year owing to the pressure upon agriculture.

The delighted tithe payers tackled the landlord's dinner of good old English fare with added gusto. After the healths of the Queen and members of the Royal Family were completed they cheerfully drank the healths of Baroness de la Zouche and all the Curzon family. [2]

At Chestham Park, Lucretia Wood also showed generosity by giving back 15% of the farm rents she had received. The farmers concerned showed little surprise. Lucretia Wood was known for her acts of generosity.

As the winter cold tightened its grip, her bailiff undertook the annual distribution of beef to the poorest families and gave them an added gift, a large stack of extra firewood.

Hard as the times were, poor crops and potato blight were not the greatest worry. A recurrent killer was again at work across the country – cholera.

The government sent the Steyning Union a set of instructions to be followed throughout their area if cholera struck. Inspectors were to report unhygienic nuisances. Parishes had to ensure facilities were ready for any outbreak of the disease.

The instructions were put to one side.

Rev. Dunlop and Dr. Morgan took up Henfield's cause with the Union; an inspector of nuisances should be instituted. The guardians discussed the matter at their next meeting and unanimously agreed that it was not advisable to appoint one.

It was the fear of cholera that drove Mrs. Longley to write to the Union asking them to make enquiries about stagnant water in the ditches on Henfield Common so that a decision could be taken to have them cleansed.

The guardians informed Mrs. Longley that a letter signed by two Henfield residents would first be necessary.

The letter was sent stating how the ditch caused great offence by its smell and was a health hazard.

Back came the guardians' considered reply; the Henfield Surveyor had inspected the ditch and found it was on private property. As it adjoined her property she had better remove the nuisance herself.

Mrs. Longley had the ditch cleaned. The nuisance persisted. She informed the guardians. They sent the surveyor again and informed Mrs. Longley that if she had the ditch properly cleansed and made a little deeper the nuisance complained of would disappear.

Mrs. Longley fought no more. She did as she was bid.

The people of Henfield could console themselves that the person promoting their cause, Rev. Charles Dunlop, was now vicar of St. Peter's. Their late long-serving but ever absent vicar, Rev. Guy, had passed away peacefully at his rectory in West Stoke. They prayed that Rev. Dunlop's indifferent health would allow him as long an incumbency.

At the Congregational Church, Rev. Hall was certainly enjoying a lengthy time as minister.

A large number of visitors came up from Brighton at the next Anniversary Celebration keen to support the village Independents. They settled to hear special guest speaker Dr. Morrison of London preach on "God is love."

At the close of the service they made their way up the High Street and down to the meadow opposite Golden Square kindly made available by James Patching.

James and Elizabeth were still regular worshippers. It was twelve years since their daughter Elizabeth had been baptised there followed so quickly by the loss of their dear son, little John Theophilus. Now, their younger daughter, Fanny, was ten.

The meadow was behind the 'Bee Hive', where James brewed his 'Genuine Farm House Ales, from malt and hops only, of various strengths; at 8d, 10d, 12d, 14d, and 16d, per gallon and Porter at 18d.'

The Independents would not sample ale. The ladies had worked hard to provide sufficient provisions for the 200 worshippers to drink tea in a splendid booth at the low price of 6d.

After enjoying tea, people listened as several members explained their part in establishing Sunday Schools in Poynings and the other nearby communities.

At the appointed time everyone walked back to the church for the evening service. Rev. Mr. Ashby had travelled over from Arundel for the occasion. At the end of his sermon the congregation went to their pockets again and gave upwards of £20 for the diffusion of the Gospel in the neighbourhood. The chairman thanked everyone. He wished those Henfield members of the larger church who gave as much as £100 for missions in foreign parts, yet never knew any good it did, had been present to hear the work of the Congregational Church's own round frock missionaries in Poynings, Small Dole and other outlying places around the village.

The anniversary celebrations were over.

James Patching could concentrate on his brewery. His Farm House Ales were as good value as ever but expenses were outstripping income. Most worrying was the mounting debt to Mr. Gilbert across at Storrington who supplied his malt.

Mr. Gilbert, too, was worried. Patching owed him £150 yet was continuing to place orders as if payment was of no matter. It was an unsustainable situation for which there was only one remedy, court proceedings.

A fiat of bankruptcy was issued.

James had to make the journey to London and face the enquiry. Mr. Gilbert was the only creditor. James knew he could have faced more.

His Honour, the Commissioner, sanctioned an accountant to make up the balance sheet and authorised James an allowance of two guineas per week until the next appearance in a month's time. James returned to his family thankful things were no worse.

At the end of March he was up in London again facing the Commissioner. More creditors were claiming money – debts in Henfield, Steyning and Brighton. James had to listen as his accounts were reviewed. They showed a liability of almost £550. The commissioner asked whether any creditor objected to the accounts. Nobody did and the balance sheet was accepted.

James explained what had happened. His uncle John Marshall had given him money many years before on the understanding that James should pay interest each year. When the uncle died, the money was mentioned in his will but not that it had been a gift. The executors claimed it as a repayable loan. Having to return that money meant he had insufficient for his bills.

The Commissioner listened and set the date for the court to consider

James' conduct and trading. Until then he would be allowed protection.

When the day came, James' creditors were granted a dividend on the money owed them. They would receive 6¾d for each £1, less than 3%.

James was granted a Certificate 2nd Class noting his degree of bankruptcy.

He had been openly honest about his affairs and was able to keep his business. The 'Bee Hive' Brewery continued to produce its Genuine Farm House Ales.

Across the road from the brewery, Harriet Harwood had been widowed. Her two youngest girls were still of school age. She continued running the grocer's shop but income was down and barely sufficient.

Her parents, Percy and Harriet Gregory, still lived with her but Percy had too little income to be of much assistance.

He determined to help his daughter. The only way was to raise a mortgage.

Most of his property was of insufficient value; the minute cottage by the parish pound in the High Street; Dogham Place way out at the back of the common; the four tenements just around the common corner.

It would have to be his shop.

Caroline Hedgecock, inheritor of much Hedgecock wealth, agreed to provide the money.

The transaction was recorded at the next Manor Court; Percy Gregory, farmer, making a conditional surrender of part of Forges to Caroline Hedgecock.

He signed that he had received £300 and Harriet witnessed it.

Harriet's ingrained careful use of money would ensure their future.

Percy's loan for his daughter proved his final positive act.

At the April Streatham Manor Court the proclamation was made of the death of "Percy Gregory, late bailiff of the manor who held certain copyhold lands of the lord but the heirs are not known."

Harriet knew she was sole heir but not until the October court could she produce probate of the will and claim her inheritance. [3]

During her lifetime everything was hers and she would provide for her mother. At Harriet's death the property would be sold and the proceeds shared between her daughters.

For the present they would continue their way of life; nothing in excess but sufficient for the day.

Chapter 20

New-shop dispute – Outlaw Lake – Deserting sailor

Messrs Tamplin, whose beer had almost knocked out the 'Bee Hive' Brewery, needed a new landlord at the George.

They appointed a local man, post-master George Starkes. He moved up the road a few places and his premises were put up for sale.

They were purchased by a 'Kentish Man', Mr. Corke of Tunbridge Wells where he already had a draper's shop.

Mr. Corke was an astute business man. His new property had plenty of potential but the place was in dire need of a facelift to make it dominant enough to ensure success.

Three solid permanent counters were positioned in the shop and prominent display areas set up. Plans for a new frontage to the street were prepared and presented to Mr. Sharp, parish surveyor for the year.

The plans were accepted and the building extension went ahead.

The new façade was impressive; a central door with the window each side glazed with large squares of costly plate glass. Mr. Corke could feel confident people would provide ready custom.

He put two of his employees, Edmund Baldwin and Richard Garrett, in charge of the new branch.

What Mr. Corke had not foreseen was the intervention of William Borrer.

Mr. Borrer felt affronted. The shop now extended out onto the footway, an unacceptable protrusion. A man procuring property in Henfield and taking such liberties could not be ignored. The extension must be removed.

Mr. Borrer contacted Mr. Sharp and it was agreed that a case should be made out against Corke, answerable in court.

Mr. Corke was informed.

The case was heard at Steyning. Mr. Sharp stated his complaint. Mr. Borrer gave supportive evidence.

The defence lawyer questioned the validity of the statement about the right of way being infringed. Mr. Borrer acceded that he was not fully conversant with the legal position.

Mr. Corke maintained that he had followed correct procedures, that the parish surveyor was fully informed and knew exactly what was being built. The boundary of his property reached further towards the road. If the court found him guilty he would appeal against the decision.

The justices consulted. It was a case fraught with difficulties. That the building narrowed the pavement was clear. If the defendant's deeds confirmed the true boundaries, the infringement would have to stand.

They decided the charge could not be made out; case dismissed.

Mr. Corke returned to Tunbridge Wells triumphant.

He later proposed that Baldwin might like to go into business at the shop. Attractive terms were offered with fixtures and fittings included.

Edmund Baldwin was keen to accept.

The following months were difficult for him; the deal seeming probable and then frustratingly out of reach as an expected partner withdrew. Finally he persuaded Garrett to join him.

Another good friend agreed to provide security of £500 and Mr. Corke sealed the agreement.

The stock was valued to them at £1200 calculated as 15% below the selling price.

The men were in business; a great step up from being counter assistants. They knew it was a challenge. The long established shops with their narrow leaded window lights had the loyal support of many inhabitants but a challenge was a challenge and the new pair were ready for it.

The Baldwin/Garrett partnership enjoyed a profitable first year of trading with almost £400 between them but the next year was bad. Income did not cover outgoings. Certain bills were outstanding, debts mounting.

Mr. Corke was owed upwards of £2000. Both men wrote to him, thanking him for his support and wishing him good comfort.

The debt proved more persuasive than the good wishes. Mr. Corke felt obliged to press them over repayments.

They did their best to work out a survival strategy and were forced to the conclusion that their only way was to suggest Mr. Corke should demand the £500 security Baldwin's friend had put up. It would be hard on the friend but he was not facing the consequences of bankruptcy.

The news reached one of the other creditors who was told how times would be better because Mr. Corke was decreasing the men's debt to him by calling in £500 security money.

The man feared it could mean all other debt recovery procedures being stopped and he reacted by immediately starting bankruptcy proceedings.

Assets were seized. Trading ceased. The London Gazette recorded Baldwin and Garrett in the list of latest bankrupts.

It was the start of long drawn out legal proceedings in London, the pair travelling there for each sitting.

Mr. Corke explained his agreement. Arguments ensued.

The shop fixtures and fittings, including the three counters secured to the floor, had been sold by the men. Mr. Corke claimed they were his.

The pair's balance sheet of transactions was disputed. Mr. Baldwin was adamant that at the original stock taking he and Garrett had taken an inventory of the stock while Mr. Corke had written it down. Mr. Corke produced the book proving much of the writing to be Baldwin's and Garrett's.

It all ended with two ruined men and bruised creditors who received just a few pence for each pound they had lost. [1]

The shop was taken over by Henry Colgate, an East Sussex man from Withyham. He would have to prove himself able to supply as wide a range of products at prices very competitive with his rivals. Happily married, Henry determined that with the support of his wife he would make a success of the business.

There was a second shopkeeper, grocer William Lake, attempting to improve his lot by taking on a shop in Henfield.

He, too, did his best but within a few years of trading he found himself in deepening trouble.

Try as he might, income was never matching expenses. Bills for his stock could not be settled. Creditors pressed for payment.

The major creditor, a Mr. Perkins of London, seemed very threatening; polite but persistent. William did his best to fend him off.

It was to no avail. Mr. Perkins took out a fiat of bankruptcy.

The shop stock was listed and auctioned. Worse was scheduled to follow.

Two dates were fixed for William to appear at the London Court of Bankruptcy.

He considered his options and decided the best way forward.

His plan was pragmatic. Sell his property and get away smartly with the money and all his books and papers to keep them from prying eyes.

With the help of a friend he managed the sale.

Books, papers and William Lake disappeared. Mr. Perkins and the Court of Bankruptcy could whistle in the wind.

The Court duly met on the dates set aside.

At the second sitting his non-appearance was dealt with as the law demanded; William Lake was proclaimed an outlaw.

Outlaw Lake, safe within his secret location, had no idea he was branded. He was miles away from Sussex concentrating on survival; plenty more were doing likewise.

Along the back of Henfield Common at Dogham Place, James Newland was somehow still managing to make a living from tin.

With him was his son James, now an able seaman, who had been without a ship for some time and was enjoying a quiet break ashore – visitors were few at Dogham Place.

Surprise and considerable dismay were caused one day when there was a knock at the door and it was answered to reveal a uniformed constable standing on the step.

He had come up from Shoreham briefed to contact able seaman James Newland and take him into custody for deserting his ship.

James was taken away.

On the Monday, he appeared before Steyning magistrates charged with desertion under the Merchant Navy Act.

The ship's captain recounted events;

"I made an agreement with the prisoner to serve as a sailor on the barque 'Claud' for two years and to sail from London to San Francisco in California and to other places. On the 27th May while the ship was in San Francisco the prisoner left the ship without leave and never returned.

I produce the original agreement bearing the prisoner's mark and also the log book in which the prisoner's desertion was entered. At the time, nine of the crew deserted."

He stood down and James was called upon to explain himself;

"I left because the others did. I worked a ship to Calcutta and another to London. Then I joined the navy."

James was given a month's hard labour for his concise confession. He would be a hardened man by the time he saw Henfield Common again. [2]

Halfway between Dogham Place and the High Street stood an L shaped set of six tenements.

Pork butcher James Greenfield and his wife had moved into one with their young family – two girls, a boy and two more girls. The more the family grew, the tighter became the living space.

Rosina, the eldest, had a good reputation as a dress maker by the time she was 20. Henfield families were pleased to procure her services.

Mrs. Randle at Kentons on the Woodmancote Road hired her and had an order nearing completion. It meant long hours of work for Rosina and her sister Maria finishing by lamplight and not leaving for home until late evening.

The walk home across Henfield Common was a lonely one; best foot forward in as quick time as possible; past the school, past old 'Lossam' and over to the north side and home.

They were well on their way one September evening when there was a greeting call; "Holloa, my dears, I want you."

Out of the darkness stepped a man.

The girls ran.

The man grabbed Rosina and threw her to the ground. She screamed but he put his hand across her mouth; "Damn you, don't you shout so."

Maria ran on, screaming; "Murder! Murder!"

Rosina felt her clothing lifted, the man attempting to handle her. He lay beside her.

"I'll give you all my money," sobbed Rosina.

At the school house Obadiah Hall heard screaming and the cry of "Murder."

He grabbed a candle, opened the door and stepped out onto the common.

Maria saw him; "Run. A man is murdering my sister."

They had only a hundred or so yards to go.

Obadiah could see a girl on the ground, a figure lying close by her.

He shouted.

The man stood up making no attempt to run. He offered all the money he had to be allowed free.

Obadiah Hall grabbed him.

More help arrived; the screams had carried loud across the common.

The two frightened sisters were escorted home.

Their attacker was taken to P.C. Buckwell and placed shoeless in the lock-up.

The next day they all made their depositions before a Steyning JP and signed their statements. [3]

The accused man turned out to be a labourer from Poynings, William Coppard.

His trial at the Chichester Quarter Sessions was on a charge of attempted robbery; a far less ordeal for those required to give evidence.

Coppard made no defence and was given six months hard labour with two of the weeks in solitary confinement.

Rosina and her sister would need all that time and more to come to terms with their ordeal.

William Piper also had one of the L shaped tenements. His was not quite so crowded; just him and his wife with their own two small children, Emma and Frederick, plus their two year old granddaughter, Harriett Dale – the little girl who had begun life in Shoreham Workhouse.

William kept geese on the common. They ranged the length and breadth of it obtaining food where they could – which included visits to the Hope Cottage garden of 'Lossam' and Mahala.

'Lossam' was a keen gardener, proud of his flower display and particularly his vegetable patch like any man who wanted decent crops for his family.

William Piper had offered more than once to put a protective fence around the vegetable patch but as far as 'Lossam' was concerned the trouble was nothing to do with fences, it was the geese pinching his crops. His answer was always the same, a threatening; "No. I'll kill 'em."

Things came to a head about 4.00 a.m. one summer night, or morning, when the geese congregated noisily around the garden gate.

The house door suddenly opened. Out stormed 'Lossam', down the path, through the gate and into the geese. He kicked out and connected with one, booting it into the garden.

His blood was well and truly up. He went for the goose, stamped his anger into it and threw the body onto the common with an oath; "------------ 'em. I'll kill 'em all."

'Lossam' returned to the house satisfied he had made his point; his vegetable patch was for him and his wife, not for anyone's geese.

When William Piper discovered his goose had been slaughtered, he wanted compensation.

It became a Steyning Petty Sessions case, the magistrates listening to yet another neighbourhood squabble. 'Lossam' could not deny the act, only explain the reason for it. He was ordered to pay a one shilling fine and one pound costs.

'Lossam' fumed; his opinion of geese more entrenched than ever.

Chapter 21

The Henfield Band – A fire engine – The village omnibus

Not everything on the common was confrontational.

Henfield's cricketers were happily going from strength to strength as more Sussex players participated and more true villagers like gamekeeper Bushby proved their worth. Bushby was a force to be reckoned with – bat, bowl or fielding – who would prove talented enough to play for his county.

When Storrington came over they announced their arrival by a reverberating bugle call in the village guaranteed to draw attention.

Of more concern to interested onlookers was the fact that Storrington's star man, Hammond, who often played for Henfield, was set to oppose them in his home team.

When all was ready on the common, Henfield batted first.

Hammond set to work and took three quick wickets but opener Skinner was still there and the man joining him was Bushby, a firm basher of the ball.

The partnership ended when Skinner was bowled on 42.

Bushby kept on as partners came and went until the last man was out for a duck closing the score at 150 with Bushby not out on 33.

Storrington now faced the might of Henfield bowlers. Not a wide was delivered. One ball scattered the stumps, seven catches were held (two by the safe hands of Bushby) and a man was run out. Total 56.

Henfield's second innings was academic, there was never going to be enough light to dislodge Storrington again. It closed at 129 and the only thing to do was adjourn back across the common to the George Inn – without a clarion bugle call.

The Henfield band was already there briefed to ensure the day's cricket finished on a high note. Players and supporters joined together in an evening of song, jokes and tasty Tamplin's beer; the perfect way to end a day's cricket.

By kind permission of Henfield Museum. All rights reserved.

The Henfield Band

Henfield needed to be at full strength for their match away at Southsea against Hampshire. A village side against a county eleven; David against Goliath except that ten of Henfield's team had played for Sussex. The one exception was John Penikett, the hairdresser from Nep Town.

The match made club history because at Shoreham most Henfield players left their horse drawn vehicles and bought tickets to continue on the railway. What an experience – the amazing speed of train travel.

They arrived in good order, better order than the weather which produced half a gale and made play difficult, especially on the second day.

Hampshire went ahead on the first innings, disappointed their followers in the second and set Henfield 119 to win.

Four men were out. 35 runs were needed with six wickets to fall. Bushby was still at the crease and about to be joined by Penikett.

Between them the pair could well clinch the game. There was plenty of time remaining; they were in with a good chance.

The team's hopes were dashed when somebody reminded people how they had travelled to Southsea. The last train home would be leaving without them unless they got to the station in double quick time.

Cricket ended abruptly. [1]

Belongings were gathered and lifts given to the station.

There they caught the train and had time to ruminate. Surely Bushby and Penikett would have secured the victory. How could anyone doubt it?

A year later the team had the chance of another train journey.

The London, Brighton and South Coast Railway (L.B.S.C.R.) had completed the final spur of the line from Brighton to Eastbourne in May. In August, Eastbourne Cricket Club hosted Henfield.

An advert appeared in the Sussex Express naming the teams and stating a special evening train being laid on to take people home.

CRICKET.

ROBERT PICKNELL begs respectfully to inform the Public, that a Match will be played on the Eastbourne Cricket Ground, on Thursday and Friday, August 9th and 10th, between 11 Gentlemen of Eastbourne Club, and 11 Gentlemen of Henfield Club.

EASTBOURNE.	HENFIELD.
G. BAILLIE, Esq.,	A. SMITH, Esq.,
H. M. CURTEIS, Esq., M.P.,	H. SMITH, Esq.,
— HUMPHREY, Esq.,	G. W. KING, Esq.,
Mr. J. W. PAGDEN,	W. NAPPER, Esq.,
— D. GREEN,	E. NAPPER, Esq.,
— G. DOUBELL,	Mr. HAMMOND,
— G. PICKNELL,	— BUSHBY,
— W. EAGER,	— PENIKETT,
— HODSON,	— SKINNER,
— DEAN,	— SONGHURST,
— ROBERT PICKNELL.	— WOOD.

Wickets to be pitched at 11 o'clock.

A Good Ordinary will be provided at two o'clock, by the public's obedient servant, Robt. Picknell.

☞ There will be a special train leave Eastbourne, on Friday evening, at half-past six p.m., to meet the last up train at Polegate.

Eastbourne versus Henfield [2]

The match drew plenty of spectators, train receipts were good.

Bushby did not travel too well and made a duck in each innings. Penikett was admired for his batting. It helped his team to a comfortable victory and still left time to catch the special train back to Brighton – with the everyday speed of horse transport from there to home.

The train journey could have continued to a Steyning terminus if only L.B.S.C.R. had not reneged over building the branch line from Shoreham. Influential Steyning inhabitants who had pledged money for the project kept agitating for its construction. Nothing happened.

Henfield, three or four miles outside the plan, was pleased to keep its

'Royal Victoria' stagecoach with London, happy that it had survived when the railway swept away the coaches along other routes. It was restricted to alternate days but the routine was the same.

As the 'Royal Victoria' crossed Henfield Common, the guard blew a blast on his horn which brought increased activity down at the White Hart. The ostler brought the new team of horses out from the stable and kept them ready at the roadside for a quick change over.

The driver slowed the team round into Golden Square, up past the George and down to the White Hart. The Brighton horses were unhitched, the new team put in place and the coach was away again for Horsham.

One cold February morning the routine was broken.

When Coachman Clarke crested the High Street he could see there were no fresh horses ready.

Clarke brought the coach to a halt beside the inn, impatient at the delay. He waited a few moments, climbed down from his seat and crossed to the stable.

In the yard stood the horses partially harnessed but unattended.

He strode over to them and stopped abruptly. On the ground lay ostler James Wood, face down and very still.

Clarke called for help.

The landlord came and together they bent over the man. They both agreed; from his very posture he must surely be dead.

A servant was sent to fetch Dr. Caudle.

Clarke turned to the horses – James Wood could no longer concern him; his coach was late, he had to make up lost-time.

He completed harnessing the horses, changed the teams and climbed back to his driving seat. Whip in hand, he headed the coach for Horsham. They would cross Mock Bridge at a very smart pace.

In Steyning, a handsome new vehicle, a string carriage for two horses, was occasionally seen driven along the roads at high speed. It was a patent fire engine costing £105 raised by subscription in the town and neighbourhood.

How far the neighbourhood stretched would have to wait for a providential blaze.

Months later at Thomas Wisden's New Hall Farm, wisps of ominous smoke rose above the barns; a stack of about 50 loads of fresh hay had overheated.

The foreman mounted the farmer's horse and headed for Steyning.

Farmhands ran to the equipment for pulling hay from the stack.

It was slow work. At first little headway was made.

Men shouted and counter shouted advice to each other.

Gradually the stack parted but the more it did so, the more the air got to the fire. Bucketfuls of water thrown on were having little effect.

Suddenly the blaze intensified.

Flames threatened the nearby buildings. Men were put to saving equipment.

Thomas Wisden knew he was a beaten man, the roaring fire about to engulf his livelihood.

A new sound was added to the noise. Men turned to look.

Into the yard clattered Steyning's patent fire engine.

As it halted, firemen leapt off in well rehearsed drill to prepare the pump. Soon, jets of water were hitting the stack.

It was a long, hot task but the crew persevered.

Flames wrinkled and dulled. Glowing embers paled to wet ash.

At last the fire was out.

The men reckoned damp hay must have been in the stack.

The whole lot had gone but the intervention of the firemen had saved the farm buildings. It was hats off to the Steyning Fire Brigade.

A fire brigade answering a call had to travel fast. For the ordinary traveller, respect for other road users was the expected norm.

One afternoon the village sweep, James Humphrey, and some of his mates were heading down the new Oreham Common Road seemingly without a care in the world for anyone.

Fancy-free James Humphrey! Among his Nep Town neighbours were those who felt their sweep should be showing more of a care or two.

They sympathised that his 11 year old son James was deaf. Their concern was that the household now included a six year old nephew, George Handmore, from Maidstone in Kent. The six year old was learning his trade as sweep's boy despite a letter in the Sussex Express from 'Humanitas' cautioning how the employment of boys in chimneys was banned by law and reminding readers how injurious it was to the growth and health of the children. 'Humanitas' was aiming his remarks at the managers of Union Workhouses which supplied such children – the neighbours felt James Humphrey could well be party to such an arrangement.

At the top of Oreham Common, James' sole concern was the enjoyment of the afternoon. He flicked the reins, the horse responded and for a few minutes their descent became fun.

Suddenly James realised his horse was setting the speed; he was no longer in control. He commanded the horse to stop. His mates joined in loudly and the horse simply went faster.

It would have been all right if there had not been a cart ascending the hill at the same time, but there was. The road was narrow enough to hardly have a left or right hand side. Their horse's canter was almost a gallop. The ascending carter pulled tight into the side and stood back. James' cart careered past – almost, except the carts' wheels touched

The mates found themselves in a bruised heap beside the road; the stricken cart on its side minus one wheel. Down the hill the horse was heading away at speed trailing broken harness.

Only the driver of the other cart had any voice. His was a distinctly angry voice. He explained that he would be taking the matter further, as far as the next Petty Sessions Court.

They met again at Steyning to explain their version of events to the magistrates.

James Humphrey did his best. He was short sighted, the harness had broken and he was prevented from controlling the horse.

The magistrates sided with the complainant and imposed a fine of ten shillings with costs or in default 14 days imprisonment. James begged for time to raise the money and was allowed a fortnight.

For sensible controlled transport, travellers could depend upon Charles Stoner's omnibus plying between the George Inn and Brighton.

Tamplin's had appointed Mr. Stoner as replacement for landlord Starkes and he was determined to make the George Henfield's foremost inn.

One dark December evening just before Christmas, the omnibus was heading home almost out of Brighton when a passenger remarked on a shuffling noise coming from the roof.

Another passenger pointed out parcels bouncing on the roadway.

Barrow Hill farmer John Martin did better by noticing a figure on the roof. He leant out and grabbed hold of its clothing but the roof rider wrenched free, leapt for the road and was away into the darkness.

Charles Stoner halted the horses. Passengers recovered the parcels and climbed aboard again.[3]

The rest of the journey was as uneventful as usual and everyone finally reached home with a little Christmas story to tell.

It was not many months before landlord Stoner came to the conclusion that he had enough on his hands promoting the George without running an omnibus. He looked for someone willing to purchase it.

Not far down the High Street was Edward Pattenden. He had made his name driving Brighton to London coaches on the fast five-hour route through Hickstead. His father had run coaches through the village itself.

Here was the chance for the Pattenden name to be linked with Henfield transport again even though a two horse omnibus hardly compared with the old 'four-in-hand' days.

Charles and Edward readily came to an agreement. The Henfield/ Brighton service was now in Pattenden hands.

Smartened with a few coats of paint and a fresh name-board, the omnibus was soon on the road again.

The Henfield Omnibus when taken over by Edward Pattenden

Chapter 22

Horse cruelty – Petition to Her Majesty – The missing ring

Constable Buckwell encountered an acutely disturbing transport incident one Sunday evening the following summer when he went on duty in the High Street.

His notice was drawn to a horse shaking and trembling in the shafts of a fly outside the George. He discovered five wounds on the animal; two on the back under the saddle, another on its right side as long as his finger, one on the left shoulder by the collar and one under the front leg caused by the strap. On the side of the fly was the name, JOHN BROWN, NO 2, HOVE-TERRACE, HOVE.

Constable Buckwell called for the ostler and had the horse taken to the stables. Feed and drink were ignored. When the horse attempted to lie down it tumbled to the ground.

Buckwell turned his attention to the driver and entered the George. A group of chatting strangers were seated enjoying their drinks, four adults and three boys. Amongst them had to be the driver.

Buckwell ascertained who it was and questioned him. Constable Charles Buckwell found he was in conversation with James Buckwell, a coincidence which could not be allowed to affect the outcome.

The man said the fly had come up from Hove; the group were just about to return. They had travelled that afternoon. It was the horse's second job of the day.

Charles Buckwell was disgusted. He charged the driver with cruelly overdriving and torturing a horse.

He went back to the stables. The horse was lying down and appeared to be dying. There was no way it could be taking the fly anywhere that night. The group had to hire one from landlord Stoner to take them home to Hove.

At the Petty Sessions the driver claimed he did not know the road to Henfield and the passengers took him such a bad way that old wounds on the horse opened up again. The children had caused a new wound by poking the horse with the butt end of the whip.

The magistrates did not comment.

John Brown, the proprietor, had also been summonsed. He explained that when the horse went from his stable that morning it was as bright as a button without a sign of raw flesh about it.

Their Lordships declared the case as cruel as ever was brought before them. The driver was given two months hard labour at Petworth.

Proprietor Brown was fined £3 and 18s 8d costs for allowing an animal in such a poor state to be put to work. Such cruelty to horses would bring retribution whoever was the perpetrator.

With careful attention by landlord Stoner's ostler, the horse recovered.

Down at the White Hart, four licenced silk and shawl hawkers arrived by foot; a man and his wife, his brother and a colleague. They dined there and asked to be shown rooms for the night.

The landlord apologised explaining he had only one room vacant.

The hawkers agreed the married couple should have it.

The rest of the evening was spent happily enough at the bar until closing time. People were asked to leave.

All but the bedless pair made ready to go. The two stayed put and demanded accommodation.

The landlord tried firm words to no effect; the men were not budging from their seats.

Other customers sensed an interesting situation developing. They lingered outside.

Further up the High Street, P.C. Buckwell was on duty ensuring people kept the peace.

Voices within the pub became louder.

The door opened again.

It was the landlord. He called for assistance from the constable.

Buckwell crossed the road and went in.

The appearance of authority was enough. The two men followed Buckwell out of the pub.

His duty was done. He moved to cross the road again.

As he did so, there were shouts;

"Knife, knife; look out!"

The brother was wielding a knife and heading for the constable.

Buckwell twisted round, truncheon in hand, and struck out warning him to put the knife away or face prison.

He calmed down sufficiently to close the knife and put it back in his pocket.

Buckwell moved forward to arrest him.

That was too much for the man. He kicked out violently, his studded boots hitting hard against Buckwell's legs.

Onlookers rushed forward and overpowered him. They bound his legs together and carried him down to the lock-up.

Buckwell took the knife; a large clasp one with a long blade.

He considered the matter; threatening a life with a knife. The prisoner would be charged accordingly.

When the brother appeared at court the next month he was contrite. He deeply regretted the evening's outburst claiming it was because he had been pushed out of the White Hart to spend the night on the street.

It cost him a month's imprisonment. [1]

There was a bigger threat hanging over the village; a religious assault on the Church of England.

The threat was nationwide emanating from Rome where the Pope had taken upon himself to divide England into portions and allot a Roman Catholic bishop to each. The Protestant Faith was under attack. It was a threat against Queen Victoria who at her coronation just 13 short years earlier had become head of the Church in England.

In December 1850, Rev. Charles Dunlop and his churchwardens aligned themselves with the thousands of other English parishes who knew the Pope's design was akin to an invasion of their land and the overthrow of their Queen's religious authority.

They were determined not to stand idly by. A carefully phrased petition was prepared and signed on behalf of Henfield's ever loyal parishioners;

> That by your Majesty's coronation oath, your Majesty has solemnly engaged to maintain the free profession of the Gospel and of the Protestant religion in these realms --- have been insolently assailed by the nomination of a Cardinal Archbishop of Westminster and Roman Catholic Bishops by a foreign Prince and Potentate, the Pope of Rome --- who hath not any jurisdiction in this realm of England --- do protest against the act of insolent usurpation and humbly implore --- Parliament to enforce the defence of the Protestant faith. [2]

It was humbly forwarded for presentation.

If Drake and his men could repel the Spanish Armada, Rev. Dunlop and his parishioners could surely help repel the Roman Pope.

What actually befell was far more mundane and sad. Just months after the humble petition, Charles Dunlop's health deteriorated rapidly and in September 1851 he died. The parish was again without a vicar.

In due course a new man was inducted, Rev. John O'Brien, of Ireland; a family man who took up residence in the vicarage opposite the church.

Mrs. O'Brien played her part as the vicar's wife and was considerate to everyone.

She was pleased to give a shilling to the traveller who knocked at her front door seeking alms. He explained how he had been walking for almost 60 miles without being fortunate enough to obtain anything and was thankful to be received by her with such kindness.

With his shilling in his pocket, the traveller left the vicarage in a far happier state of mind. Finding nobody around to bid the time of day with, he carried on to his next call, again the vicarage but round at the back door. There he explained himself to a servant who went to her master and returned with a pair of shoes. Again his thanks were profuse.

When Rev. O'Brien and his wife compared the two callers, the vicar sought help.

Constable Buckwell obliged, found a hearty young man of similar description hawking brooms and brushes around the village without a licence and accosted him.

The outcome for the hawker was a fortnight of hard labour at Petworth.

Rev. O'Brien worked hard for the parish, hard enough to decide he and his wife should have a September week's holiday together in Brussels leaving the two children in the care of the head nurse. The safety of the vicarage itself would be in entrusted to the good hands of their exceptional guest, affable young Mr. John Hamilton.

They enjoyed their holiday and returned home much refreshed. All was well in the house except that young Mr. Hamilton had to report the loss of a ring, a ring of considerable monetary worth apart from the more important sentimental value it held for him.

The O'Briens were very upset that their guest should have to suffer the loss of his ring. The distinct possibility was that the nurse who had seemed so trustworthy when they appointed her earlier in the summer was in reality dishonest.

Rev. O'Brien felt great empathy for his servant parishioners but young Hamilton had proved himself a friendly, reliable man in looking after the vicarage. His ring had to be recovered.

The nurse disclaimed all knowledge of a ring declaring she had never seen one on Mr. Hamilton's finger. Rev. O'Brien felt he had no alternative to discharging her immediately with a month's wages. Before she left, he sent for the constable in order to have her box inspected.

The constable opened it and searched thoroughly. There was no sign of Mr. Hamilton's ring but three items in it indicated the nurse as a possible thief; three pounds of moist sugar, ½ a pound of tea and ¾ of a pound of soap. Although there was no mark by which they could be positively identified, Mrs. O'Brien was able to ascertain the tea and sugar were similar to that issued in the nursery for the two children.

It was no good the nurse protesting innocence; the evidence was there. The constable charged her accordingly.

At the petty sessions she continued to protest that the soap was hers and the tea and sugar had been saved from her own allowance.

The magistrates considered the evidence; the vicar's fears and the woman's denial. They announced their decision; prisoner discharged.

The vicar would need to review his ethics on empathy.

The O'Briens knew they were losing a good friend when their ever sociable visitor left for a vicarage in Suffolk with the mystery of his missing ring unsolved.

No mystery required solving when four young boys – deaf James, the sweep's son amongst them – decided to spend a Sunday afternoon exploring the Brookside Farm buildings opposite Rye.

The old farmhouse stood empty amongst farmyard rubble.

There were enough stones in the rubble for the boys to decide on a target competition. A successful throw at the house would be heralded by tinkling glass.

Success was a bit intermittent but the score rose steadily until the tinkle of glass was replaced by the bellow of an angry farmer.

Stones dropped to the ground. Stephen Stammer commenced a lengthy chastisement.

At its end, four deflated boys headed for home; secret prayers buzzing in their heads.

On their departure, Stephen Stammer inspected the damage.

It was serious; 11 panes of glass broken and a door frame damaged – a matter for the police.

Constable Buckwell prepared charges.

Parents and children appeared at Petty Sessions. Pleas that the windows were small and not used held no weight. Fines plus damages were imposed with the alternative of 14 days imprisonment.

The chairman added a severe reprimand; on Sunday afternoons parents should be taking their children to divine service instead of allowing them to wander the village causing wanton mischief.

The fines were paid and the parents took their children home, rankled more than humbled by the chairman's insulting words.

Constable Buckwell returned to his nightly High Street duty of patrolling for drink offenders.

The Plough kept him reasonably busy.

On a moonlit August night, John Wood, the bailiff at Backside Town Farm, stepped out from the Plough with a group of agricultural labourers, William White and Peter Browning among them. They had enjoyed a long evening of give and take convivial drink and banter until the landlord called time; their time for home.

Out in the influence of fresh air, conviviality ceased. William White shook his fist in John Wood's face and threatened him. Peter Browning struck him on the back knocking him to the ground. His hat fell off and that was the last he saw of it.

The incident was witnessed by Constable Buckwell who was close by but not close enough to intervene.

All he could do was ensure the case came to court.

There, his account was challenged by Peter Browning who had two witnesses able to swear point blank that he had not struck any blow.

The magistrates turned to Buckwell. Could the constable establish that Browning was the right man?

Constable Buckwell was adamant. The moonlight had been bright and clear. There was no doubt.

At that, any doubts in the magistrates' minds were removed. Browning and White had to pay the inevitable fine and costs of more than a week's wages. They were also called upon to amend their ways and not remain at an inn drinking until Sunday morning. The words fell on deaf ears.

Charles Flint was another with deaf ears when follies of drink were being propounded. He was a family man with four children in one of the slate hung cottages of Barracks Row off the narrow Blackstone road near the White Hart.

Charles preferred the Plough, especially on a Saturday night. His pint or two or three of beer, the camaraderie and the give and take of banter between the men uplifted him. He could go along with the best of them – and did.

P.C. Buckwell had him twice in a week for being drunk and disorderly.

At the Petty Sessions, the constable labelled him an inveterate drunkard, very troublesome and continually causing a disturbance.

He was admonished by the magistrates for his intemperate habits but it was of no interest to him.

What did give him concern was the fine of 5s 0d for each offence with costs amounting to 15s 0d which would become a month's hard labour if he did not find the money within a fortnight.

Charles turned over a new leaf and kept off his beer until the account had been settled.

Peace did not last long at the Plough. A scissors grinder turned up one evening, drank his day's takings and decided to settle down for the night in the warmth of the pub stable.

The landlord tried telling him to leave but the scissors grinder was quite content to stay where he was. In fact there was no way he was going to give up stable warmth for a night of coldness in the street.

It became another case for P.C. Buckwell followed by yet another 'drunk at the Plough' case for the magistrates. They fined the man 5s 0d.

His worldly wealth amounted to 11d so he was given a week to earn the rest. He set to with determination grinding as many pairs of Henfield scissors as owners could be told needed sharpening.

When Steyning Petty Sessions next held court for renewing licences, the Plough application was opposed by Constable Buckwell.

He declared the Plough was badly conducted, particularly on Saturdays when drinking men gathered in front to watch others fighting to prove their prowess. The all too many cases of drunkenness were generally from there.

The magistrates felt they could rely on the constable's assessment. The renewal was refused. [3]

At the next sessions the landlord promised better conduct in the future and regained his licence.

The magistrates' sense of duty in withholding the licence had completely ignored the better aspects of the landlord's conduct.

The Plough had a well run Friendly Society and a helpful service for the poorer households by stocking coal for purchase in small quantities.

Ann Martin took advantage of it.

She walked down from Nep Town to buy eightpennyworth. Her household comprised just husband Henry and youngest son John, both agricultural labourers.

She tapped at the bar window to attract the landlord's attention but he made no response.

Fortunately a customer was entering and he asked if he could help. She gave him a shilling for the landlord explaining it covered eightpence for her coals leaving fourpence to be returned to her when the coal was brought out.

The man took the money and went in to find the landlord.

Ann waited as long as she could but no coals came. She had to leave without any; her menfolk needed their meal.

That evening, she went back to the Plough and attracted the landlord's attention.

She discovered nobody had spoken to him about any coals. Her shilling had been purloined. She described the man.

The description fitted William Knapp who lived up in Shermanbury.

Knapp was taken and had to appear in court.

He willingly admitted being in the Plough and spending sixpence but he had not gained any money by false pretences as charged.

Ann was asked to explain how the prisoner had obtained the money from her. She answered honestly

The magistrates considered the two accounts. Which was the true one? They decided it was not possible to be certain enough.

William Knapp walked free.

Chapter 23

An outlaw's Mecca – Baccy & a pint – Basket makers' strike

Henfield's outlaw, William Lake, safe after three years of anonymity in his hideaway, did not have to concern himself any more with the merits or otherwise of British justice. Safe from his creditors, he walked his chosen streets with confidence and concentrated on building a new life. London; vast, bustling, with ever-in-a-hurry millions intent on living, indifferent to those around them – William's Mecca.

More precisely, Mecca was the streets around Euston Station, the London and North Western Railway's gateway to the north.

November freedom was tainted by a penetrating damp coldness. William did his best to ignore it. He stepped out briskly.

"Aha, Mr. Lake!"

William was taken aback, stunned. There stood Perkins, his arch enemy and number one creditor. At his side stood a lady.

A spontaneous reply was needed; one to confuse the man – to not recognise, not know him.

"You have the advantage of me," limp and ineffective.

Perkins was not to be distracted. Here was his one chance to nail the man who had cheated him of so much money. Lake would not defraud him of justice this time.

"Yes," he retorted, "and you had the advantage of me in 1846."

William knew he was cornered. His only course was to appease the man.

They talked and came to an agreement. William would accompany Mr. Perkins to his warehouse some three miles away and there they would come to some mutual agreement about settling the outstanding account.

First, though, Mr. Perkins' wife had a train to catch at Euston Station. That done, they made their way to the warehouse. There, Mr. Perkins had to ask his son and a shopman to entertain the guest because there was a call Mr. Perkins could not avoid making.

Before long he was able to return with company; Alderman Sir George Carroll and the City Superintendent.

Mr. Perkins explained to William that there was no longer need for discussion as the superintendent would determine proceedings.

With that, the meeting ended. William Lake was taken into custody.

On the first of December he stood in the dock of the crowded Guildhall Police Court. The case had excited intense interest.

He was charged with not surrendering to the fiat issued him on the 20th August 1846.

The evidence was heard and the prosecuting barrister, Clarkson, proposed the prisoner should be remanded to the next Monday when the depositions of the bankrupt and the creditors could be read.

Defence lawyer Kennedy objected. Either the prisoner should take his trial there or the court should allow him bail.

Back came the prosecution. The prisoner ran away from the fiat. What he might do with regard to his bail was impossible to say.

Listeners laughed at the thought.

The magistrate resolved the matter. He was satisfied the August fiat had been served in the correct manner. Lake had been at large since October 1846. It was his duty to commit him for trial. The question of bail was beyond his powers.

William Lake was returned to his cell with no knowledge of when his next appearance would be.

He had three weeks to wait. The next venue was the Central Criminal Court to answer a charge of removing his business books and papers to defraud his creditors.

Even there he had to endure a long delay while a similar case was being tried. Unknown to him, prosecution and defence counsels, Clarkson and Kennedy again, were in court arguing points of law. A man stood charged under the Act of Parliament decreeing that if any bankrupt should destroy, alter or falsify any of the books or papers with a view to defraud his creditors he was liable to three years prison with or without hard labour. If found guilty there was the probability of an associated charge carrying a further two year sentence.

The question at issue was the interpretation of that law. Clarkson considered it was unequivocal, its intent and wording were clear. Kennedy maintained it was flawed and that no case could be made with it.

The judge listened attentively as each point was argued. Finally he was ready to deliver his findings.

He favoured the reasoning of defence lawyer Kennedy, a flaw in the law. Clarkson acceded. The prisoner was found not guilty.

Kennedy declared the next case should be decided on the same lines. Clarkson felt bound to agree.

At last William was brought to the bar. No evidence was offered.

The judge formally announced the verdict; "Not guilty." [1]

Outlaw Lake was a free man. He wisely chose not to return to Henfield.

For the genuinely free men in Henfield there was a new interest; a branch of the Useful Knowledge Institution which would widen horizons over a range of topics.

The first meeting was at the Boys' School where a lecture very applicable in a farming area was given on 'Meteorology, with special reference to weather predictions'. The lecturer was enthusiastic and included several instructive experiments as he explained how all distant weather forecasting must necessarily be fallacious.

His audience saw no reason to doubt his findings. They had spent years being aware of weather's fickleness and were relieved he was imparting his knowledge free of charge to help their infant society.

Chairman Rev. Hall thanked him profusely and said the money saved would be put to good use in purchasing more books for the library set up in their Reading Room where the latest Sussex and London newspapers were already on hand for the use of subscribers.

At their second meeting the lecturer was Charles Longley, the respected High Street grocer. He spoke on 'The Progress of Man' from the beginning of civilisation and followed it with entertaining descriptions of the customs and employment in bygone days.

When the clapping ceased, Rev. Hall announced that the following meeting would be chaired by Charles Longley and be a discussion class debating 'Public Opinion'. The venue would be the Girls' School.

The idea proved popular. Members arrived early to ensure a seat.

Mr. Longley gave a short introductory talk and the debate began.

Members were keen to contribute although the merits or otherwise of Public Opinion had a tendency to wander into personal opinions on a range of issues until guided back by the chairman.

At the meeting's close, all agreed on their chairman's merits. He was a man of character.

Mr. Longley's next engagement was with the Inspector of Weights and Measures at the White Hart next door to his shop.

All tradesmen had to attend with their scales and weights; a yearly event that was a time of apprehension for them. The inspector was not an understanding man.

That year Charles Longley came to grief; a 4lb weight 4½ drachms light, a 2lb weight 1½ drachms light and 12 smaller weights all inaccurate.

He had to appear at Steyning Magistrates Court as did butcher Benjamin Cornford; his 7lb weight 1½ drachms light, butcher John Cutress; meat scale ¼ ounce out, grocer Henry Colgate; flour scale ¼ ounce out against the purchaser, and grocer James Frost; flour and counter scales defective.

Charles Longley confided he did not dispute the inspector's evidence but his weights had all been adjusted by the inspector the previous year.

He discovered it was no good casting doubt on an official how ever firm his own mind may be. His fines reflected the number of deficient weights, £2 plus 18s 0d costs.

The others had all proved themselves reliable in serving their term of public office as Parish Overseer but that was of nothing compared to using inaccurate weights. Each offender incurred similar fines. [2]

For Henry Colgate, the weights fiasco was the final straw. His move to Henfield had not proved beneficial; he returned to Withyham.

His shop was taken over by another incomer, Samuel Tobitt.

Mr. Tobitt takes over the BALDWIN & GARRETT emporium

William Keywood at the New Inn had an inspection of a different type, the constable's – not by appointment but by stealth.

It was a Sunday. Up in the village, people were at worship. Out at the New Inn, people were socialising – the day of rest enabling them to relax with a pipe of tobacco and a pot of beer.

William busied himself ensuring everybody's needs were being met until someone gave him the nudge; Constable Buckwell was approaching, nearly on them.

The company continued smoking and joking; landlord Keywood heading at speed into the next room.

When the constable walked in, not a pot was to be seen.

He took it all in with a sniff and a glance. He went to the next room and found beer.

Constable Buckwell demanded to know what had been going on.

William next heard the constable at Steyning giving evidence;

"I went there about 10 o'clock. There were several smoking and I saw the defendant run into another room with the beer, someone having given the alarm of my presence."

William paid his fine and returned home, the expense just part of an innkeeper's life. [3]

Stephen Ward suffered similar intrusive visits.

Stephen did not have a Henfield Settlement but he was self sufficient and made no requests for parish Poor Law assistance.

He worked at the Broadmare Common brickworks for Alfred Richardson who lived on site in the house fronting the pond; a house with everything a man needed.

Stephen was content with the small cottage and garden he rented from James Trussler the new Nep Town miller.

Life suddenly became stressful when Trussler issued a notice to quit.

Stephen was paying his weekly 1s 6d rent regularly and had no intention of being thrown out without proper cause. He refused to budge.

Trussler took the matter to court and requested a warrant to oust his tenant.

Stephen explained to the magistrates that he was not going to move out unless Mr. Trussler found him another house to go to.

The clerk to the court explained the law to him. It was not the task of a landlord to find new accommodation for a tenant. If he did not quit the house within 21 days, he would be put out on the street.

Stephen was evicted.

For him, home became a tent big enough for one.

At the end of the working day Stephen made his way to his chosen site for home, a sheltered spot on the common.

He pitched his tent and settled in for the evening. All he wanted was a meal and a night's rest.

At times he managed it. At times he was interrupted by Constable Buckwell carrying out his duty as instructed by the vestry committee – confront Stephen Ward and order him to move off Broadmare Common.

Broadmare Common with copyholders' cattle

It continued that way on and off for several weeks, Stephen moving away for a short while and quietly returning, until the vestry decided Ward should be prosecuted under the vagrancy laws.

He was taken to court and had to accept a fortnight of uninterrupted nights at Petworth House of Correction.

In the cottages alongside the road by Broadmare, 'Sunny' Woolgar was concentrating on keeping his basket making solvent. 'Sunny' could be a hard master suspicious of his workforce; four men employed at 12s 0d a week, the average labourer's money.

Peter Cragg was a voluble member pleased to act as union man for his mates should the need arise.

His chance came one autumn after the men had been out on Broadmare cutting osiers for the season's rods.

'Sunny' had boiled most of the rods to give the buff colour his customers expected. The men were going through the next process of stripping the bark.

They had completed a good two hours or more work by 8.00 a.m. when 'Sunny' decided he needed to talk to his men.

He talked what he expected of the men and what would otherwise happen. Peter replied, talking what the men expected and what would otherwise happen – at which the men downed tools and walked out.

That was too much for 'Sunny'. His employees had left their service without leave. They would face him in court.

By the time that happened, two of the men had made it up with him. They returned to work and agreed to pay their share of the forthcoming court expenses.

At Steyning Petty Sessions, 'Sunny' and Peter came head to head.

The charge was put and 'Sunny' stated what had occurred.

Peter gave his evidence. He disputed the agreement altogether in as many words as he could muster. The court found them to be abundant.

The magistrates endeavoured to elicit the true turn of events. They decided the parties should be allowed to withdraw and settle their differences. It would include the payment of court costs.

The men withdrew and agreed that no one should be outright winner or loser; work would be resumed by all and costs would be paid by the men.

'Sunny' Woolgar could feel quiet satisfaction. [4]

Peter Cragg decided to quit basket making. He would buy a horse and van and be a huckster; 'Sunny' Woolgar was a storm cloud best avoided.

'Sunny' had more trouble when he gave temporary employment to a travelling basket maker.

The man stayed about four months before suddenly announcing during work that he was moving on. He gathered up his tools and went.

It happened very quickly, so quickly that it was several hours before 'Sunny's' son Henry realised he was short of one of his father's bodkins.

Constable Buckwell was called in. He was briefed; the alleged crime and the suspect's description. He set off on his investigation.

Brighton was top of the list for likely refuge. The next morning Constable Buckwell was there visiting probable pubs and lodging houses.

He found his man at the Royal George Beerhouse in Middle Street.

Among his belongings was a likely bodkin. The man expressed surprise and denied he took it with felonious intent. He had been using the bodkin four or five weeks, it must have been by his side when he packed up his tools. He had not been alone, other workers had watched him.

Constable Buckwell noted the statement and arrested his man.

Steyning magistrates heard all sides; that the value of the bodkin was eight pence, that it had not been taken intentionally and that the prosecutor's son had been present when the traveller packed his tools.

"Not guilty," was the decision. The happy traveller travelled on and this time it was 'Sunny' Woolgar who paid the costs.

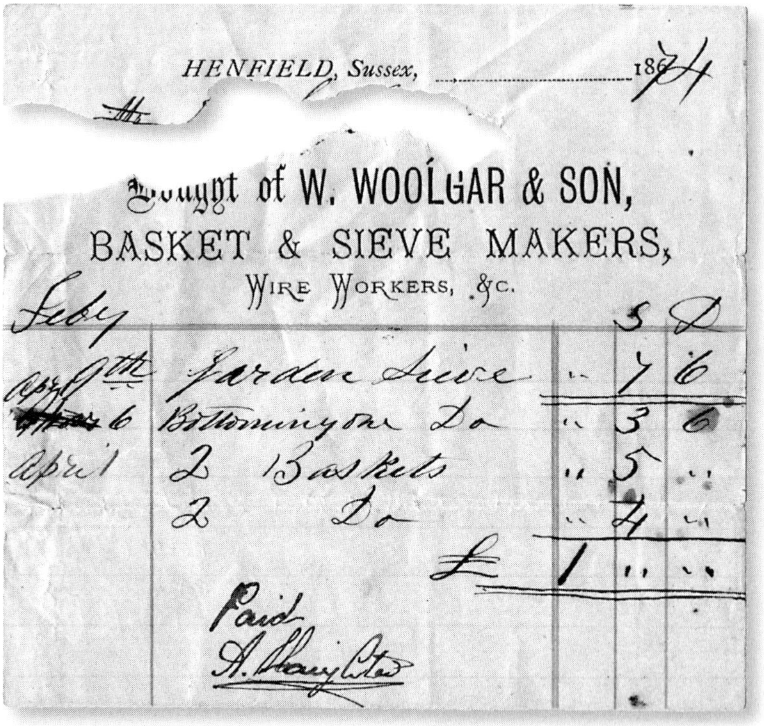
HENFIELD, Sussex, 1874

Bought of W. WOOLGAR & SON,
BASKET & SIEVE MAKERS,
WIRE WORKERS, &c.

			s	d
Feby				
Apl 9th	Garden Sieve	..	7	6
6	Bottoming one Do	..	3	6
April	2 Baskets	..	5	..
	2 Do	..	4	..
	£	1	..	..

Paid

'Sunny' Woolgar's bill to Rev. J. Goring of Wiston House near Steyning

About a mile beyond Broadmare Common stood Woods Mill, its large water-wheel obvious from the road. In the fields opposite was West Mill, not such a big wheel but a large pond.

Both industries were working to full capacity; Woods Mill with three pairs of stones producing flour, West Mill concentrating on oil cake.

Owner John Botting had died and the mills were advertised for sale.

In the unlikely case of the properties not being disposed of by private contract, an auction would be held at the King and Queen Inn, Brighton.

Woods Mill was freehold. The sale included the dwelling house, piggeries, cart lodges, a hovel and outhouses with about four acres of meadow.

The stones and machinery would be paid for at an agreed valuation.

Although there was no railway through Henfield, the advertisements guaranteed trade covering a wide area because rail services were within seven miles at Hassocks Gate on the London line and four at Kingston Wharf, the station for Shoreham Harbour.

West Mill was in production both day and night supplying the many local farmers feeding oil cake to their stock.

The current occupiers, Vallence and Wickens, had been there for 13 years of a 21 years lease paying an annual rent of £50. It was copyhold with a cottage in two tenements and four acres of pastureland.

That sale included the whole of the gear.

For the would be miller, the list comprised the essentials of oil cake manufacture; two very large oil tanks, meal and seed bins, a reservoir with pipe, tap and pump, stirring tackle, presses and six wrought-iron stampers.

A value would be agreed for the mill's boat, van, cart and casks.

The advertised advantages of nearby rail links proved ineffective. Nobody bought the mills by private contract. Nobody bid enough at the auction. Son Jonathan Botting remained master miller at Woods Mill with his son as assistant.

Messrs Vallence and Wickens remained undisturbed at West Mill supplying their oil cake to grateful farmers.

Chapter 24

The ploughing match – A horse race – Harriers and hares

The local farmers formed a Farmers' Club bringing social and business matters together for the benefit of them all.

They held their first meeting at the end of May in the best room of the George. There they enjoyed the food of landlord Stoner and drank their way through the healths of as many patrons as they could.

Thus fortified, they decided that in the autumn they would hold a ploughing match.

The rest of the evening was given over to singing, some by members but many by the comic singer from Brighton, Mr. Simmonds, who found just the right songs to make the evening yet another memorable occasion.

The year reached its climax; haymaking and harvest.

At Parsonage Farm, Alfred Mitchell was enjoying a good season. His hay dried well and proved a bumper crop neatly stacked in the yard; the August corn harvest was safely gathered and brought home.

He threshed his corn the modern way, hiring a threshing machine powered by a steam traction engine.

Men who once flailed wheat now confidently operated machinery; so far without loss of employment.

Weather permitting, work began as soon as daylight allowed. Breakfast was a short break. By 8.30 they were threshing again.

They had been back at it for about ten minutes one morning when the men noticed flames at the base of a haystack in the yard. Threshing stopped abruptly.

A normal day's hard work became frantic battle. If the fire took hold, the blaze would spread to the barns.

Threshers were put to fetching water from the yard pond. They formed a chain passing bucketfuls along the line to be thrown on the flames.

Fortunately the fire had been noticed before it took could develop into a blaze. The men worked fast. Flames were doused.

More water ensured nothing would reignite.

Yet something was amiss. A short trail of blackened straw led away from the fire. In which direction had the flames travelled?

The mystery required a solution. Farmer Mitchell sent for Constable Buckwell.

By the time he arrived, the workmen had decided a probable reason – the young boy, William, who normally spent most of his day around the place.

The cottage where he lived was searched. His grandfather, one of the threshers, was unable to say why he was missing. Constable Buckwell set off in search.

Buckwell found the boy playing with his mates on the common. He did not have anything to say for himself but his friends said plenty. William had told them how he found some Lucifer matches and had taken them outside to the yard. He struck one on the heel of his boot and lit a bundle of straw. The fire went along to the stack and started up the side. It frightened him and he ran away.

Constable Buckwell had his suspect. They returned to the farm.

The grandfather explained that the boy's father was away at sea and had asked him to look after the child.

The matter was sorted out at the Petty Sessions, seven year old William Piper in the dock.

Farmer Mitchell stated that he did not want to press charges because when the boy lit the match it was purely out of mischief. There had been no malice in the boy's actions but the fire had come near to consuming several barns containing farm produce. However, he could not allow the boy to continue living at the farm with his grandfather.

The magistrates felt they had to accede to Mr. Mitchell's wishes which left one conundrum, where would the boy be accommodated?

After careful deliberation they came up with the answer; the Steyning Union Workhouse at Shoreham – a secure haven for a young arsonist. [1]

That October the promised ploughing match took place at Mr. Randle's farm 'Kentons' beyond the common, luckily in good weather which encouraged a fair number of spectators.

There were five classes and each competitor had to plough half an acre within the time limit of four hours. Prizes would be from £2 or £1 10s for first and 15s for second; each prize much more than a week's earnings.

All competitors completed their half acre in about 2½ hours, enjoyed the refreshments provided for them and awaited the decisions of the judges – wisely men from outside the area.

The judges compared notes and the choices were made.

Awards for the three-horse, two wheel turn-furrow plough went to men from Beeding and Saddlescombe.

First prize for the three-horse, turn-furrow went to Woodmancote. Second place was gained by Henry Nye, ploughman at Betley.

The final three-horse event was with a round plough; Peter Pesterfield of Backside Town Farm ploughed his way to victory with Henry Banfield from Mr. Arthur Smith's Bilsborough Farm second.

Brother Alfred Smith's ploughman Henry Freeman was first with the two-horse round plough worked without a ploughboy driver. To everyone's satisfaction, host farmer John Randle's man came second.

The last class was for young men under 18 using a two or three-horse round plough. Success went to a 15 year old from Albourne.

The ploughboy driver for each successful man won 2s 6d. The unsuccessful ploughmen also received 2s 6d and their ploughboys had 1s 0d.

Prizes were awarded. The contestants set off to return the ploughs to the farms. The farmers made their way across the common to the George Inn.

There they enjoyed another of landlord Stoner's excellent dinners.

When the cloth was removed, loyal toasts were drunk.

Next, the president of the club formally announced the prize-winners. He was pleased to commend the ploughing of Henry Browning from Mr. Alfred Mitchell's Parsonage Farm – a satisfying mention for Mr. Mitchell.

Opinions about the match and the merits of the different ploughs were exchanged. On one point there was full agreement; although there had been modern ploughs in use – Howard's, Ransome's and others – the old round or half-swing plough performed the work very much better. [2] Henfield farmers knew what was what.

Alfred Smith, the Wantley farmer, qualified for Esquire in the cricket club scorebook. It was well deserved because he was putting more resources than anyone into keeping the club healthy. He also gave hunting enthusiasts a lot of pleasure coursing with his harriers.

Unknown to him, a group of his friends decided some sort of tribute should be made. They decided upon a dinner at the George where they would present him with an inscribed silver tankard. Contributions were sought from acquaintances who might like to attend the dinner.

Before long they had sufficient response and had to close the books; 60 people had subscribed, the absolute maximum the George could cater for. Enough money had been raised to include an extra gift, an inscribed hunting whip. The tricky part was to invite Mr. Smith without him sensing what was in the wind.

This was managed and the dinner took place, yet another of landlord Stoner's wonderful spreads prepared by his wife and enjoyed by everyone. It was followed by toasts being drunk which to Alfred Smith's great surprise culminated in one for himself.

As the guests settled to their chairs again, a visitor from Hove kept to his feet and began a speech in praise of Alfred Smith.

He listened in astonishment; magnified when he was called forward amidst thunderous cheering to receive the tankard and whip.

He now had to reply. It was difficult, an unexpected emotional moment that had to be overcome. He coped, made his reply and sat down thankfully as the evening moved into song and chat until the early hours of the morning.

Another village benefactor was Mr. Randle, host of the Ploughing Match. He provided a popular outing on the common for the working man's family. There were pony and donkey races interspersed with rural sports. Mr. Stoner provided ample refreshments from the George. It proved a day to be remembered.

It may have been Mr. Randle's festivities that spawned the wager of a horse race on the common between two local rivals who had never been astride a horse. Word spread around.

A good crowd assembled to watch the spectacle hoping for amusing entertainment. Would either man keep mounted long enough to ride the length of the common from the cricket pitch to the village corner?

The horses stood saddled and ready. The men were helped to mount.

The starter set them off.

People grinned. Neither horse did more than walk, its rider holding tight to the saddle and looking distinctly unhappy.

After a few minutes one of the competitors summoned up courage to wiggle the reins and persuade the horse to break into a gentle trot. The other man felt the walk was movement enough.

The crowd gave encouragement, the leading man gained confidence and his horse began a lolloping canter. The second man was left far behind, his spirit down among his boots.

Across the common they went. The canter became respectable, the rider still tight kneed against his saddle, one hand gripping the pommel. Half the course had been completed.

Before too long the common corner was reached, the horse stopped and the triumphant winner was helped dismount to the cheerful acclaim of the spectators.

The second rider stuck to his task. He too was acclaimed at the common corner and assisted to the ground. Horse racing was over for the day.

Another spectacle was assembling on the common. The Brighton Harriers had chosen the same March day for their sport; killing hares.

They set off full of optimistic enthusiasm. By mid afternoon it was waning; the hounds had not located a single hare.

It was early evening before one was disturbed. The chase was on.

The hare headed away past New Hall and round to the brooks, hounds and harriers in hot pursuit. The hare lost in the end and Brighton Harriers returned home. Henfield's hares had been disappointing.

Until summer the common was quiet. That changed with the start of the cricket season.

Petworth visited in glorious weather for a match said to include several of the best players in the county.

It attracted a large number of spectators who saw some excellent play on a pitch extremely lively for the bowlers. In Petworth's second innings Penikett wreaked havoc bowling seven overs to take six wickets for 5 runs; Henfield winning by an innings and 2 runs.

Bushby for once played a minor role being bowled out for 6 and taking only one catch. Perhaps his mind was on other things. His wife had just given birth to their first child, Ruth. Baby Ruth was still less than a month old.

The match that had most coverage in the Sussex Advertiser was the fixture over at Lewes where the reporter picked out gamekeeper Bushby for particular praise.

Lewes batted first. The reporter recorded progress. With the score on 79;

> Mr. Pagden made a hit to Bushby at the point, which he thought out of reach, called Picknell, who was, amidst great regret, run out; 5 wickets, 79 runs.

Gilbert came next – runs scarce; he had a narrow escape from the claws of Bushby, a hard hit and a little too high for the great Sussex player.

Lewes were all out for 102.

Henfield gentlemen took possession of the wickets --- 2 wickets – 12 runs. Bushby, the pride of English batters, came forth and was applauded. --- Mr. Payne sent a sky-scraper as high as a rainbow, which Carpenter missed. Bushby played carefully and obtained 2 singles, a two and a three. ---Bushby gave a fair catch to Cooley at cover point which he missed, a damper for Lewes. Bushby, grateful for his escape, soon sent the ball to the wall for three." He scored 32 and then yielded his wicket to one of Picknell's trimmers (rounds of applause).

Henfield just managed a three run lead.

When Lewes batted again, hairdresser Penikett scalped them taking eight wickets. His amazing bowling meant Henfield needed just 58 for victory.

They had scored only six of them when the second wicket fell bringing cheers from Lewes supporters;-

Bushby, that formidable Bushby came next; everybody admires the man and his play, but many wished him on this occasion disposed of – a very unusual wish in Sussex. --- Mr. Wynch sent a fine ball to Bushby, the wicket keeper caught it beautifully and cried out "How's That!" "Can't say" responded Mr. Umpire – a pause – and Bushby was – not out. Bushby made a two and a few singles before being run out, "bravo" for Lewes and an unfortunate end to the leviathan of the bat. [3]

Henfield's lesser men managed victory in the end. The team returned home and resumed the chores of the working day.

Back in the village the two heroes' ways diverged.

Penikett's father followed the example of several other manor tenants. He took advantage of the Government's Copyhold Act to negotiate for his property to be enfranchised to become completely free of manor control – his Nep Town house and garden, 90 feet by 34, at the corner of Windmill Lane.

The manor valuer set the compensation price at £2 19s 1d. [4]

Charles Penikett paid with alacrity. The land, John's inheritance, would become Penikett land, no strings attached; no manor customs to adhere to, no more quit rent or heriot, no allegiance owed to any bishop.

Edward Bushby with his wife and baby daughter, Ruth, lived in a tied cottage. If he changed his employment they would have to move.

During the autumn his health declined. He became almost lethargic, lacking his normal energy although still fully committed to his duties.

On one of the drab post-Christmas days a shoot was organised. Bushby had an important part to play as gamekeeper in ensuring birds would appear for the guests' guns.

Underkeepers beat the woods. Birds duly flew.

Guests and Bushby took aim; triggers were pulled.

From most guns, shot pellets peppered the sky but not from Bushby's – the gun exploded shattering his hand, spilling blood and flesh.

They helped him to the house, sent for the doctor and did what they could to ease the pain. Bushby would need all his determination to recover.

The wound slowly began to heal but nothing would restore the use of his hand.

Bushby's spirit had been shattered too.

In March 1856, the Sussex Advertiser carried the news;

DEATH OF BUSHBY THE CRICKETER. He was just 39. [5]

Chapter 25

Gingerbread scrambles – Violin variations – Sleepy carter

The gun accident and death of Bushby, a significant event in village eyes, paled to insignificance the following month when Her Majesty proclaimed a Thanksgiving for Peace in the Crimea. 45,000 British soldiers had lost their lives – vast numbers from depredation and disease; Florence Nightingale's men.

The vicar led the parish in heartfelt prayer and remembrance.

That done, village life continued.

The George Benefit Club held their 30th anniversary enjoying a hilarious day followed by an evening of food, drink and song for which several wives arrived to enhance the gathering. Landlord Stoner, provider of the meal, proved to have a capital baritone voice pleasingly conspicuous. Other members contributed numbers but undoubted star of the evening was again humorist and comic singer, Mr. Simmonds of Brighton. Who else could entertain so well?

For September a non-anniversary event was planned, Henfield's first ever Horticultural and Floricultural Society Show.

Preparations by the organisers had taken months; committee meetings, ideas shared, contacts made, the decision to proceed agreed, a venue arranged, the various classes of exhibitor and exhibits decided and prize money guaranteed.

Classes would be 'Professional' for market gardeners and gardeners of the gentry, 'Amateur' and finally 'Cottagers' restricted to those in houses paying less than £6 Poor Rate in furtherance of the show ideal to encourage the poor to cultivate their gardens.

Interested amateurs and cottagers had begun working towards it as soon as winter allowed digging to commence. Seed had been sown, plants nurtured and promising specimens coddled. Gentlemen's gardeners had chosen eye catching plants to enhance their reputations.

The show took place in the School Room on the common. All the elite and fashionable attended.

Inside, a patriotic red, white and blue coloured motif announced 'Cottagers, Gardeners and Amateurs'. On the far wall was a motto picked out in coloured stars 'In all labour there is profit', the handiwork of Infants' School Mistress, Miss Wallington.

The judges considered the cottagers' vegetables were very good. They also praised the displays of wild flowers, all being thoughtfully arranged. Extra prizes were awarded to two outstanding entries; V.R. in pink thistle heads on a moss ground, and an array of colourful blooms in a miniature garden.

Some excellent fruit was shown:- apples, pears, plums and greengages of the amateurs with mouth watering peaches and nectarines from gentlemen's residences.

Wonderful specimens of garden flowers were in abundance; hollyhocks, roses, asters, dahlias, tropical gloxinias, Indian pinks....

Mr. Borrer kindly showed a selection of his Barrow Hill plants, excellent examples all labelled in Latin as befitted an eminent botanist.

Everyone agreed the show was a truly wonderful first exhibition with the added enjoyment of brass band tunes throughout the afternoon.

The committee could feel justifiably pleased and look forward to another show in 1857. [1]

To many parents' regret, Miss Wallington was leaving the Infants' School at the end of the year.

A farewell ceremony was quietly arranged for the prize-giving afternoon before the children began their Christmas Holiday. It was an occasion the vicar, his wife and village dignitaries regularly attended.

That special year, Rev. Glubb, the Rural Dean and Diocesan Inspector of Schools, joined them together with many of the mothers.

Rev. John O'Brien addressed a few guiding words to the parents. Rev. Glubb talked to the children in a homely and pleasing manner and asked a few simple questions by way of inspection.

Now came what the children were waiting for, the prizes awarded to almost all of them depending on the regularity of their attendance according to strict school protocol.

They were all valuable awards, warm and useful articles of clothing – blessings for their money-stretched parents.

After the prize-giving, the children enjoyed the thrill of large pieces of good, rich cake with an orange to follow.

The final treat gave an opportunity for a few minutes kind hearted amusement among visitors as the youngsters scrambled for gingerbread, nuts and sugarplums.

Scrambling completed, there came the climax of the afternoon. Rev. O'Brien turned to address Miss Wallington thanking her for her constant dedication, skill and kindness whilst at the school.

She was than presented with several elegant and useful gifts as a mark of the esteem in which she had been held.

Finally the vicar turned to the mothers and expressed his appreciation of their exemplary conduct the previous week when they had banded together and visited the school to show their gratitude with little gifts to Miss Wallington. [2]

Miss Wallington thanked everyone and gave her sincere Christmas wishes to the children. The holiday could begin.

Before Christmas Day the Useful Knowledge Institution Discussion Class held their regular evening meeting. This time the speaker was Mr. Henry Longley, the High Street draper, whose chosen subject was "The Character of Oliver Cromwell."

Mr. Longley championed him as a great statesman and general to whom the nation should be truly thankful.

Society members were divided. Opinions were expressed in a frank and friendly manner to such an extent that the meeting had to close with a number of people still wishing to speak. It was agreed to meet again the next day.

The reconvened class kept the subject going well into the evening with two amendments by members favouring the Royal Cause of King Charles. Members voted. Both amendments were rejected and the Discussion Class came out Republican in a very democratic and gentlemanly manner – no heads would roll.

One head was in danger – that of a 23 year old man with accrued debts of £2900 appearing at the Canterbury County Court in Kent having spent the previous year at a Suffolk rectory and, before that, as a guest at Henfield vicarage.

In Suffolk he had acted as a clergyman although not ordained. He nevertheless signed his name as Rev. when ordering goods – Rev. Hamilton, J.C. or J.T. was uncertain.

The court proceedings ran into the evening and they too had to be closed until the next day.

Reassembled, the court heard the extent and nature of John Thomas Hamilton's debts. He had claimed to possess considerable landed property whereby he obtained £62 value of silver plate. He ran up a debt of £376 at various silversmiths plus £24, gunmaker; £78, draper; £28, wine; £30 for a horse and on until he had amassed a total of 33 debts.

Defence argued that tradesmen had no right to trust a young man on expectation that his friends would pay.

The judge ignored him and summed up. Hamilton's debt to the silversmith bordered on criminal misrepresentation. For the worst offences the sentence was 14 months with another six months for the lesser debts. John Thomas Hamilton's easy tongue would have to stay tight lipped. [3]

Perhaps the terrible loss of his ring whilst looking after Henfield vicarage was not such a mystery as Rev. O'Brien had thought. Perhaps the nurse's word should have been accepted with a little more trust.

Rev. George Hall at the Congregational Chapel had an opportunity to feel pleasure. His only child, Cornelius, – just five years old when they moved into the village, and now grown to manhood – had become a pupil of Doctor Adolphus Caudle. Cornelius proved a zealous pupil and had recently studied for an examination in midwifery. He passed and the achievement was reported in the Sussex papers – penned by surgeon A. Caudle Esq.

Barely a month later, there was an opportunity for people to enjoy musical entertainment at the White Hart. It was provided by a solo performer from across the wide Atlantic, violinist Mr. Athlic Smith.

His performance was in the big club room at the back of the inn. Drinkers and music lovers filled the room. So did the exquisite playing of Athlic Smith. His bow bounced to buoyant rhythms, sauntered softly in sweet melody, tinkled tuneful ditties and brought guffaws of applause as it imitated bagpipe and hurdy-gurdy. [4]

What a performance to extol; White Hart beer and Athlic Smith's violin. A perfect evening.

Concert goers returned home quietly uplifted under the watchful eye of Henfield's new regular police constable. Parliament had decreed that every county should have a properly constituted Police Force. West Sussex duly complied and the new Constabulary appointed Police Constable George Egerton to Henfield – still with three parochial constables as assistants if needed.

P.C. Egerton was keen to make his presence known. His chance came during night patrol.

A regular on the roads was huckster John Browning. He seldom rushed his horse; certainly never at night on the way back to Henfield.

The horse was quietly walking John and his cart homeward from Cowfold at 11.00 p.m. one warm July night when they came upon P.C. Egerton.

John, being fast asleep, did not notice anything; certainly not that his horse was being led the rest of the way to the village. There he finally managed to rouse himself and became aware of the constable.

P.C. Egerton repeated the events to the Steyning Magistrates and John had to pay a 1s 0d fine with 14s 0d costs. He was warned of the serious accidents which could befall when drivers acted the way in which he had done. [5]

Despite the warning and unwelcome expense, he continued his quiet ways particularly returning from a hard day's trading in Brighton. The constable on duty along the Brighton road vowed he frequently complained to Browning about his conduct in getting intoxicated and being asleep on his cart.

Another night the horse kept on walking as they approached the Terry's Cross Turnpike Gate. The wooden gate stopped them but it cost John another petty sessions visit with a 5s 0d fine, costs increased to 15s 6d and severe words from the magistrates of how the final outcome would be Petworth if he failed to mend his ways.

Chapter 26

Why the heathen rage – Railway promise – Dishonest miller

July became harvest August giving way to September; time for the second Horticultural and Floricultural Show.

Three linked marquees were needed to provide a single covered space for the great number of entries expected in the extended range of classes.

The evening before the show saw intense activity. Charles Nathan Stoner superintended the erection of floral arches outside and decorative foliage inside. Competitors carefully arranged their exhibits and the gardeners of village gentry prepared displays to enhance the occasion.

All knew the weather was unfavourable, they could only hope.

The morning's dawn was ominous with a wet westerly wind. Shoulders were shrugged – weather was weather.

By afternoon, weather was still weather – as fine as could be wished. Over 600 people visited the show to glory at the wonders of the English Garden.

Murmurs of admiration came for Mr. Borrer's achimenes and cipus biscolu; Lucretia Wood's black grapes, hollyhocks and China asters; the German asters from Newtimber Place; the melon and African marigolds from Dutch Miss Melvil at Henfield Lodge.

There was praise too for the cottagers; the 'Device of Wild Flowers' from Charles Parsons and his 'Pot Herbs'; of 'Garden Flowers' by Henry Hills and the general high standard of vegetables that the entrants had grown.

The organisers' hopes had been exceeded; the receipts a mark of true success.

Four weeks later the devout people of Henfield assembled in St. Peter's Church for the nation's 'DAY OF SOLEMN FAST, HUMILIATION AND PRAYER' proclaimed by Her Majesty Queen Victoria at Balmoral Castle because of the terrible situation on the vast continent of India.

The British East India Company had changed the native people's way of life and increased taxation. Indian soldiers objected to biting off the fatty seal on a new type of cartridge because for Muslims to ingest pork, or Hindus beef, was against their faith. Some mutinied. Punishment was severe. Mutiny spread and barbarous acts were being committed.

Rev. O'Brien selected his text from Psalms; Why do the heathen rage?

He spoke with feeling, his words painting scenes of distressing sorrow:- members of devoted missionary groups being murdered as they worked to spread Christianity among the heathen millions; soldiers' wives and children butchered and their bodies thrown down a well at a place called Cawnpore.

Collections were made morning and evening for the Indian Relief Fund. The cause justified compassionate response. [1]

The enlightened British Army on actual service in India decided that what the cause really justified was strict military response. They were doing so.

Useful Knowledge Institution members in their Reading Room could read eyewitness reports of further events in Cawnpore:- eighteen mutineers under sentence of death – ten at the gallows, three kneeling to be shot, five lashed by their hands to the wheels of ready primed cannon facing away from the assembled troops. At the given order, ropes tightened, muskets blasted and the cannon boomed, recoiling to leave a scene of dangling corpses and scattered body parts. The wicked mutiny would be stamped out.

Useful Knowledge members could ponder; 'Why do the heathen rage?'

Safe in Henfield, Miss Mary Stringer felt a degree of Christian annoyance one November afternoon at her Berlin Wool Shop close by the Plough.

She was sitting alone in her inner room ready to serve anybody entering the shop. Two men, strangers in the village, were gazing intently at her window display.

Apart from a few books and penny-papers, her display comprised ladies' handbags, patterned cushion and furniture coverings, canvas pattern designs and colourful embroidery wools.

Her customers were almost always ladies from the better class of family. She could not envisage such ill dressed men reading, let alone stitching. They were undoubtedly suspicious characters.

Mary kept her eye on them.

The pair finally entered the shop.

She went through to serve them.

They asked to see some of the books.

Barely waiting for an answer, they moved forward and picked several up.

Mary told them that she would prefer to find whatever they wished to see.

The men put the books down but showed displeasure by ill manneredly pushing back past her.

"Do you have the book Dread?" asked one.

Mary knew of no such title. She assured them she did not.

Thereupon they bought a penny-paper and left.

Mary returned to her inner room to recompose herself.

About an hour later she put her hand to her pocket for her purse. It was missing. She knew it had been safely there earlier with fifteen shillings in coins. She was convinced one of the men must have taken it.

Although upset, she did nothing until well past nine o'clock when P.C. Egerton was on duty in the High Street.

P.C. Egerton listened to her tale and her list of missing coins; two two-shilling pieces, two threepenny pieces, two fourpenny pieces and the rest in sixpences and shillings.

He decided it was a genuine enough complaint to warrant enquiries. He would begin at the pubs; always a worthwhile source of information. Closest was the Plough.

There, landlord Tidy described a man who had arrived that afternoon about two o'clock and two brothers arriving about an hour later. All three had left together and shortly afterwards had come back in and asked if they could have a bed. He told them beds were available and one of the men ordered a pot of sixpenny paying for it with two threepenny pieces.

P.C. Egerton was convinced he had traced his suspects.

Tidy took him upstairs to the room the men were sleeping in. They were given a rude awakening and told to get out of bed. P.C. Egerton informed them of their situation and searched their clothing. One of the men had fifteen shillings wrapped in a handkerchief. The other two had just a knife and a comb each and one had a leather bag containing a shirt.

In the constable's police eyes two friends with nothing whilst the third had fifteen shillings was akin to them being guilty. They were marched off to spend the rest of the night amongst the straw in the lock-up.

Next morning P.C. Egerton questioned other shopkeepers in case the men had visited them too.

At Charles Longley's grocery the shop boy told of serving a man between four and five o'clock the previous afternoon. First the customer bought a loaf of bread for which he paid a fourpenny coin and received three farthings change. He had then asked for a quarter of a pound of butter costing 3¼d for which he produced another fourpenny coin. The boy had the rest of the morning off because P.C. Egerton took him along with landlord Tidy, Mary Stringer and the three suspects for the legal examination by a Steyning J.P.

Each gave their version of events. The two brothers were let down a little by the third man swearing he had not gone into the shop but had only put his head in at the door.

One of the brothers complained of being taken out of his bed at 11 p.m.

He made a defiant challenge;

"If the woman can swear to any of the money let her swear to it."

They then went their separate ways; four to Henfield, three to the Steyning lock-up.

That same fortnight John Browning, the huckster prone to sleep driving, took a cartload of potatoes down to Shoreham.

On the way back he called in at a pub for a few drinks. With his drinks safely down he offered one of the Beeding bargemen a lift back.

Near Old Shoreham Church they passed a group of men, a lone soldier amongst them, heading the other way.

John called a jocular greeting. One of them called back turning the meeting into a sovereign bet on what money they had.

The man held out his hand.

John reckoned himself to be in money enough to take the bet on; two sovereigns, two half sovereigns and the silver change from the pub. He put his hand in his pocket and held out his money.

The man straightway knocked John's hand up.

The coins shot in the air to lie scattered on the road except one sovereign. John was convinced it lay hidden between the stranger's closed finger and thumb.

"Hey Old Fellow, you've got my sovereign." He moved to recover his money.

The man swung his fist hitting John a wallop on the side of the head.

John continued to insist on having his money back.

In reply, the man swung his stick, struck John on the hand, called for his mates to come and help him and stooped to pick up the fallen coins.

The soldier stopped him.

The bargeman got down from the cart, collected the coins and gave them back to John. They left the group to continue their way.

Once the men were out of sight, John asked the bargeman to take the cart on as far as Beeding while he went back to Shoreham for a policeman.

The bargeman was happy enough and set off home.

John found a constable in Shoreham and told his tale.

The constable considered he would have noticed a group containing a soldier. The men must have crossed the toll bridge over the Adur and made off that way.

The pair set out over the bridge and enquired at the Sussex Pad Inn.

Yes, the landlord could recall five men in the Tap Room about 6 p.m. He had served one of them with a pot of beer and three large measures of gin. Three of the men had shared it. They left soon after seven.

John and his constable continued to Worthing reaching the railway station about 9 p.m. There on a bench outside lay their quarry deeply asleep.

John roused him.

"Hey Old Fellow! Where's my sovereign?"

"Hallo," mumbled the man.

"Are you going to give me back my sovereign?"

"I don't know anything about your sovereign. I came over the hill to Worthing."

"Didn't you meet me the other side of Old Shoreham?"

"I did."

"I should like to have my sovereign."

The constable had listened to enough. He took the suspect into custody accused of robbing John Browning of one sovereign.

The man insisted it was his own sovereign.

"I had three sovereigns when I left home."

He was searched and found to have only a few pence.

The three of them walked back to Shoreham.

John continued alone to Beeding, found his horse and cart, climbed aboard and headed for Henfield. This time he was wide awake and negotiated his way with no difficulty.

Both Miss Stringer and John Browning had to wait for justice until the January Quarter Sessions at Petworth.

There the magistrates had to be convinced beyond doubt before they could reiterate P.C. Egerton's "Guilty" verdict on the shop customers.

Miss Stringer could not swear to the coins being the ones in her purse. The magistrates found in favour of the man who had challenged her to identify them. Mary's 'Christian Annoyance' momentarily raised its head again; men treating a lady with contempt and being supported by authority.

The ill mannered customers went on their way with no further stain on their characters.

John Browning's betting opponent may have done better if he had made a similar challenge. He did not and was sentenced to six weeks' hard labour which left John still short of his sovereign; a wager lost by them both.

Back in Henfield there was gossip far more interesting than encounters with petty robbers. Rumours of progress on the railway front were widespread – of the train speeding passengers and produce to far off destinations.

Steyning landowners made it official. Their projected branch from Shoreham was to be extended via Horsham to Dorking.

Promises of financial backing came from as far as Knepp Castle in West Grinstead.

People warmed to the idea; a passenger service right up to the Waterloo Station in London.

A petition was begun at Steyning for Parliament to legislate the line.

Several prominent Henfield men signed their support; - Vicar Rev. O'Brien, shopkeeper/churchwarden George Longley, registrar William Challen and solicitor Stephen Coppard. All were delighted at the prospect of a railway through the village

In December a meeting was held at the White Horse in Steyning. Walter and Percy Burrell of Knepp Castle and Rev. Goring of Wiston were chief among the landowners. Several Henfield residents attended including Dr. Morgan, a sceptic of the new line fearing it did not involve Henfield at all.

Rev. Goring took the chair. He knew everyone there wanted the line because it would bring great benefit to the area. Indeed, such was the support for it by those owning property that the line was being referred to as The Landowners' Line.

He did, however, have one late development to announce. Since entering the hall he had been handed a notice from the solicitor of the London, Brighton and South Coast Railway informing him that the Brighton Company had a scheme for their own line through the district. He recalled how the Brighton Company had let Steyning down in the past by failing to construct anything although an agreed line had been pegged out. They had afterwards intimated they were not really interested in a Steyning Branch. He was sure that even if the Brighton Company did build a line they would run as few trains as possible in order to serve the interests of shareholders rather than of the public. He was certain his listeners knew which line would serve them best; the Shoreham, Horsham and Dorking.

Listeners echoed their approval.

The next speaker explained the routes, a circuitous zigzag by the Brighton Line but by the Landowners' a direct route of shortest mileage to keep down costs and reach London within 47 miles. He assured his Henfield listeners they would be given choice about the actual site for their station a short distance from the town itself.

Dr. Morgan rose to say how pleased he was. He had come expecting to be told Henfield was to be left entirely out of the line and that they were to hear trains pass yet not be able to use them. Now that he knew how well Henfield was to be served he would be going home in better sprits than when he had set out.

Votes of thanks ended the meeting and people dispersed homeward.

Just one week later there was a second meeting, this time at the George in Henfield. Although no major landowner was there, it was attended by numerous Henfield landlords and traders. There were invited visitors, too; a high powered group of London, Brighton and South Coast Railway Directors led by their chairman Mr. Leo Schuster.

On the motion of solicitor Mr. Coppard, Rev. O'Brien took the chair. He explained how previously at Steyning he had given his name to a petition to Parliament on behalf of the Horsham and Dorking Line that had been described to him as having a station in Henfield not more than a mile from the church. He had since learnt that the station was not to be in the parish at all but the other side of the River Adur in Ashurst – a station two miles off in a direction almost impassable where not even £20000 would make a good road to Henfield. He was therefore prepared to listen to the London, Brighton and South Coast Railway proposal. He believed several people wished to speak so would say no more.

Solicitor Mr. Coppard explained that he had been requested by his fellow townsmen to ask the chairman of the Brighton Company if they really would make the railway if Parliament rejected the opposing Landowners' Line.

Mr. Schuster first assured him it would be completed within twelve months. He then compared the two routes in detail taking great pains to deride the Landowners' Line. He read a letter stating there was no agreement for the South Western Railway's Waterloo Station to be used by the Steyning, Horsham and Dorking Railway. Such an arrangement was out of the question. The Steyning meeting had mislead Henfield people.

His carefully chosen words went down well and were greeted with applause and laughter. Henfield was for the Brighton Company's line.

Registrar Mr. Challen rose to propose a resolution; 'because so many gentlemen present at the Steyning meeting had been induced to sign a memorial in favour of the Dorking Line under the misrepresentation of it passing close to Henfield, the meeting should record such a misleading statement having been made'.

George Longley explained how after the Steyning meeting he had written to one of the legal advisers of the Landowners' Line requesting the withdrawal of his name from the memorial. The reply asked him to await developments. He therefore wished to second Mr. Challen's resolution.

The motion was carried.

Mr. Coppard had another resolution, one of paramount importance. He felt confident the London and Brighton Company would actually build their line once it had Parliamentary approval and he proposed that the meeting should pledge itself to use every endeavour to ensure that company's success. Agreement was almost 100%.

Rev. O'Brien thanked everyone. Henfield residents had made their position clear. The L.B.S.C.R. line was the way forward. Parliament should take notice and reject the Landowners' Line. [2]

The meeting closed and people returned to the business of everyday life.

For journeyman miller James Randall, everyday life included an increasing problem.

It was James who years before had noticed the fire raging at the barn across the brooks when he had been disturbed in the middle of the night by his baby daughter Nancy falling out of bed.

Life had dealt a vicious blow to James since then in the loss of his wife which left him fully responsible for bringing up six children.

He married again, widow Sayers, becoming step father to her young son. James switched employment to the mill on Henfield Common and moved into one of the L shaped tenements there.

The Henfield Common Windmill from Broadmare Common

Home life became increasingly crowded as the children grew. Two of the girls left home but the boys remained; the youngest at school, the others bringing in money at the lowest rung of the pay ladder.

James gradually became a familiar figure in the village pubs. His drinking became a topic for gossip.

He tried not to let it affect his work at the mill.

Large orders still went out on time. The daily purchases of villagers continued; small quantities of flour and by-products that were recorded by James in the day-book.

Many customers were men he knew, agricultural labourers coming in for just enough flour to tide them over a few days.

Thomas Smith came in from Nep Town for half a bushel of flour and a bushel of sharps – from the hard parts of wheat ground a second time. Thomas handed over the money his wife had given him.

James checked it and Thomas walked off home with his purchases not having the foggiest notion of how much he had paid for them. He was content enough that his wife would mix the flours just right to bake her family's bread.

Richard Luxford, a near neighbour, went to the mill about six o'clock that same evening. His order was similar; a half bushel of flour, half of sharps and two gallons of pollard – like bran but not so coarse. Richard was a widower lodging with his brother's family. He knew he paid 5s 4d.

Things became difficult when the mill foreman, Henry Barringer, checked the day-book.

The only entry for that day was; "Peter Cragg, half bushel of bran 5¾d"; Peter Cragg, the one-time basket maker come huckster, whose waggling tongue meant he could never keep things to himself.

It was almost incredible that nobody else had been.

Mr. Barringer questioned other members of staff.

Deaf John Harmes had news to impart. Thomas Smith and John Luxford had been in and paid for what they bought. Henry Dale had been served with a bushel of flour and went off without paying for it.

Henry Dale was confronted at his house up the alley in Nep Town. He was surprised because he had not been to the mill that day.

Mr. Barringer doubted the surprise.

Mr. Stephens, owner of the mill, was consulted at his Shiprods Farm.

He was told how Randall appeared to be serving people without recording it in the book, that he must have pocketed the money and had doubtless been doing so before.

Mr. Stephens had always trusted his men, especially his foreman.

The scant entries in the book suggested a dishonest employee. Such a man would not be tolerated.

James Randall was dismissed.

Mr. Stephens also prosecuted him for embezzlement.

The case was heard at the Quarter Sessions.

Thomas Smith and Richard Luxford told of their purchases. Henry Dale also appeared and remembered that he too had visited the mill.

James Randall disputed nothing. At the end of the trial he was taken to Petworth for three months hard labour which would be spent without any taste of beer. [3]

Beer was an important part of life for husband and wife John and Philadelphia Budgen who arrived at the village from miles away, West Hoathley, for harvest work. They were seasoned travellers equipped with essential items.

John had his reaping hook, Philadelphia a basket of tinware, a saucepan and a basin.

It had been a hot journey. In the evening they had a few beers at the Plough.

They were supping their drinks and enjoying the good company when there was an unnecessary interruption by a police constable who proclaimed he was performing a duty, the eviction of an obdurate drunk.

The drunken man was too far gone to understand that he had to go home. The constable, P.C. Egerton, was obliged to arrest him and take him out.

John and Philadelphia Budgen were people of principle, unprepared to stand aside and watch a man being ill treated in such a manner. They gathered up their belongings and followed.

The constable forcibly marched the man down the road and put him in the lock-up. Philadelphia intervened. She insisted on being given entry to offer the man some beer.

P.C. Egerton refused but she stood her ground, thumped him with her saucepan and threw the basket of tinware at him.

John leapt to assist and did his drunken best to stick the constable with his reaping hook. P.C. Egerton collared him. Philadelphia ran for it.

An assisting parochial constable, set off after her.

Even if Philadelphia had been sober it would have been a poor contest. In her beer befuddled state he was on her in no time. Cornered, she struck him as well as she could and threatened to smash his head with her basin.

It ended with the constables in complete control and the lock-up very full.

Next day, the Budgens appeared at the Petty Sessions, stated who they were and what their background was. They were remanded and had more captive days to sort themselves out.

They were sober and contrite when they next stood before the magistrates.

One of the bench was a military man, Colonel Lloyd. He had read the case report and questioned Budgen: -

"You have been in the army?"

"Yes, sir. I have been in the 22nd, 28th and 48th regiments of foot, a long time in India. I came from West Hoathley to harvest for Mr. Pannett."

"Then as an old soldier you should have known better."

"It was the drink, sir; we didn't know what we was about."

Colonel Lloyd was satisfied that he had made his point as an officer. The man was a good soldier at heart.

Sentence came. John Budgen was fined 4s 0d and 9s 0d costs; fighting Philadelphia, 6s 0d and 10s 0d costs. [4]

It could have been far, far worse. Perhaps the magistrates had borne in mind the Indian Mutiny – military version.

John and Philadelphia gathered up their belongings and went. They still had some way to travel; there was no Farmer Pannett in Henfield.

Chapter 27

Smithfield heifer – Christmas tree lamps – Taxation debate

In April 1858, shopkeepers Charles and Henry Longley and miller William Brooks made a journey up to London to appear before a Parliamentary Committee at Number 11, Downing Street.

The committee was assembled to determine who should be given the right to build the Shoreham to Horsham line.

Large maps covered the walls of the room showing the competing routes; Landowners' Line in red, London, Brighton and South Coast in green. The committee should have no difficulties in that regard. It was in considering the opposing opinions that they would have to concentrate their minds.

The Landowners were heard first. Mr. Hope Scott QC outlined their case strongly point by point until he had to state that the line being planned along the best route did not go close to Henfield. He suggested a good bridge would bring Henfield within easy reach. He chose the moment for brief humour at the village's expense;

"Henfield has either the good fortune or the misfortune of having only one legal gentleman residing in it."

Landowners' Line supporters laughed. What type of men were these villagers who sang for the Brighton Company?

Rev. John Goring of Wiston was now called as first witness.

He explained how their line would be of more benefit in the area, especially for the deteriorating stock and corn markets. Although going nearer to Ashurst than Henfield, it would also serve Cowfold.

Traders from those places confirmed they favoured the line. The Cowfold man lamented that not a single coach now passed their way because of the London to Brighton Railway.

Sir Charles Burrell spoke not only in favour of the Landowners' Line but also to oppose the other route as being only a half-musket shot distance from Knepp Castle. The noise of trains rattling past would be a continual annoyance.

At last it was Henfield's William Brooks' turn to speak. He said he preferred the Landowners' Line because it would give cheaper transit.

The Brighton Line solicitor questioned him;

"Do you not know that in Henfield 300 favoured the Brighton Route with only 30 or 40 against it?"

Mr. Brooks confessed his ignorance.

The solicitor moved in; "You like the line further away then," he taunted.

"Yes," came the simple reply.

Scornful laughs enlivened the room.

The Landowners' Line completed their hearing. The turn of the London, Brighton and South Coast Railway came.

The representatives willingly accepted their line was more circuitous and had two bridges as against the one of the Landowners', but it served far more people. Henfield alone had some 1600 inhabitants, Cowfold very few. The L.B.S.C.R. stations for both Henfield and Steyning were far nearer those places than the stations of the Landowners' route.

Land would be purchased for a double track but it would first be built as a single track.

Construction would begin immediately. Knepp Castle would be half a mile from the line therefore there would be no problem with noise.

Finally, Brighton would use old, light rails not heavy enough for main line trains at a saving of £3 per ton.

Witnesses were called.

Charles and Henry Longley both pointed out how useless the Landowners' Line would be for travel between Steyning and Henfield because both stations would be so far from the towns, a total of three miles.

Nobody sought to ridicule them.

The chairman summed up and announced their findings. They would inform Parliament that the committee favoured the London, Brighton and South Coast Line.

The House of Commons duly passed an Act for a Railway from Shoreham terminating in a certain field adjoining the carriage road from Henfield to West End with another line from there to Itchingfield.

With the Act passed, the line was stumped and marked out.

Shafts were sunk to ascertain the type of soil where cuttings would be excavated. It just remained for the Company to find agreement with property owners over the value of their land.

Henfield and Steyning, at loggerheads over the railway, came head to head again at their annual cricket fixture – sunshine all day, spectators numerous, competition fierce, cricket top class and the match going to two innings with a nail biting finish.

Henfield v Steyning on Henfield Common

Steyning's final pair came together needing an unlikely 15 runs to win against the bowling of Penikett – already with nine wickets to his name.

Nothing ruffled the pair. The runs came. Just three more needed. Penikett bowled, the wicket fell. Henfield's game by just two runs.

With the match decided, camaraderie could commence. The evening was a convivial one.

There was even more camaraderie at the annual Market Dinner. About 50 members and friends gathered at the George and sat to a mouth watering 2 o'clock dinner provided by landlord Stoner and his wife.

At the end of the meal, with the cloth withdrawn, miller Mr. Stephens and butcher Mr. Thorns were installed as chairman and vice-chairman. Loyal toasts, local toasts and special person toasts were given and drunk.

Toasts completed, it was time for song and for special entertainment by Mr. W. Windebank from Brighton.

Entertainer Windebank had only one arm. It would not affect his voice but he had a flutina accordion as well.

Mr. Windebank began. It took but a short time for the gathering to accept that he was amusing. Soon they were in fits of laughter. Windebank excelled with character pieces and songs.

He took up his accordion. How on earth was he to work the bellows?

He did and he amazed them with lively tunes and an evocative rendition of the cuckoo solo. What a man! [1]

All too soon, he concluded his performance. The dinner drew to a close but the name of Windebank would remain, surely to perform again.

In December, London's great Smithfield Show exhibited farmers' prize stock specially fattened for Christmas. Mr. Dennett, several times successful with Southdown sheep from his Woodmancote farm, showed a four year old pure Sussex heifer. To his delight it was awarded the silver medal, the £10 prize as best in its class and the accolade of the judges who declared it as complete an animal of the Sussex breed as ever was fattened.

The prize-winner was brought back to Henfield. There it was entrusted to Mr. Thorns the butcher who took great care in slaughtering it; 168 stones and 21 lbs of beef – just over a ton of it – for celebrating village families.

Mrs. Lucretia Wood made her annual gift of a generous 70 stones weight of beef for the families too poor to afford meat – Christmas should be enjoyed by everyone.

During the last week of school before the Christmas Holiday, little Lucy Wood made her normal morning walk from her tenement home across the back of the common, through the twitten by widow Harwood's shop, up the High Street, along the lane past Potwell, up the narrow path by Red Oaks and round to the Girls' School.

The day was cold, the school room slightly warmer with its rationed heat from the great iron stove. The chants, recitations and sand tray sums and letters of morning school were completed. The teacher went out of the room for her lunch and the children remained, restrained and chilled, awaiting her return.

Somehow, for some reason, seven year old Lucy went to the stove. Somehow her dress caught fire.

Her screams brought the teacher rushing to her aid. Flames had raced up her clothing, leaving severe burns. [2]

The doctor was called and he attended the child as well as he was able. The next day she died. It was a terrible event for the school children to witness, a devastating day for her parents and sisters. The Christmas edition of the Sussex Express recounted the event for its readers.

Sad as the tragedy was, the vicar could not allow it to affect the great missionary celebration planned for January at the Girls' School.

Rev. O'Brien invited devoted ladies of the parish to make the event a success. They did so.

It involved a large Christmas Tree left in place beyond Twelfth Night. No longer part of Christian Christmas, it now stood in celebration of the jubilee of the Missionary Society for the Jews.

The tree was magnificently decorated with elaborate flowers and coloured draperies. A floral V.R. above a crown showed people's loyalty to their queen. A jaunty flag tipped every laden bough bent low with an array of saleable gifts; cushions, bags, baskets and other practical items. In the evening the whole tree glowed with coloured lamps and tapers.

The tree was not the only eye catching display.

Along the end of the room were the larger articles to be sold. There was a marvellous collection of photographic views and panoramas to enrapture everyone and the room was enlivened by familiar tunes from a musical box.

The event continued for three days from Wednesday through to Friday. Secretary Rev. O'Brien was pleased with the parish effort that enhanced the wonderful missionary endeavours begun by the late lamented vicar Rev. Charles Dunlop. [3]

January proved a long, cold month for Peter Cragg with his huckster's van. He could talk his way through most things but persuading trade away from John Browning's cart proved almost impossible. The discordant days of basket making seemed an irredeemable Shangri-La.

Peter had to make the most of any opportunity to improve his lot. Such a chance came when he was approaching Small Dole in the evening dark on his way home from Beeding.

On his outward journey he had passed a sheepfold right beside the road with several trusses of hay laid out. When he reached it on his return he stopped his van and climbed into the field.

Bleating sheep huddled to one corner. Peter seized as much hay as he could, carried it back to the road and pushed it into his van. At least his horse would be well fed.

As he went back for a second load he was given the surprise of his life. Unseen in the dark, a patrolling policeman had been quietly observing proceedings. He accosted Peter and charged him with felony.

Peter begged forgiveness. He would pay willingly; he wanted to pay – anything but being taken before the magistrates.

The constable noted the remarks and carried out his duty.

Peter and the hay became another Petty Sessions case.

Mrs. Cragg accompanied her husband to court. She would support him all she could.

The charge was made.

Peter Cragg explained what he had really meant about payment. He hoped the magistrates would understand.

The Chairman answered with a question:

"Have you anyone here from Henfield to speak for your character?"

"I was not aware it would be required."

"There are many persons here from Henfield today."

Peter looked around the court. No great friend seemed to be there but his eye alighted on one man with whom he had many years acquaintance, his old basket making boss. 'Sunny' Woolgar could speak for him.

'Sunny' was very happy to speak and answered without hesitation;

"I can't say anything in your favour."

Peter was dumb struck – but not his wife.

"Then you had better have said nothing," she retorted.

Her comment proved only too true. Peter Cragg was found guilty. He would spend the next month cranking water at Petworth.

During Peter Cragg's monotonous weeks of water cranking, there was a sale at Mr. Randle's Holedean Farm of animals specially selected for the occasion.

Sale day saw increased traffic moving across the common, turning away from the cricket ground into the lane opposite and down to the old farmhouse set around with apple trees in the valley.

Holedean sales had a good name. No one doubted Mr. Randle's claim that the heifers had been reared entirely on the farm and were perfectly clear from any prevalent complaint. When he said they were of large size and most would calve during February, potential buyers could rely on his word.

The stock fetched good prices; a satisfying day for Mr. Randle with money to bank.

There could be no feeling of satisfaction for Rev. O'Brien. He was once more confined to the vicarage feeling uncomfortably indisposed instead of chairing the annual meeting of the Useful Knowledge Institution.

His place was again taken by Rev. George Hall. He stated how pleased he was to be able to announce that they now had 94 members among whom 1500 books and newspapers had been circulated. 13 new books had been added to the library including "Livingstone's Travels" and "The Life of George Stephenson". The new season of lectures would begin at the Girls' School with one on Comets by the Rev. Holland of Shipley.

The lecture attracted a packed audience including Rev. O'Brien, happily recovered from his indisposition.

Rev. Holland illustrated his lecture with instructive diagrams showing how all comets revolved about the sun. He explained that many uneducated persons clung to the erroneous ideas of comets affecting earthly events as in 1066. His audience were stirred. They were on more familiar ground; brave Saxon Harold versus cruel Norman William.

Rev. O'Brien expressed the meeting's sincere thanks and announced the subject of the next lecture, "The Steam Engine" a subject of intense topical interest now that Henfield's railway was no longer just a dream.

The Brighton Company encountered longer delays than expected in gaining landowners' permission for the line crossing their property.

Farmers made strong complaints about the embankment planned along the low fields around the Adur that were subject to flooding. People's livelihood would be jeopardised.

The company undertook to ensure all streams and outlets had clear passage. Farm tracks would be kept open by bridges or crossings.

After intense consultation, agreements were made and the route mapped out.

Soon, the railway was in course of construction.

Doubtful looking men with strange accents from far off places were working across the brooks – navvies, bricklayers and carpenters.

Local men were being recruited as well.

Peter Cragg, home from his Petworth gaol sentence, applied and was accepted but he would be no simple navvy; he was Peter Cragg, excavator. William Piper from the L shaped tenements on the common was content to be plain navvy. His wife had died, daughter Emma was in service and son

Frederick had gone off navvying at the West Grinstead section of the line. William was on his own except for 12 year old granddaughter Harriett Dale who was now housekeeper for him.

Up in Nep Town, Philip Lelliott, brought up as a bargeman's son, decided his future was with the railway.

Others did likewise.

The prospective route took the line close to the old Streatham Manor House and across the River Adur on a bridge named Stretham by the company as if avoiding confusion with their Streatham stations in London.

It would continue along the marshy land past Pokerlee and Brookside Farms.

The railwaymen sought lodgings as near their work as possible.

Two navvies, one of them Irish, were welcomed by agricultural labourer William Simmonds at the old house with its roof half tile and half slabs of heavy Horsham Stone down the lane past Nep Town windmill. William was a family man with three boys – his namesake eldest son being just 11 years old and bringing in a pittance as carter's boy. For Mrs. Simmonds the navvies' lodging money was almost a pot of gold.

The old house beyond Nep Town Windmill

Another four men, again with one from Ireland, were willingly found space at the old Brookside Farmhouse, now home of Mary Joyce and her seven year old son.

Mary Joyce was thankful to house them – her income as a stay maker would never be enough to bring up her son decently. The extra money meant less poverty; a better chance in life.

The men were equally pleased. That their living conditions were squashed and somewhat spartan was of no account; they were better off than those of their mates living in the temporary huts alongside the line, and almost as close to their work.

Brookside and the huts were well within the sphere of Pokerlee where farmer Stephen Woolgar had a popular beerhouse brewing enough beer to satisfy any thirsty visitor whatever the work in hand.

Stephen took a relaxed approach to drink. He was well away from any prying constable's late night beat. If drinkers liked to linger longer than official hours he was willing to oblige them.

The stretch of completed line steadily increased as the days lengthened into June.

In the village, the 'Lodgings to Let' notices for clients of acceptable class were fast disappearing as summer visitors arrived anxious to avail themselves of the picturesque beauty of the village.

Dr. Morgan had a chance late-evening meeting with one summer visitor who had taken up residence in the High Street by lying in helpless intoxication on the road at the front of his house.

Butcher John Cutress, serving his year as one of the parochial constables, had the task of rehousing her. She was so hopelessly drunk he had to pitch her in the lock-up for the night.

When she sobered up enough to appear before the magistrates she explained how she and her blind husband had been put into lodgings by the relieving officer. Her husband had slept in the stable. The landlady had insisted on giving her some beer and making her drink it.

The magistrates did not bother to doubt her story; they simply imposed a five shilling fine and allowed her a week to find the money.

For visitors and villagers alike, the summer weather proved fickle with strong winds and heavy rain.

Farm crops were badly damaged. Ripening corn was beaten down to such an extent that farmers were paying as much as £1 5s per acre to their harvesters.

The attractive farm rates lured navvies off the railway. Pickaxes were set aside in favour of sickles.

Men not accustomed to wielding a sickle found harvesting to be a time of fathomless thirst.

One night, Stephen Woolgar was kept busy at Pokerlee providing drinks for his customers until well past 11.00 p.m. It proved an evening of bonhomie with everybody happy and content; a good to be alive time.

Next day Stephen discovered that one his erstwhile revellers had chosen to report him to the constable. It cost him £2 at the Petty Sessions. He accepted it resignedly as part of life.

It was well into September before the final sheaves were carted home. Navvies returned to the railway.

Farmers Alfred Smith and John Randle were glad to have their corn safe in the barns no matter who wielded the sickles. They held a joint Harvest Home. Both were happy for their men to enjoy themselves provided it did not become drunkenness and profanity.

Masters and workers met up in the middle of the village on the Town Field. Cricket was the order of the day, a gloriously sunny one.

Cricket paused for an hour or two while a generous dinner was eaten washed down by a measured sufficiency of goodly beer. Once that had been allowed to settle, play continued until evening when another pause was made for supper and more draughts of beer interspersed with plenty of farming healths.

The match was now forgotten. It had been more a cheerful relaxation than a match to be won. The rest of the evening was given over to song; old favourites sung as they should be sung with everyone in harmony high, low or a little off tune.

In the darker nights of autumn, the Useful Knowledge Institution held a discussion class to debate national and local taxation.

The meeting was lively from the start. Members had plenty to say about taxation in general but before long the focus moved to local taxes.

The statistics were startling. Members were soon made aware that in the Steyning Union's fourteen parishes no less than six, comprising 5971 acres of the best land, paid not an iota to county, police or Poor Rate although the costs of any labourer in them falling on bad times was met by the taxed parishes.

The injustice of the current system became even more obvious in a comparison of Hove's 4104 inhabitants, rateable value of about £600000 providing a yearly £216, with Henfield's 1664 inhabitants, rateable value £6000, paying £579. It was iniquitous inequality. [4]

The discussion class was unanimous; Henfield ratepayers must make a vigorous effort to achieve a more equitable distribution of the Poor Rate.

With the call for equality ringing in their ears, members made their way home. It had been an exhilarating meeting.

Chapter 28

Disappearing onions – Failing barges – The Rifle Corps

That winter, John Gardener, who ran a tailor's business with three of his sons in Church Street, found he was losing his onions. For John it was serious. He had cropped about three bushels of them, a special sort of underground onion different looking from the normal sorts planted by most people. He had strung them in his pig pound. Somebody had discovered them – twice.

That was too much; it needed positive action.

John got his oldest son, dumb George, to help him. They set a large vermin trap among the onions and nailed some boards over them. The onion thief would have a nasty shock.

On the Thursday the thief struck again. Nothing was heard during the night but next morning they discovered one of the boards broken off and another bushel of onions gone together with the trap. John was left with just a scattering of onions to show for all his endeavours.

It was time for P.C. Egerton.

The constable arrived and took stock of the situation. Church Street led not only to the church but beyond, well beyond, as far as the navvy huts beside the developing railway.

P.C. Egerton was not to be taken in with current sentiments of good behaviour by railway navvies. He set off to inspect the huts.

One was kept by Mrs. Jane Paul. She was a willing talker. Two of the men in her hut had been out when she went to bed about half past nine, John Brown and John Ward.

At the name John Brown, P.C. Egerton quickened. John Brown was 'Johnny Broome' to the drinkers of Henfield; 'Johnny Broome' with his strange accent and willing fists – self exhibiting pugilist. It had to be him. Mrs. Paul kept talking. The men had come home at some time during the night. The next morning she saw onions on the floor beside their bed. When she asked whose they were, Ward told her he bought them for two pots of ale.

The onions were still in the room. P.C. Egerton took them and made his way to the site where the navvies were working. There he arrested John Brown. Ward was not there.

Brown hazarded the man might be found at the part of the line further on towards West Grinstead.

A messenger was sent to inform the West Grinstead constable.

When Ward was confronted he explained that they had bought some onions at Henfield Thursday night.

At the Petty Sessions, Ward was able to explain more fully how he had bought them off a man at about 11 o'clock on his way home and had given a shilling for them.

Brown avowed he knew nothing about the onions.

The magistrates took considerable time in determining the case. Their consensus was imprisonment with hard labour for one calendar month. [1]

For two strapping navvies the hard labour would come easily. The rub would be the silence, particularly for 'Johnny Broome'. It would be hard to take; impossible to forget.

Work on the railway from Steyning to Streatham was progressing again. Bricklayers were busy building the bridge over the river. Between there and Henfield, navvies were constructing an embankment high enough to allow farm roads to pass under by timber bridges. Loads of earth for it were brought from the deep cuttings being dug between Bramber and Steyning.

One morning the navvies arrived to continue work at the embankment only to discover that most of the earth they had piled on during the previous day had gone. It was as if they had been doing virtually nothing.

They piled more on but it was two steps upward and almost two back down again. Each night the embankment settled – they had hit the Pokerlee marsh.

Work stopped completely during severe February frosts. Men turned up each morning only to be sent home again.

Stephen Woolgar's Pokerlee beerhouse became a regular port of call for the returning men. They lingered over a pint or two through the morning hoping for a thaw, called for another pint to have with their dinner and stayed through the afternoon until dusk.

Navvy Joseph French's lingering continued until six o'clock one Saturday; well past dusk. He called a cheerful goodbye and set off back to his Nep Town lodgings.

Up near the windmill he somehow fell over a fence and crashed down into the ditch the other side. He lay in pain, unable to move, shouting for help.

Luckily he was heard by sawyer John West.

He and his sons found Joseph and asked what the matter was.

He could only manage by answer;

"Oh! My back! Oh! My belly!"

They lifted him onto a hand cart, pushed him home to his lodgings and helped him to bed.

One of them set out for Doctor Caudle.

The doctor now had a partner in the practice, his son Dr. Adolphus William Wisden newly qualified at London and aged 21.

Doctor Caudle knew that French would be a good case for Adolphus to inspect. The man had been treated several times for abdominal disease and could be be in a serious condition.

Both doctors went immediately.

They examined their patient and knew little could be done.

Several further visits were made on the Sunday.

On the Monday, Joseph French died.

Doctor Caudle carried out a post-mortem examination.

At the White Hart inquest he explained his findings to the coroner. Joseph French died as a result of complications from a severe hernia.

To the navvies it was just one more way the railway could do for them, accidents were never far away.

When the weather eased, the men resumed their task of attempting to build the Pokerlee embankment.

The contractor decided to use chalk. Load after load was brought from the hill behind Steyning.

Navvies spent the day piling it on the embankment.

Each new day the level was more or less at the previous morning's mark.

After a few days the contractor accepted the task to be impossible.

Landowners were contacted and plans altered.

The embankment would be kept as low as would still allow for flooding on the brooks. Farm roads would be raised to the same level as the railway line. Gates on the roads would protect farm stock.

At last progress could continue.

Work at the Stretham Bridge had continued with minimum interruption. For William Lelliott, the bridge was a major obstacle. He had valuable contract work with the Adur authorities carrying Beeding Pit small chalk at 8d a ton for riverbank repairs.

The bridge work meant a delay each time 'Lion' or 'Stag 'went through. He had to moor the barge, unhook the tow rope, move the horse round the obstruction, take the tow rope through and link it to the harness again; a loss of time and money twice for each load carried.

William's greatest worry about the railway was the loss of trade that could occur when the train service began.

He had once felt assured that both barges would carry full loads; constant coals for distribution to his customers, farm produce, Horsham bound cargoes up the western branch to Partridge Green, timber down river to the coast and road gravel coming back. He had always been busy.

Those days had gone, speeded alarmingly by the opening of the railway between Three Bridges and Horsham which linked the town with the London to Brighton line.

Horsham shopkeepers had quickly switched to far quicker rail transport that would not be subject to delay by difficult tides or offloading from barge to wagon.

Trade did not recover. Apart from the chalk contract, 'Lion' and 'Stag' were too often lying empty at their Henfield moorings.

Low income caused inroads into William's capital. Outgoing financial commitments could not be met. Bankruptcy became a spectre approaching ever closer. He tried to conceal it but one March morning it was there, a brief entry in the London Gazette;

> William Lelliott coal merchant and dealer in wood having a wharf at Mock Bridge, insolvent debtor to appear for first examination touching debts and estate and effects. [2]

He was spared the London visits of earlier bankrupts. His journeys were only as far as the Brighton Insolvent Court.

In March his debts were made public, £221 17s 11d against assets of £28 10s 8d. The newspapers reported that he was accepted in his examination.

The next month they reported his final order which was passed without opposition. As his debts were below £300 the inquisition was over. He now had to start life again.

William was a practical man. He moved his family into a tenement at the bottom of the High Street just past gun maker Peter Ward and obtained work as a railway labourer. At 55 he could still turn in a fair day's work. His 19 year old daughter, Louisa, brought in money as a dressmaker, 16 year old Leonard was a labourer. Three lodgers ensured adequate income.

If William's finances had been in better shape he could have attended the meeting just up the road from him at the White Hart to promote the formation of a Henfield and Mid-Bramber Rifle Corps.

Parliament had legislated for a Volunteer Force the previous year.

Rules were strict. A corps could be formed only at the behest of the Lord Lieutenant of the county. Members had to swear an oath of allegiance before a justice of the peace, attend a set number of drill days, and pay for both uniform and rifle. They had to achieve military efficiency.

The payment issue ruled out any working class participation. Were other men of Henfield interested?

Guest speaker at the White Hart meeting was Robert Loder Esq. from Handcross. People listened intently as he expounded the importance of a Volunteer Corps.

He was frank. France and Russia had far more men under arms per 100 inhabitants than England where the army never reached the numbers set for it – the army that had to defend the scattered empire including India where such destructive losses had been encountered.

The Navy was in as poor a state. In the last ten years the French had built 85 steamships of the line. England had added 12.

The militia which had provided men by ballot for the war with Napoleon was now a failure.

Just three options were available:- increased taxation for funds, the failed militia or volunteers.

The obligations of volunteers were great; discipline, drill and developing rifle skills. Let not the men of Henfield be behind their neighbours but be up and doing.

The speaker sat down to applause by his listeners.

It was resolved to establish the Henfield and Mid-Bramber Rifle Corps.

By early April, the Rifle Corps had struggled into existence. Prejudices and organisational difficulties had been overcome. There were forty members and the Lord Lieutenant of the county had offered their services to her Majesty The Queen. They had been accepted.

A different form of service was being legislated at the Steyning Petty Sessions. New overseers were being sworn in for the coming year.

High Street draper Henry Longley and near neighbour chemist William West were the vestry nominations. Henry Longley was willing but chemist West objected. The requirements of his business meant he was frequently called upon to dispense medicines in the absence of the surgeons. It did not enable him to carry out an overseer's duties in a satisfactory manner.

The bench of magistrates listened carefully and overruled him. A man could not use the circumstances of a business to shirk his duty as a rated parishioner. William West took his turn as overseer.

P.C. George Egerton held a much sharper image of duty. High Street propriety was in his charge. He would maintain good order there.

He was dutifully patrolling the street about 8.30 one April evening when somebody asked him to buy them a drink. It was a forceful request made in a strongly accented voice.

P.C. Egerton had no need to look. He knew at once who it was; John Brown, 'Johnny Broome', in circulation again following his recent imprisonment for stealing the pig pound onions.

John Brown was insistent. There was an old grudge outstanding with the constable who had turned him in for a month of Petworth silence. He wanted a drink as settlement.

Egerton told Brown to move on.

There was instant transformation to 'Johnny Broome': fists flying one, two, three into Egerton's face, kicks following.

Egerton called for help. Assistance was willingly given and the onslaught ended. 'Johnny Broome' spent the rest of the night in the lock-up.

He appeared before the magistrates next day and was offered a choice; £2 4s 6d paid in cash or another three weeks of Petworth silence.

There was no 'Johnny Broome' left. John Brown paid the money.

P.C. Egerton had a quiet six weeks before the next call. It came well after 10.00 p.m. when two servants reported an attempted break in at their master Mr. Heisch's house.

One of them explained that she went to bed a little after ten and shortly afterwards heard a scraping noise outside. She was frightened but crept to the window to find out what was causing it. To her dismay she could make out a man on the slates of the larder close to her room. She screamed an alarm and the figure made off.

P.C. Egerton accompanied them back to the house. He examined the larder roof. Fresh earth was scattered on it and two slates were broken. He remained in the vicinity quietly reconnoitring, ears alert for any sound a returning intruder might make.

Suddenly there was noise, soft but repetitive. P.C. Egerton proceeded cautiously, seeking the source.

His caution was rewarded. Partially concealed in a ditch lay the suspect, his breathing a gentle snore as he slept, bootless, reeking of beer.

He was prodded awake; surprised to be out of his bed. He was not aware of any cracked slates on anybody's larder. In fact he was not really aware of anything except being uncomfortably cold and achy.

Bootless, he was conducted to the lock-up. He was James McVey, worker on the railway having some drinks and remembering nothing.

In the morning Egerton found a pair of boots in Mr. Heisch's garden. McVey was pleased to ascertain they were his.

Booted, he appeared before the magistrates and was sentenced under the vagrancy act; six weeks' hard labour at Petworth. [3]

It was P.C. Egerton's last case. He was moving to a new location.

By the time of the next investigation, P.C. Goldring would be in charge.

Chapter 29

School inspection – Stoolball – Ginger beer & a dud shilling

It was June, an unsettled June with too little sun following a May of too much rain.

Rev. John Glubb had an important duty to perform as Rural Dean, the inspection of the National Schools ready for his report to the bishop.

The Infants' School proved pleasing. It had an efficient certificated mistress full of energy and acting on the best motives. There was also a Pupil Teacher. The results were apparent. The children seemed happy, orderly, clean and intelligent. They sang and marched well, even the youngest ones, barely three year old, who had been at the school only a few days.

The Girls' School was also efficient. In arithmetic, the top class did well in reduction while the other classes were efficient in simple rules. English dictation from memory was good and original composition was done reasonably. They answered well in the examination on the scriptures and catechism.

The sewing, darning and knitting were neat. Most noteworthy were the six girls, average age 13, who could cut out and make a gentleman's shirt without previous fitting or any other help.

The most difficult was the Boys' School.

It had just been reopened after a six week shut down because the vicar and committee had been obliged to dismiss the master for ill conduct. Added to that, most of the oldest boys had left to begin work. Only seven of the 22 in the class were there – with an average age of 11. The best work came from the lowest class where the children had just come up from the Infants' School which showed the importance of those schools.

Rev. Glubb had one deeply held conviction concerning children in the Rural Deanery. The older ones were leaving school too early with the girls going into service and the boys being employed in hard work before their bones and sinews received sufficient firmness and strength. He should like to see appropriate legislation passed similar to that for the manufacturing districts.[1]

B

Diocese of *Chichester*

ARCHDEACONRY OF *Lewes* *RURAL DEANERY OF* *[illegible]*

PARISH OF *Henfield*

INSPECTOR'S REPORT OF *Infant* ~~BOYS'~~ ~~GIRLS'~~ ~~MIXED~~ **SCHOOL.**

The *15.* *day of* *June* **185***8.*

POPULATION OF PARISH OR DISTRICT *1664.*

			1st class	2d class	3d class	4th class	5th class	6th class	7th class	Last class	TOTAL.	General Remarks.
	Number on Books	B	9.	1.	5.	15.	11				41	
		G	4.	7.	12.	8.	5.				36	
	Number present at Examination	B	9.	1.	5.	14.	9				38	
		G	4.	7.	12.	7.	4.				34.	
	Average Age in each Class	B	5 8/9	6	5 3/5.	4 2/15.	2 6/11					
		G	5 1/4	5 4/7.	5 1/12	4 [illegible]/8	2. 2/5					
DEGREE OF PROFICIENCY IN: Knowledge of	Elementary or Church Catechism		B.	B.	C.	C.						
	Prayer-Book											
	Old Testament		A.	B.	B.	D.						
	New Testament		A.	B.	B.	D.						
Reading	*Monosyllables		B.	C.	C.	C.						
	Easy Books		B.									
	Books of greater difficulty		C.									
Writing	On Slates only		B.									
	In Copy-Books											
Exercises	From Dictation or Memory		B.									
	In Abstracts or Compositions			B.								
Arithmetic.	Simple Rules											
	Compound Rules											
	Higher Rules											
Knowledge of	Secular History											
	Church History											
	Geography			B.								
	Map-Drawing											
	Grammar											
Singing	From Notes											
	Needlework (1), or other Industrial Work (2)		A.									

* The degree of efficiency to be marked by the letters A, B, C, or D, in the compartment under each Class, and in line with the respective subjects—A denoting the highest degree, or very good; B good; C moderate; and D bad or deficient. No figures to be used, except in the first three columns.

The Infants' School Inspector's Report

He also noted that the older children who had been through the Infants' School were markedly superior to those from Dame Schools and the like.

Widow Harwood's daughters at Part Forges would have vehemently disagreed. The three of them now ran a school for young ladies, some very young, including a boarder from Brighton. They were confident their facilities were of an excellent standard, certainly above those of any village school. Their school was of great importance to them; the sole source of income.

Widow Harwood decided it should be supplemented by an alternative source, the property of her late father, Percy Gregory.

The sale took place in June down at the auctioneer's Brighton premises to ensure good prices. Although it was the end of the Gregory property it ensured a future for Widow Harwood and her girls.

SALES BY AUCTION.

HENFIELD AND WOODMANCOTE, SUSSEX.

MR ATTREE is instructed to Sell by Auction, at the Estate Auction Mart, 136, North Street, Brighton, on Thursday, June 7th, 1866, at Two for Three o'clock,

A PIECE OF FREEHOLD ARABLE LAND, known as "PIGEON HOUSE FIELD," situate on the north side of Henfield Common, containing 1a. 3r. 5p.

A FREEHOLD MEADOW, in the parish of Woodmancote, known as "MIDDLE FIELD," situate at the east end of Henfield Common, containing 1a. 1r. 14p.

TWO COTTAGES, with small Gardens, situate on the north side of Henfield Common, known as "DOGHAM PLACE."

A RESIDENCE with Garden, desirably situate in the High Street, Henfield, distinguished as "THE FORGES." Let at the very moderate rental of £16 per annum. Early possession of this lot may be obtained.

FOUR WELL-BUILT COTTAGES, situate on the Brighton Road, corner of High Street.

Also a TENEMENT with a SLIP OF LAND, situate in High Street, having a frontage thereto of sixty-four feet, known as "THE POUND HOUSE."

Particulars may be obtained ten days prior to the sale of Messrs. Black and Freeman, Solicitors, Ship Street, and at Mr Attree's Offices,

The ESTATE AUCTION MART, 136, North Street, Brighton.

Percy Gregory's property up for sale [2]

July saw the anniversary day of Henfield Odd Fellows.

In the morning, members from all quarters of the parish assembled at the George and lined up behind the Brighton Band.

Eye-catching Lodge Banners were held aloft, the band struck up with a march and members began their annual parade of the village.

Stops were made at select houses for the band to play a special tune. Surprised occupants expressed delight at both the music and the array of banners.

The parade reached the George again. Banners were furled and the band put away their instruments ready for one of landlord Stoner's acclaimed dinners. Members were joined by the main traders of the village and the gentlemen of the houses that had been so surprised by the parade's visit.

Charles Stoner's wife lived up to her reputation – the meal proved as excellent as ever.

As soon as the dishes were cleared and the cloth removed, Chairman Henry Longley proposed the first of the toasts.

When the last was drunk and the glasses emptied, members took their guests across to the Town Field for the afternoon's entertainment.

Prime attraction was cricket organised by John Burtenshaw of Rye Farm.

Some tried stoolball; a sensible round bat, softish ball, small head-high square-of-wood wicket instead of stumps, simple underarm bowling and not so far to run – but still great fun.

Others were happy with trap and bat; knock the bat on the trap to make the ball pop up, whack it and hope nobody catches it or hits the target when they throw the ball back. A successful whack would score a run for the team and another go for the batter.

For those wanting something more energetic and physical, there was football.

Gradually, wives arrived – necessary for the next part of the day, the dance.

The games ended and refreshments were produced. A suitable break was taken to regain breath and exchange tales of the afternoon.

The band struck up again, gentlemen took their partners and the dance began.

It continued until evening's dusk crept in. The final dance ended and Myrtle Lodge members and guests made their ways home allowing peace to return to the High Street.

The afternoon's cricket had given rise to a wager between farmers Burtenshaw and Randle, Rye v Kentons, as to which of them would be the victor in a single wicket match.

A date was fixed; a fortnight's time on the Town Field.

The match was watched by supportive friends. It finished with Mr. Burtenshaw victorious. He returned home a richer man despite celebratory expenses – the wager had not been small money.

Mr. Randle went home beaten but neither ashamed nor remorseful. A losing wager between friends was of little matter – here today and gone tomorrow.

A far more memorable event was about to be enacted by the Volunteer Rifles.

Numbers had increased. 50 rifles had been supplied and drill had taken place twice weekly on the common with increasing improvement.

The men were now in uniform, the green and grey of riflemen. The time had come for public parade.

It took place in the High Street. 30 members meticulously turned out, rifles at the slope, marching in step and going through drill sequences with military precision. At the end of the display, the crowd of onlookers raised a cheer; the volunteers of Henfield were surely as good as volunteers anywhere.

Farmers had a greater concern, the poor weather's ill effect on their crops.

The year's general absence of sunshine had left oats sickly, of no height and with the grain thin in the ear. Some fields of peas were being ploughed in. Potato blight was developing.

A fortnight of sun enabled a quantity of hay to be stacked but a lot still remained in the fields when the weather broke again.

Two days of wind and heavy rain brought deep floods across the brooks. Ungathered hay floated away to finish up draped across uncut grass and on other farmers' land. Fields of wheat and barley were beaten down.

There was no way the August harvest could begin.

Farmer Sydney Street invited fellow farmers and the principle tradesmen to an afternoon's cricket up at his Kidders Farm behind the Bull Inn. Almost 20 decided they could afford the time. They played their cricket, ate the dinner prepared for them by the family cook and settled in the farm chairs to enjoy Kidder's beer, exchange news and sing favourite songs.

The next week, farmers could at last begin harvesting corn. On Rye Farm Leonard Davey's wheat proved of better quality than expected.

Up at Fieldlands beyond Chestham, Thomas Wisden did not fare so well. None of his barley was good enough for malting. The whole crop would have to go for grinding, a loss in market value of almost 50%.

At Rye there were peas in good condition.

Three boys spent part of their Sunday afternoon in harvesting them. Nimble fingered, they were able to pick quickly.

They worked willingly with an intense concentration that proved their undoing. P.C. Goldring confronted them.

Pea pods fell to the ground as the boys ran for it.

P.C. Goldring let them run; he would recognise them. He gathered up some of the pods and decided there must have been a quart or more.

The pickers proved to be 14 year olds James Brooker, Mark Woolgar and Henry Newland.

They met again at the Petty Sessions.

Butcher John Thorns and basket-maker 'Sunny' Woolgar were also there ready to affirm the boys' good characters.

Mr. Thorns spoke well of James as a servant at the butchery. 'Sunny' Woolgar vouched for Mark and Henry.

Good characters or no, the verdict was guilty. The magistrates valued the stolen peas at 3s 6d which together with costs made a total of 13s 6d due from each defendant. Non payment would mean a prison term of seven days for each of them.

John Thorns and 'Sunny' Woolgar ensured there was enough money. Parents thanked them. Other parental duty could come later. [3]

Sunnier days heralded September but on some farms the white wheat had spiked, the ears sprouting for new growth ruining its value. Brown wheat and slower ripening crops fared better. Potato blight proved bad and grapes were claimed a complete failure – sobering news for the Flower Show organisers.

The 5th of September had been chosen as Show Day. The choice proved good for weather; bright sunshine and a gentle breeze.

Soon after three, the familiar family names of Henfield society began to arrive.

They paid their entrance fees and walked inside. The marquees were bigger, the arrangements better.

The exhibits of the professionals shone with unabated lustre, the amateurs' productions although not numerous were of rare excellence but the cottagers' produce, certainly numerous, still had room for improvement – so claimed the Sussex Express.

Unread newspaper opinions would not diminish the delight of the cottage ladies gaining prizes:- Harriet Smith's onions, Betsy Woolgar's tray of flowers, Ellen Parsons' device of flowers, Mrs. Gander's apples, Louisa

Tugwell's tray of herbs, Ellen Ward's apples, Sarah Foreman's tray of wild flowers and Ellen Elmalie's parsnips. Eight ladies issuing a challenge to the menfolk; the Flower Show embraced everyone.

Of grapes there had been none but potato blight had not caught everyone. The show of both kidney and round potatoes had proved of good enough quality to gain eight prizes; peas had just one.

The show's fine weather continued into the weekend.

On the Sunday the rifle corps, now fully credited as the 18th Henfield and Mid-Bramber Rifle Corps, went on parade. They fell in at the White Hart and marched in full uniform to St. Peter's Church for the afternoon service. There they occupied the whole of the west gallery and heard Rev. O'Brien preach a suitable sermon for the occasion. The service over, they marched back to headquarters – their first church parade complete.

Well before the end of the month, bad weather returned to heighten farmers' worries.

Harvest was still being gathered in early October. More wheat and oats were sprouting. Barley was so poor everywhere that there would be little good enough for malting. Second cut clover still lying out in the fields lost its quality and some was completely spoiled.

Although the year's harvest was proving so difficult and disappointing, plans were in place to provide a bigger room for the corn market.

The present room was far too small to accommodate the increasing trade. A search for suitable premises had been going on for some time.

Mr. Stoner came up with the answer; rebuild the upper storey of the George to form one large hall as both a market room and a centre for village events.

Messrs. Tamplin the Brighton brewers, were consulted as owners. They agreed.

Plans were drawn up.

Alterations began with no disruption to the sale of beer and spirits. Daily trade was too important.

All was going well with men at work completing the new roof when there was a sudden shout as one of them slipped and fell over the side 30 feet to the ground.

It was Charles Martin. He lay groaning.

Friends rushed to his aid but there was nothing they could do other than attempt to comfort him.

A man ran for Dr. Caudle who lived just six houses down the street. Father and son were both at home.

Young Adolphus accompanied the man back to the George.

A quick examination showed Charles Martin had broken ribs.

Friends fashioned a stretcher and carried him home; his future in the balance, dependant on the skill of the two doctors.

Work on the roof continued.

The sale of beverages also provided a side line and additional income for James and Mary Dear at Crouch Hill Toll-house. They were not licensed for alcoholic sales but they made a very palatable ginger beer. Thirsty travellers were keen to take advantage of it.

For James, being keeper at Crouch Hill was the ideal job because an accident had resulted in the amputation of a leg.

One Saturday afternoon he was out beside the house enjoying the day's good weather and watching three travellers make their way up Crouch Hill from the village.

As they reached the gate one of the men called to him; "Do you sell ginger beer?"

"Yes," replied George, "it's a penny a bottle."

"Then give the woman a bottle," commanded the older man.

James headed off to fetch it. He was too slow. By the time he reached the door his wife was already handing a bottle to the woman.

The man paid with a shilling. He carefully counted his eleven pence change.

Satisfied, the three moved off.

Mary passed James the shilling and asked him to check it. James took the coin, placed it in his mouth and bit. The coin bent – counterfeit.

He stumped to the door and yelled for the travellers to come back because the money was bad.

They did so. The man was very apologetic and gave another shilling. He explained how he had changed a half-crown at one of the village shops and had failed to notice he had been given a bad shilling.

James expressed his satisfaction and the travellers went on their way towards Horsham.

They were barely out of sight round the curve of the road when Mary Dear set off heading to Henfield for P.C. Goldring.

She found him and began recounting the incident.

Crouch Hill Toll House

P.C. Goldring listened to her tale. He reckoned the men were probably regular smashers living by counterfeit coinage. He would set off in pursuit.

Mary Dear returned home.

Goldring collected one of the parochial constables and they set off at a smart pace.

The pursuit was a lengthy one right through Cowfold to the Crab Tree Inn halfway up the hill at Lower Beeding where the constables saw a woman waiting out on the road.

They held back hoping men would appear. They did, two emerging from the inn for all three to continue up the road in Horsham direction.
The constables set off again, purposefully closing in on them.

One of the men turned.

The constables saw something quickly thrown into the hedgerow.

Nobody tried to run, nobody hurried.

P.C. Goldring stopped the three of them. He searched the older of the men and found 2s 3d in good money. He left the parochial constable in charge and retraced his steps to search the hedge.

He recovered a glove. In it were paper wraps. Each contained a coin.

Each coin failed the biting test.

The woman was enraged. She vented her anger at the man;

"You villain, you have brought us into trouble as well as yourself!"

She explained how she and her husband had fallen in with the other man on their way up from Brighton.

P.C. Goldring was unmoved. All three were suspect.

On the Monday they appeared before the magistrates and were remanded to the Wednesday. A message was sent to the Solicitor of the Treasury to determine whether the mint would prosecute.

Word came that it would.

On the Wednesday the three stood before the magistrates again. The justices assessed the case and declared it one for the Quarter Sessions – but for the older man, James Talbot, only. The other two were discharged.

James Talbot, 40 year old labourer, appeared at the next sessions charged with unlawful possession of counterfeit coin – ten pieces resembling half-crowns and six resembling shillings. He pleaded; "Not guilty."

Silversmith Charles Steadman witnessed that he had tested the coins. All were counterfeit.

George Dear was called to give evidence.

Prisoner Talbot poured a torrent of questions at him. None was effective.

In final exasperation he made his ultimate challenge;

"Well; let somebody go out and bring in a cup of water and mingle it with some earth from the church-yard and drink and see who drops down dead first."

Laughter answered him. Judgement followed; twelve months hard labour.

James and Mary Dear returned to their toll-house assured that their ginger beer revenue would be safe from itinerant money smashers. [4]

Chapter 30

Riding a windmill – Mercury for geese – Wait for the Wagon

In the village, the alterations to the George were complete enough by mid October for the corn market to be held there.

Landlord Mr. Stoner was careful to give full credit for the rebuilding to Messrs. Tamplin. They had provided a much needed venue for public meetings and concerts with a room 52 feet in length, 18 feet wide and 13 feet high equipped with the great feature of a domed ceiling specially designed to provide good acoustics. The entrance from the street was up an easy flight of stairs past the new bar and through an anteroom. [1]

The rebuilt George Inn

That Friday, the grand opening dinner was held. Between 60 and 70 gentlemen attended, including several from Brighton and Hurst, plus all the principal tradesmen and farmers. John Randle of Kentons took the chair with John Thorns, farmer and butcher, the vice-chair.

The food was served up in the first-rate style Mr. and Mrs. Stoner invariably achieved.

Post-dinner, as ever, were the loyal toasts and speeches.

At their end it was time for merry making and song.

Mr. Stoner had planned thoughtfully. To entertain and amuse the guests he had acquired the services of professional singers including none other than Brighton's one and only Mr. Windebank.

Mr. Windebank excelled again, the clarity of his voice enhanced by the new domed roof.

There were jokes to roars of acoustic laughter, tunes from his flutina accordion and climactic choruses of communal songs. The end came all too soon.

Guests made their way home commending Messrs. Tamplin, landlord Stoner and, above all, the one and only Mr. Windebank.

One Henfield lad was set on providing his own amusement.

The Wednesday after Mr. Windebanks's entertainment, 14 year old Richard Foreman was up by the Nep Town windmill watching the miller prepare for his day's work: - rotating the mill to face the wind, ascending the wooden steps and disappearing inside to set the sails in motion.

Richard took his chance to clamber over the barrier, nip across to the mill and grab hold of a sail as it began to rotate – a short but exciting ride.

Somehow the slats trapped his hands. It was impossible to let go.

As the turning sail lifted Richard higher off the ground he screamed in terror.

The miller raced down the steps and round to the front of the mill. He glimpsed the figure on the sail already descending again.

He raced back round the mill, up the steps and inside to the brake.

The sails stopped. There was another scream and a thud as the freed boy hit the ground.

Horrified, the miller walked over to the body. There was a moan, the boy was alive.

A man went for Doctor Caudle. Again young Adolphus responded.

Examination showed Richard to have bad chest bruising but fortunately no broken ribs. Dr. Caudle was confident the outlook was encouraging.[2]

Charles Martin was still recovering from his broken ribs fall at the George. With careful nursing, both should make a rather painful recovery.

November came in like a March lion with a severe gale of wind that kept the mill securely battened down and people thankful to stay indoors.

At the far end of the High Street among the old houses beyond the road to the church lived retired watchmaker Richard Lashmar and his daughter, Frances.

The old houses by Church Street

Beyond them were gunsmith Peter Ward, tenant of Lucretia Wood, and long established shoemaker Stephen Yeates who had inherited his shop from his father. From there, it was open road as far as the Bull Inn by Mock Bridge.

The night of the gale, Frances and her father sat each side of the fire listening to the wind wail and roar around the chimney.

A sudden, startling crash sounded.

The ceiling disintegrated and Frances sat screaming in alarmed fright among fallen wooden joists jumbled against the wall. Lodged in the joists, were large sections of broken chimney.

Her father helped her work free and they thankfully accepted shelter with Peter Ward.

Their house seemed a ruin but fortune had smiled on Frances, indelicately squeezed yet little hurt. [3]

Gale force winds were of no significance on the railway.

The new alignment of the track past Pokerlee overcame the problems of the bottomless marsh. An ever stretching line of rails was heading for the village.

A noisy six wheeled engine hauled a daily 'muck train' of wagons filled with stones for packing along the newly laid sections.

The sight of a steaming engine crossing the brooks was sobering or exciting for whoever was seeing it – the end of a way of life or a vision of the future.

One morning the navvies found a metal obstruction placed on the line. They cleared it in time for the 'muck train' and knew they had prevented a probable derailment.

When it happened again a few days later the men knew it was being done with evil intent.

Notices were displayed round the village promising a reward to anyone with positive information about the culprits. [4]

The miscreants remained undetected but the line was left clear.

John Cosslet, one of the foreman of the railway contractors discovered he had been robbed of £4 1s 6d. He named the perpetrator as Sarah Stanford, a woman quite familiar among the navvies. He had been in her company the night of the 22nd. He remembered the occasion well; knew he was not mistaken and was positive about her identity.

The woman was brought before the magistrates and had to answer for her actions.

She utterly refused to accept there had been any theft on her part. Yes, she had been with the man. He had asked for her services and had paid. Nothing had been stolen.

The magistrates had no wish to delve deeper. Case dismissed. Sarah Stanford should tramp her services to a different area.

All that time the November weather had been rain.

The brooks flooded to become a lake over a mile long with Rye Island isolated in the middle.

When the rain ceased, there were calm days with temperatures plummeting.

Freezing conditions heralded the Christmas season.

Benevolent families bore gifts of clothing and blankets for the needy.

By Christmas Day the floods had frozen with the ice several inches thick.

Boxing Day was kept as a general holiday with all shops closed. The frozen floods were dotted with skating villagers.

As evening darkness settled, the skaters held flaming torches to light their way making an ever changing pattern across the ice. Numerous slower flares tracked the slides of the skateless determined to enjoy themselves to the full.

When temperatures rose, cloud filled the sky and snow began. Deep drifts formed in fields and along roads.

Railway work stopped. Edward Pattenden's omnibus to Brighton was snowbound. Coalman Richard Morley set off for Shoreham to replenish supplies only to be forced to leave his empty cart at Beeding and make for home with his horse.

On Henfield Common, 'Lossam' was having difficulty coping with the combination of winter weather and his neighbour Anthony Hole's geese.

Geese and 'Lossam' just did not go together.

One afternoon, Mrs. Hole was outside with her son Thomas when she noticed 'Lossam' by the geese pound. She called over to him;

"Is there anything there belonging to you Master Ward?"

'Lossam' turned and hurried away without answering.

Mrs. Hole went over to the pound. Four pieces of bread lay there; a goose nibbling at one of them.

She gathered up the bread, wary of 'Lossam's' unusual kindness.

Something had been pasted on the bread. She took it inside to show her husband.

Both were suspicious. Three geese had mysteriously died since September. The pasted bread could have a bearing.

They took it to P.C. Goldring.

The next day two of the remaining geese ate nothing. The following day they were dead.

Anthony Hole took the bodies to P.C. Goldring who set off for Brighton with bread and birds to consult an analytical chemist.

The chemist found mercury in the paste, within each bird's gizzard and in the intestines.

The whole sequence was recounted at the Petty Sessions Court.

Another witness described how 'Lossam' had been to him wanting some arsenic for a troublesome rat.

'Lossam' could find nothing adequate to say in defence. His counsel argued that the charge had not been proved according to law.

The magistrates considered the case.

When they announced their findings, 'Lossam' winced; fines totalling almost £4 or three weeks at Petworth. He chose home life. The money was paid. [5]

Just along the common from 'Lossam', at the Boys' School, a concert was being held in aid of the new organ being installed in St. Peter's Church.

The leading light along with the vicar was Ernest Pattenden the church organist.

A lot of effort had gone into arranging the schoolroom tastefully. Banners and flags brightened the walls. Extra chandeliers reflected on evergreen decorations. Behind the special platform for the performers was a sign in coloured cloth letters stating what everyone knew; "FOR THE ORGAN".

Dignitaries from West Grinstead and Brighton attended with the village gentry and traders in an audience a hundred strong.

Hand written programmes were handed out.

A section of the Brighton Harmonic Society was providing support for local participants. One item would be sung by seven Henfield schoolgirls.

Although for church funds, the concert proved more secular than religious.

At the finish of several pieces, polite hand clapping became enthusiastic and encores were sung

The seven schoolgirls took the stage all identically dressed. The audience were impressed.

The chosen song was unknown to most; "Wait for the Wagon," a song straight across the Atlantic from the United States.

The girls sang sweetly, their diction clear;

"Will you come with me my Phyllis dear to yon blue mountain Free,

Where the blossoms smell the sweetest, come rove along with me.

It's every Sunday morning when I am by your side,

We'll jump into the wagon and all take a ride."

The vicar may have been taken aback by such sentiments but a catching chorus was coming;

With acknowledgements to the late R. B. Buckley

"Wait for the Wagon" chorus

After four more verses with echoing chorus, the song came to an end.

The applause was rapturous. There just had to be an encore. [6]

Ernest Pattenden went home a very satisfied organist. Rev. O'Brien had his reservations.

The next social event was at the George Hotel the following Monday when visitors from Brighton, Hurst, Cowfold and Steyning gathered for the Farmer's and Traders' Ball.

Landlord Stoner and his wife made sure the viands were acceptable, the band made sure the music was acceptable and some forty couples danced the hours away to 4 a.m. before accepting it must be time for home or hotel bed.

Down at the White Hart, landlord Martin and his son had been doing their utmost to promote the Rifle Corps. Disagreements within the ranks had seen attendances dwindle as low as four.

Gradually absentees returned. Drill sessions recommenced three times a week in the large Club Room behind the inn. Finally the 4th of February was selected as the first outdoor drill.

By the end of the month they were parading up to the Town Field each Thursday for firing practice under the strict control of Ensign Stanford.

Morale lifted and a tempting carrot was floated before them; the Grand Review with sham battle to be held at Brighton that Easter Monday. The 18th Henfield could be part of it if they achieved a high enough standard.

On Sunday the 12th, those of them joining the worshippers at St. Peter's had the pleasure of hearing Mr. Winsor of Brighton playing the new fine-toned organ in its own tiny gallery above the west gallery. He proved himself complete master complementing the excellent sermon preached by Rev. Carey Borrer the rector of Hurstpierpoint – the controversial devotee of the Oxford Movement with its celebration of Holy Sacrament each week aping Romanism.

Rev. O'Brien thanked them both, delighted that the organ fund had benefitted by collections of £20.

Charles Stoner's delight was a fine new building under construction close to the site for the railway station. Once finished it would be named the Station Hotel with its licence held by his son.

Even more satisfying for him, he was able to manufacture the bricks at his field close to the hotel, a field heavy with clay. His men shaped the bricks, left them in loose mounds to harden, and fired them; good bricks obtained at minimal cost.

The railway was progressing well. Navvies were carrying out their tasks efficiently with health hazards rigorously ignored.

Shafts were sunk to begin the excavation of the deep cutting beyond the station. Men balanced on narrow ledges to widen the shaft. Two men fell and sustained serious injury.

A few weeks later a man slipped between the muck wagons of the train bringing ballast stone. His thigh was broken.

A man using his sickle severed a finger.

Messrs. Caudle dealt with each and reported on their patients' recoveries.

One accident was beyond the skills of the Caudle doctors. Navvies forgot to set the rail points correctly for an empty muck train. The engine ran out of rails and came to a stop with the front wheels buried in the ground. It took eight hours to position rails and set the train on its way again.

The navvies finally finished laying the rails to Partridge Green.

People began badgering for the line to be opened unaware that it could not happen until officials had inspected the line by foot and by train.

Chapter 31

Easter battle – Food adulteration – 'Rough Music'

The weeks passed and Easter Sunday was celebrated at St. Peter's with a service of Holy Communion. It was the eve of the Grand Review at Brighton.

Over 30 Rifle Corps members were listed to take part. Supporters would travel with them. Their transport had been arranged.

Easter Monday dawned warm and clear. Members and friends gathered at the station where the empty muck wagons train stood, engine steaming, the driver ready to depart.

Everybody clambered aboard the wagons. The train moved forward. Henfield's railway was opening well ahead of any inspection. They all enjoyed the thrill of their ride to Shoreham where they caught an official train of covered coaches to Brighton. [1]

Special trains had been arriving with artillery and riflemen not only from across Sussex but also Hampshire, Kent, Surrey, Middlesex, the City of London, Tower Hamlets, Highgate, Bloomsbury and the Cinque Ports.

Brighton had declared a general holiday with all shops closed.

Spectators thronged the streets to watch the troops march down Trafalgar Street and along to the Level.

There, each volunteer was issued with a day's rations and 25 rounds of blank ammunition. The Sussex Artillery had four six-pounder cannon lent for the occasion by the Government.

At 10.30 the parade of ten thousand men set off to the Race Course where seats for a view from the grandstand cost half a guinea.

The troops arrived and military bands set the pace for a grand march past; the Lord Lieutenant taking the salute. That the riflemen came last took none of the honour away.

The men marched on, away from the Race Course to the empty hills and valleys of Ovingdean followed by expectant spectators unable to afford grandstand comfort – those in the seats exclaiming dismay as the troops disappeared.

The opposing armies deployed among the hills. Battle began and raged. After fierce fighting the attackers' onslaught was repulsed by the defenders forming squares – Duke of Wellington squares that had repulsed Napoleon at Waterloo.

The climax came in a furious fusillade of canon fire echoing across the Downs. The enemy retreated. Brighton was saved. [2]

Spectators were thrilled; so this was battle – minus injury and death.

Fighting completed, troops were marched back to Brighton, trains rejoined and combatants returned home.

The 18th Henfield and supporters changed trains at Shoreham and boarded the muck train wagons. What a day it had been.

The Useful Knowledge Institution concentrated on the more ordinary side of life. They were now listed in the County Directory as a mechanics' institute of more than 80 members with Mr. Henry Longley as secretary.

At their annual meeting, Rev. George Hall took the chair in the absence of the vicar who was again indisposed. Membership was better than for several years. Chess sets and drafts were now available and the library was to have a fresh supply of books in addition to the many so generously contributed by Mr. William Borrer. It was hoped funds could be improved by staging a concert. A committee was even then working to arrange one.

At their monthly meeting they had an enlightening lecture; "On the Adulteration of Food."

The room was full. People were anxious to discover what they might be consuming.

The speaker held their undivided attention with explanatory diagrams and clear illustrations.

Bakers were adding alum to bleach their flour; alum caused constipation. Beer was not always simple malt and hops but was sometimes mixed with water and liquorice juice or nux vomica to give it a head. Nux vomica; the plant containing strychnine, important in so many medications by sharpening mental powers, giving a feeling of increased bodily well-being and keeping muscles in greater 'tone' – attributes seldom appreciated by people passing the Plough Inn on a Saturday night.

Family drinks were suspect too. Tea was mixed with leaves of sloe, ash or elder; coffee with ground up peas and beans.

There were so many sharp dealers; so much to be aware of.

Members thanked the speaker for his enlightening lecture. They would return home and instruct their wives to shop with extra caution.

The institute's plans for a grand concert came to fruition at the acoustic Assembly Room above the George. The Lay Vicars of Chichester Cathedral were visiting specially for the occasion. They had a worthy audience to please with most of the nobility and gentry of the area attending.

The Lay Vicars rose to the occasion with a carefully selected programme starting with a charming old madrigal. Songs and glees followed capturing the local flavour of the day with "Riflemen Form" and a touch of national pride with "England, Europe's Glory." Institute funds benefitted.

Parish funds underwent scrutiny at the annual vestry meeting to audit the accounts of the churchwardens and the overseers.

It was held according to custom in the vestry room at the church with the vicar in the chair. All was well with the parish money; the Lay Vicars would not be called upon. Churchwardens and surveyors of the highways were re-elected and a list of five names agreed from which two would become the ensuing year's overseers.

Not quite all was well with daily life in the parish. There was conjugal infidelity within a particular family; or so it appeared to disinterested neighbours who felt bound to confide in other disinterested neighbours.

The situation became so unacceptable that a group of the offended felt it incumbent upon themselves to make their feelings public – although without naming the guilty parties.

It was agreed to mark people's concern the accepted way with a short demonstration. The time chosen was after nightfall.

Neighbours and neighbours' friends gathered quietly outside the house. Each had an instrument to play – strictly non musical.

At a given signal they struck up loud and cacophonous in traditional "Rough Music" strong in its lack of rhythm, noisy to the extreme and strident in its message that echoed through the dark.

The concert did not last long but everyone in earshot understood what it meant – don't fall foul of public rebuke. [3]

In Dr. Caudle's household, one of the servants felt she had fallen beyond the days of love and marriage, happy or otherwise. She had begun service there at the age of 15 and now, at 33, there was little hope left. She became despondent and, with further thought, more depressed.

Finally she felt there was nothing left; no hope, no purpose in life. She took a razor to the breakfast room and slit her throat.

They found her on the floor.

Dr. Caudle used all his skill and knew he could not save her. Within the hour she was dead.

After a straightforward inquest, the vicar conducted her funeral. He completed the register entry and ensured she would be remembered with the words; 'cut her throat'; sad Caroline Martin.

Fred and Sarah Stillaway in their tenement at the back of the common had the awful sadness of losing their little baby, Frances, sister of four year old Harriet and two year old Hannah.

Each night baby Frances was placed at her mother's side so that it was simple to offer milk. Frances slept, took milk if she wanted, and slept again. Fred slept the other side undisturbed by Sarah's maternal duties.

One night the baby refused milk at ten o'clock. Later Sarah had to leave the bed. She returned and made sure Frances was high at her breast.

About two o'clock Sarah roused yet again. Frances lay quiet, very quiet. Sarah felt her baby's lips; cold.

She slipped Frances from her breast and the head flopped.

Sarah woke Fred. He lit a candle and they had the ghastly shock of realising their baby was dead.

Fred went for Dr. Morgan. His assistant came but nothing could be done.

An inquest had to be held with a hastily gathered jury.

Sarah told how on the previous day she had given Frances a teaspoonful of caster oil and that the following morning the baby seemed the better for it.

She then described the night.

The doctor gave his evidence.

The coroner addressed the jury and stated how such events were of frequent occurrence and the evidence generally unsatisfactory. In the present case, however, there was every appearance of the child having received kind and proper treatment. If the jury felt satisfied with the evidence a verdict might be given accordingly.

The jury retired, reappeared very quickly and the foreman announced; "Died from natural causes."

Fred and Sarah could mourn the loss of their lovely child.

Events on the common carried on.

The Rifle Volunteers, now the 18th Sussex as part of the Petworth 2nd Battalion, paraded in front of the Boys' School keen to show how the experience of the Grand Review had resulted in even greater efficiency.

They had formed their own brass band which was proving very promising. With a little more practice they would be really proficient.

Drill and manoeuvres were competently executed.

The men formed ranks to march back to their White Hart headquarters.

They reached the common corner and began ascending the High Street with the band playing a lively march.

Approaching from the other side was a four-wheeled chaise, the horse at a smart trot.

In an instant the horse turned and bolted back down the High Street.

Unaware, the 18th Sussex marched on.

The chaise driver brought his horse under control and turned it to continue. He made sure the horse understood who was master by using his whip.

As the band breasted the hill, the horse bolted again. The chaise capsized throwing the driver to the ground, the horse kicking its way to freedom and completely wrecking the vehicle.

The march finished without music.

Young Dr. Adolphus Caudle attended the driver, dressed his wounds, which proved superficial, and drove him home to Edburton. Henfield had a doctor who really cared. [4]

The Rifle Corps also encountered somebody who really cared.

The 18th Sussex had to attend periodic battalion parades commanded by a high ranking officer.

Colonel Luard proved a stickler for detail. His eagle eye noticed everything, his caustic tongue rebuked corps commanders.

It prompted the captain of the 14th Sussex to tender his resignation.

The Sussex Express reported the story and had more to tell;

> It is rumoured that the 18th Sussex, being in the same category, are taking similar steps, but that any observation in the present state of affairs would be premature.

In Henfield, solicitor Thomas Coppard read the report and took immediate action.

He penned a reply to the editor: - the statement was entirely devoid of truth. He happened to know that the 18th were considered as having performed their duties in a creditable manner. They were, and ever would be, good loyal subjects sensible of the responsibilities and duties they had undertaken.

His caustic pen chastised the zealous colonel and concluded with a scholarly flourish in Latin; 'fiat justitia, ruat coelum' – which fellow scholars may have interpreted as 'Let justice be done though the heavens should fall.' [5]

Solicitor Coppard signed his letter and took it to the post office. He would not have men of Henfield disparaged without good cause.

Chapter 32

The telegraph – Special Train – The Bank of Engraving

Letter writing was no longer the only means of personal communication between people.

Along the railway, tall posts placed at regular intervals supported thick wires for the signalmen's telegraphed code to ensure train safety.

The public would be able to pay for messages to be telegraphed from the station, still being built, to anywhere on the system – to London and beyond as soon as the line was completed to Horsham.

It was a wonder of technology; the dah–di-di-dah of Morse sent by wire and transcribed back to the written word.

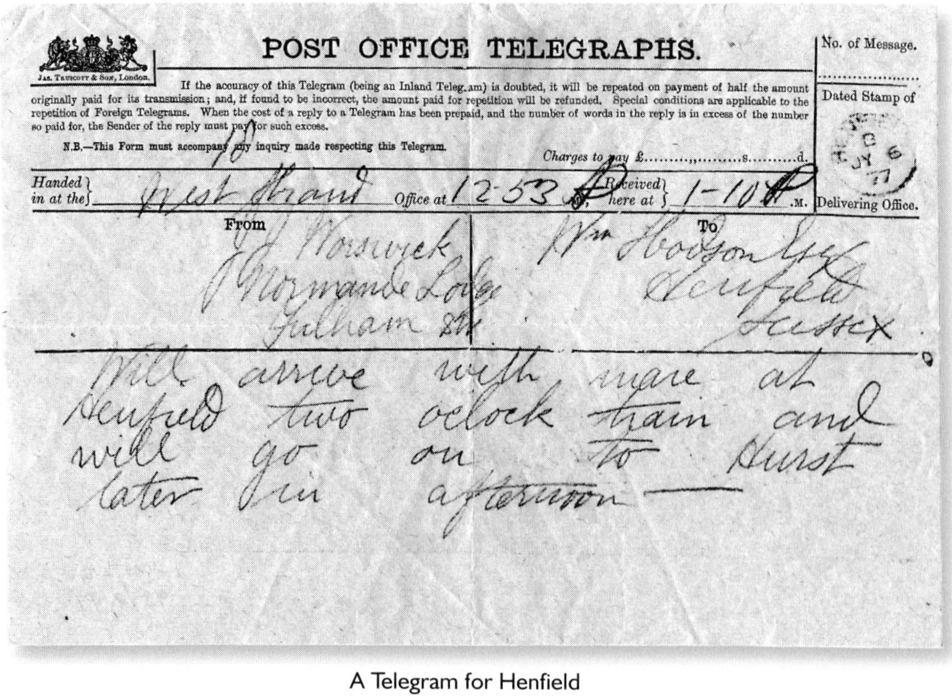

Jas. Truscott & Son, London.

POST OFFICE TELEGRAPHS.

No. of Message.

If the accuracy of this Telegram (being an Inland Teleg.am) is doubted, it will be repeated on payment of half the amount originally paid for its transmission; and, if found to be incorrect, the amount paid for repetition will be refunded. Special conditions are applicable to the repetition of Foreign Telegrams. When the cost of a reply to a Telegram has been prepaid, and the number of words in the reply is in excess of the number so paid for, the Sender of the reply must pay for such excess.

N.B.—This Form must accompany any inquiry made respecting this Telegram.

Charges to pay £........s........d.

Dated Stamp of Delivering Office.

Handed in at the West Strand Office at 12-53 P. Received here at 1-10 P.M.

From J J Worswick Normande Lodge Fulham SW

To Wm Hodgson Esq Henfield Sussex

Will arrive with mare at Henfield two oclock train and will go on to Hurst later in afternoon —

A Telegram for Henfield

Track inspections had been completed. The report was good. The station buildings were far from ready but that did not affect the line.

Services would begin on the 1st of July 1861.

There would be three trains a day at set intervals requiring an entirely new concept of time. No longer was the hour or half-hour of the village clock sufficient.

The first train would be from Brighton, timed to leave Henfield at 7.58 a.m. and reach Partridge Green at 8.05. The return train would reach Shoreham at 8.43. The clock minutes hand was suddenly of vital importance.

On the opening morning a small group of enthusiasts gathered at Henfield platform. Some bought a sixpenny ticket to Partridge Green. Others preferred to be onlookers.

A plume of steamy smoke crossed the brooks, rounded a final corner and became the train chugging up the slight incline to the station.

Henfield's first official passengers boarded for the exciting experience of a seven minutes ride. Friends waved them goodbye.

At Partridge Green the train was rearranged for the return trip.

Passengers climbed aboard again, enjoyed their homeward journey and were welcomed at Henfield by their cheering friends.

More people joined, set on the double pleasure of the excitement of train travel and a long day out in Brighton – at 2s 3d for a 3rd Class return ticket. They would not be back until 7.13 p.m.

Before walking home they could call in for a drink at the newly completed Station Hotel.

L.B.S.C.R. promoted their new line by advertising a Special Train on Wednesday the 17th July from Partridge Green down to Shoreham and west along the coast to Portsmouth. Tickets in a 3rd Class covered carriage would cost just 2s 0d, children under 12, half-price.

People thrilled at the idea; all that in a single day at less than a ticket for Brighton – and with the opportunity of taking a boat trip across the sea to the Isle of Wight.

Hundreds travelled. The weather was fine and the outing proved as good as anticipated.

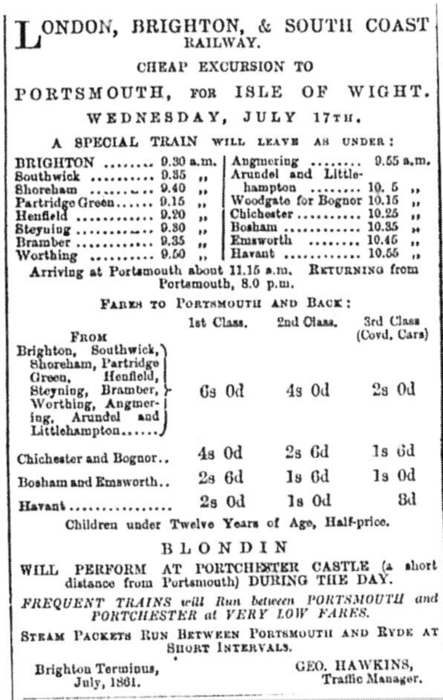

LONDON, BRIGHTON, & SOUTH COAST RAILWAY.

CHEAP EXCURSION TO

PORTSMOUTH, FOR ISLE OF WIGHT.

WEDNESDAY, JULY 17TH.

A SPECIAL TRAIN WILL LEAVE AS UNDER:

BRIGHTON	9.30 a.m.	Angmering	9.55 a.m.
Southwick	9.35 ,,	Arundel and Little-hampton	10. 5 ,,
Shoreham	9.40 ,,	Woodgate for Bognor	10.15 ,,
Partridge Green	9.15 ,,	Chichester	10.25 ,,
Henfield	9.20 ,,	Bosham	10.35 ,,
Steyning	9.30 ,,	Emsworth	10.45 ,,
Bramber	9.35 ,,	Havant	10.55 ,,
Worthing	9.50 ,,		

Arriving at Portsmouth about 11.15 a.m. RETURNING from Portsmouth, 8.0 p.m.

FARES TO PORTSMOUTH AND BACK:

FROM	1st Class.	2nd Class.	3rd Class (Covd. Cars)
Brighton, Southwick, Shoreham, Partridge Green, Henfield, Steyning, Bramber, Worthing, Angmering, Arundel and Littlehampton	6s 0d	4s 0d	2s 0d
Chichester and Bognor	4s 0d	2s 6d	1s 6d
Bosham and Emsworth	2s 6d	1s 6d	1s 0d
Havant	2s 0d	1s 0d	8d

Children under Twelve Years of Age, Half-price.

BLONDIN

WILL PERFORM AT PORTCHESTER CASTLE (a short distance from Portsmouth) DURING THE DAY.

FREQUENT TRAINS will Run between PORTSMOUTH and PORTCHESTER at VERY LOW FARES.

STEAM PACKETS RUN BETWEEN PORTSMOUTH AND RYDE AT SHORT INTERVALS.

Brighton Terminus, July, 1861.

GEO. HAWKINS, Traffic Manager.

The Portsmouth Special Train [1]

Mrs. Dunlop decided her annual school outing for the children should be a train ride to Brighton with a visit to the famous Chain Pier. Arrangements were made.

Sixty excited children reached the station bridge and bobbed down the steep steps which were proving such an obstacle to any lady encumbered by a fashionable crinoline skirt.

The steps safely negotiated, they awaited the train, boarded it and sat expectant.

A whistle sounded, the train drew away and adventure had begun.

By late afternoon they were home again recounting the amazing speed of the trains, Brighton's huge station and the distance out to sea they had been right at the end of the Chain Pier where a big steamship set off for France.

Mrs. Dunlop had provided an unforgettable day. [2]

The farmers at Rye and Betley gave their labourers, 16 in all, a day off with a paid trip by Special Train to the Crystal Palace.

The journey there was adventure enough. Arrival at the Crystal Palace brought unbelievable sights; the enormous structure itself of glittering glass and the displays within it. There was entertainment, too, a thrilling performance by Monsieur Blondin of Niagara Falls fame on the tight rope, walking, performing agilities and giving everyone momentary frights by almost falling. How he managed to recover was amazing.

Each man had the time of his life and returned to Henfield full of thanks for his master.

Through August the Specials continued; London's West End, the Swiss Gardens at Shoreham and Brighton Races.

Henfield's railway had arrived.

On the day of the Horticultural Show, a train brought 400 children from Brighton's Christ Church School for a day's outing in the country.

They walked from the station to Henfield Place for games and sports, interrupted at times by rain, followed by a filling country tea.

At 5 o'clock there was a further treat for them, a short walk to the village and free entry into the Horticultural Show.

The children wondered at such a large marquee being filled with so many flowers, vegetables and fruit just to be looked at.

Three things were worth remembering to tell about at home. Best was the soldiers' band. Second was a table of strange plants where one had bits of stuff growing on it that could be turned into real cotton. Third was a sort of big toy garden with little flowers and at the back of it some rocks with waterfalls gushing down to a pretend grass lawn that had a fountain spouting water.

Tired, the children left the show, walked back to the station and boarded the train for home and the familiar streets of Brighton.

Before the end of the month the navvy gangs had completed the railway right through to Horsham. Now England was open wide; Henfield to Horsham – five trains a day – on to the station at the junction with the original Brighton line and up to London.

Fastest was the morning express, 9.30 from Henfield, reaching London Bridge at 11.20 – a journey in unbelievably less than two hours.

Grocer James Easom took himself on an outing to London.

He was standing on London Bridge wondering at the power of the steam boats along the river when a passer by remarked on the state of the water. They began a friendly conversation.

James suggested a pot of ale and a pipe at one of the pubs.

The passer by happily accepted the idea. Fortunately he knew a good pub close by. They made their way to it.

As they smoked and drank their ale an old gentleman sat down at their table and joined in the chat. Presently he took a roll of banknotes from his pocket and in so doing had the misfortune to let a sovereign fall. Embarrassed, he explained that he was in fact quite wealthy. Indeed it was his intention to give aid to every poor parish in the country.

He also told of his interest in the local volunteer force and the pleasure he gained from being a good shot. Rather boastfully, he confided he could hit the target 17 times out of 24.

James' new friend refused to accept the boast but the old man was adamant to the point of inviting them to the Mullbery-tree public house where there was a good target ground.

At the Mulberry-tree the friend checked out the target. Unfortunately it was in use.

Somebody explained it had been booked for the next hour. They would have to wait.

The old man bought three cigars to help pass the time and gave two of them to James and his friend. His friend thanked the man and jokingly challenged him;

"I'll toss you for another and a shilling."

The old man laughed and to their surprise accepted the challenge.

He lost and handed over his money. He said he was game to try his luck another way; his £5 note and a sovereign against two sovereigns in the chance game of clapping, the best of three to be the winner.

James was invited to join in but he was not too sure.

The other two were keen enough to try and persuade him to change his mind. In the end he agreed and laid his two sovereigns on the table.

Three chalk marks were drawn.

James' friend and the old man each placed a halfpenny in the palm of their hand and closed it.

The game began. The first two calls left them equal. The third would decide.

They called.

James was the loser. His two sovereigns bound for the old man's palm.

The men commiserated and invited him to wager his watch to redeem his money.

James cottoned on quickly. What he had noticed almost tucked away in his friend's knuckles must have been an extra halfpenny. The brand new £5 note was a flash one, a forgery.

He knew he had been duped. He challenged them. The old man brushed aside the challenge with a good natured laugh.

James left, angry at himself. He walked the street determined not to be outdone.

He found what he needed; a Metropolitan Police Constable – number 81 H.

81 H listened to the tale and did not doubt its truth; sharpers were known to work the area.

They returned to the pub and the men were arrested.

P.C. 81 H searched them. On one he found two sovereigns and ten shillings in silver. On the other were nine sharping cards and five brass medals.

On their way to the police station the ex-friend took two sovereigns from his pocket and turned to James;

"Here's your money. I know you have lost it."

James ignored him.

Next day, they all appeared at the Thames Police Court.

James told his tale.

The magistrate had an important question for him;

"Was the £5 banknote genuine or of the Bank of Engraving?"

"The Bank of Engraving," answered James.

"And the sovereigns?"

"Sham ones, sir; brass medals."

The prisoners were remanded to appear at the Middlesex Sessions.

James had to make another London journey to give evidence.

He returned home a happy man. The cheats had been sentenced to two years' hard labour. [3]

Farmer and butcher John Thorns journeyed as far as Horsham market choosing horseback as his transport. He was there to purchase cattle for fattening on the farm before being slaughtered for his shop.

His bids gained what he needed and his drover was sent off home with the animals. He was instructed to go via West Grinstead where John would meet boyhood friends for a drink at the Burrell Arms.

In West Grinstead one of the bullock became restless, butting the beasts around it.

John Thorns decided to rest the animals in a field and allow them to calm.

He enjoyed his drink with his friends and decided it was time for home.

He stepped outside and called his drover to move the animals on.

When the field gate was opened, the restless bullock immediately ran amuck head down making for John.

He leapt to one side but not quite quick enough; the bullock caught him a glancing blow. He crashed to the ground semi-winded. The bullock hit the pub wall with enough force to snap off a horn.

The infuriated animal turned on John who somehow managed to kick out and avoid being immediately gored. The drover ran to his assistance only to leap for the fence as the bullock turned on him.

It next headed up the road and halted by a field of cows.

John recovered enough to open the gate and let it join them.

Help was sought from Knepp Castle.

Sir Percy Burrell's gamekeeper came to their aid with his gun and shot the animal. [4]

The interrupted drive continued to Henfield.

John Thorns' troubles were not over. His High Street butcher's shop and slaughterhouse opposite the White Hart inevitably produced liquid and semi liquid refuse charged with animal droppings. The refuse discharged into an open ditch sewer that flowed down the hill and behind the houses of Richard Lashmar, Peter Ward and StephenYeates.

Since the 1848 cholera outbreak, hygiene legislation had been tightened. The responsibility for improvements lay with the Steyning Union.

Rev. O'Brien, William Borrer and Mr. Piper of Henfield Place signed a letter to the Union stating how the drainage of Henfield and the nuisances arising therefrom were injurious to the health of the inhabitants. They requested the Union to alleviate the matter.

The Union met and set up a committee to receive notices and undertake any proceedings necessary under the latest hygiene regulations. They appointed Henfield's relieving officer, Mr. Challen, as Inspector of Nuisances.

The sewer ditch flowed on.

The Union next received a letter from Henfield's solicitor, Thomas Coppard. He pointed out how they seemed to be ignoring letters sent on behalf of a client complaining of an open ditch behind the premises of Mr. Lashmar. The client now instructed him to state that if the nuisance was not removed the case would be taken before the Court of Queen's Bench.

The Union responded with a list of ancillary questions.

They considered the answers and decided their new Inspector of Nuisances should deal with the problem.

Mr. Challen wasted no time. He measured the lengths of open ditching, prepared a plan of the properties and costed the installation of 6 inch pipes.

He sent in his report and explained that there was no alternative way to render such a nuisance free from its liability to injure the health of the public.

At last the Union acted. The expense liability of each affected property was calculated and a 6 inch covered sewer was safely installed.

Mr. Thorn's slaughterhouse refuse could flow inoffensively, financed by the very people worst affected by the old open ditch.

Along at the village's latest inn, the Station Hotel by the railway, landlord Albert Stoner and his father, Charles, had been considering ways to attract more custom.

They decided they should run their own Friendly Society; not a simple local affair but a more countrywide one like the Odd Fellows.

Charles had entertained the Odd Fellows enough times at the George to know it attracted a worthy membership. The Station Hotel could attract men to a similar one in friendly rivalry.

They contacted the Yorkshire based Foresters Friendly Society. The necessary formalities were completed and Albert Stoner had the great pleasure of announcing his hotel now hosted a section of Court Little John in the famous society of the Foresters.

He was far from pleased, however, when a weekend of incessant rain culminated in a Sunday night of storm force winds.

He awoke on the Monday to find his extensive garden wall strewn across the ground – the wall so carefully constructed of his father's own solid bricks. Thankfully the hotel had stood firm.

Charles Stoner had an even greater shock.

In the field beyond the hotel, 30000 of his moulded bricks had been stacked in carefully constructed mounds hardening in the wind ready for the kiln. Now he had 30000 shapeless blobs lying on the ground; potential sovereigns laundered into wet clay.

Chapter 33

Magic lantern – A dirty narrow lane – Brickbats and tiles

There was good news in the High Street.

On the Monday just nine days before Christmas, the Post Office would be opening a Savings Bank. People were urged to take advantage of it – the only one within eleven miles.

The idea was attractive but the first calls on people's money were for the extra expenses of Christmas.

The season brought a new entertainment to the village.

At the Assembly Room above the George there were two evening shows by Professor Buck, the wily wizard, accompanied by the music of the celebrated harpists Madame Clara Roberts and Herr Dalavanti.

The professor's illusions were perfect. Audiences clapped their appreciation, delighted to be deceived so amusingly. The harpists drew more sedate applause befitting a serious instrument.

The flooded brooks, temporary home to thousands of duck, were a draw for sportsmen who ventured out boating for Christmas meat. Alarmed ducks took to the air, guns were raised, triggers pulled – and luckless birds fell.

As labourer Thomas West raised his gun, the trigger somehow hooked on his jacket and he shot himself through the foot. His friends rowed top speed for shore and one of them raced off for medical aid.

Before long Dr. Caudle junior was on the scene. He attended to the wound and Thomas West was taken to Brighton Hospital denied his Christmas duck.

Thanks to Dr. Caudle's swift response and to careful nursing at the hospital, the man's wounds slowly healed.

Newspapers carried tidings of a death that shocked the whole country. On the 14th December, the Prince Consort had succumbed to typhoid fever.

On the 22nd, two impressive sermons were preached by Rev. Crichton substituting for the vicar who was again too ill to leave his room despite a three week Italian retreat.

The next day, being the Monday before Christmas Day, should have been the tithe audit feast of Lady de la Zouche but she sent word from Parham that in such circumstances it should be postponed.

Saddened as people were by the Prince Consort's death, they still enjoyed their festivities.

The shops' special displays were eye catching.

Butcher Thorns had half a dozen Southdown sheep fattened on his farm, a splendid heifer fattened by Mr. Dennett and a fine steer from Alfred Smith. Butcher Cutress also had his own Southdown mutton plus a heifer from Hurst gazed upon with general admiration.

Grocers' windows had seasonal arrangements of sweets and spices.

Bakers baked and stacked their bread to ensure everyone could have all they needed for the two day holiday. In the true spirit of Christmas, the traders were allowing their assistants an extra day off on Boxing Day.

Benefactors gave the children at each of the three National Schools an afternoon feast of cakes and Christmas fare. Carols and seasonal songs were sung and prizes of books distributed.

The children and parents then walked across to the Boys' School for a magic lantern show given free of charge by Dr. Lewis. He described the views and finished with humorous pieces including a hilarious donkey race. His audience loved it.

By Christmas Day, St. Peter's was decorated with evergreens and scriptural texts of the nativity displayed around the walls. At morning service, worshippers sang the Christmas Hymn once again, 'Hark, hark the herald Angels sing,' led by organist Ernest Pattenden, high above in the organ loft, and the choir in the nave.

Immediately after Christmas there was a Shakespearian evening at the George Hotel with dramatic excerpts from the tragedies of Hamlet and Richard 111. The portrayals were excellent but sadly attendance was sparse – Shakespeare did not have the aura of the Magic Lantern.

On the 28th, the day of the Royal funeral, inhabitants showed their deep sorrow and sympathy for the Prince Consort by the partial suspension of business. At St. Peter's the knell sounded the greater part of the day.

On the 30th, Lady de la Zouche's tithes audit took place at the George. Landlord Stoner filled the plates in his usual generous style and furnished wines of excellent quality. The tithe payers showed full appreciation; empty dishes and emptied glasses refilled for the coming toasts.

On the removal of the cloth, the Parham steward first expressed his sympathy with Her Majesty the Queen under her present painful bereavement. Diners expressed their concurrence.

With sentiments suitably demonstrated, the company stood to drink the loyal toast. They then adjusted their sentiments to toast lady de la Zouche and the family assembled at Parham.

The evening concluded with the good old songs to send the tithe payers home in fine heart.

The New Year came in with heavy tread. Two of Henfield's most respected men died within a few days of each other.

First was the older Dr. Caudle barely 50 years of age. At his funeral, the cortege was led by the members of the Myrtle Lodge Order of Odd Fellows for whom he had been medical officer for many years. Others of the village followed regardless of the heavy rain.

The following day, William Borrer passed away at Barrow Hill. He had been in failing health for several years.

On his funeral day all shops closed, business was entirely suspended and the blinds were closed in people's houses. 300 parishioners with visitors from a wide area followed the cortege as it made its way from Barrow Hill. Henfield's "Friend of the Village" would be much missed.

Henfield life soon got back to the here and now.

People using the railway were of accord that the 30 steep steps down from the road bridge to the platform were objectionable being a danger to anyone descending them. A petition signed by numerous passengers was sent to the company who agreed that an improved entrance would be provided.

The company knew they were on firm ground because the station building was nearing completion and had a wide, easily accessed entrance from the side road.

The station proved to everyone's satisfaction and complainants were able to turn their attention to the approach road from the village describing it as 'a dirty narrow lane – a perfect styx on a wet night to unfortunate pedestrians'. [1]

A commercial traveller added his opinion that at intervals the main road became one mass of slub (mud), perfectly disgraceful, and unless the authorities rectified things it would be a real drawback to visitors going to that pleasant neighbourhood.

The commercial traveller was unaware of one important fact. His 'main road' was an Occupation Road not repaired by the vestry who dealt only with Parish Roads – the six wider roads that were not part of a toll-road.

A meeting was held at the White Hart to resolve the matter.

Discussions were lengthy, finishing with a proposal by Mr. Piper that the road from Hackett's Gate to the newly erected Station Hotel could not be accepted legally until it was widened to the proper width and dedicated to the parish according to Act of Parliament.

There were fidgets of disagreement by a few people. Mr. Piper's property, Henfield Place, lay alongside the road. He would benefit. Was he accepting partial responsibility for the widening or seeking to have it done at other ratepayers' expense?

A vote was taken. The motion was carried.

The next month a meeting was held at the George to decide the best way to carry out the improvements. Discussion recommenced concluding with another Mr. Piper proposition; the road in question which had hitherto been an Occupation Road be now taken by the parish to be widened and repaired.

George Longley, owner of several rateable properties in the High Street, rose to make an amendment; proceedings should be adjourned for a fortnight before a decision was made.

A vote was taken. Only a few people supported the amendment.

Mr. Piper's proposition received overwhelming support. The ratepayers, not the adjacent landowners, would be bearing the cost.

The following week a letter from FAIR PLAY appeared in the paper explaining what had been going on. Prior to the meeting, the idea had been put about that there would be no motion calling for the Occupation Road to be made a Parish Road financed by ratepayers. However, such a motion was sprung upon the meeting and those not in favour were refused their request for a fortnight's adjournment to enable a proper vote to be taken. Thus the higher ratepayers were saddled with the costs of the road by a party of small ratepayers who would derive by far the greater advantage.

FAIR PLAY had the satisfaction of seeing his letter in print but could not prevent the cost falling on the rates. Mr. Piper had outmanoeuvred him.

Village goodwill and harmony were restored when landlord Mr. Stoner, a man known to have 'a soul for musical sounds', provided a room at the George for meetings of the newly formed Tonic Sol Fa Society. Membership was open to both men and women.

Enthusiasm had been aroused following a lecture given by Mr. George Debney of Brighton.

Mr. Debney happily agreed to be their tutor. He guided them through months of training until they were ready to give their first concert.

It took place in the new Assembly Room with its wonderful acoustics.

The performance proved a great success with the interplay of voices in the part-songs bringing loud applause. The audience were enthused. They wished to be part of it. [2]

Society membership grew; flourished.

To young bloods like Mark Browning, Tonic Sol Fa was a non-starter. He was fine with harmony amongst his drinking mates but what enthused him was looking after a man's rights.

Just now they were being threatened. A Brighton man was in the village laying out a new garden; work that Henfield men could do.

Mark Browning had seen him. All the man did through the day was dig the ground, plant some shrubs and trees and then go off to the Plough.

The Plough was Mark's pub, his and his mates. They made sure they were there that night.

They bought their drinks and moved near the man.

Mark broached the subject of gardening – what he and his mates were keen on.

He quickly got down to brass tacks; the man was a ------ pretty party coming out from Brighton to lay out a garden. That was Henfield men's work.

The pals joined in, chiding the intruder. Mark reckoned he would manage to do something for him.

The Brighton man did his best to say nothing; he knew better than stick up for himself in a situation like that

The four pals finished making their point and left.

The man felt uneasy about the trees he had just planted, particularly the foreign monkey puzzle that the owner was so pleased about, the first in Henfield.

He returned to the house and kept watch until past midnight. Nobody came. Satisfied all was well he went back to his lodgings.

In the morning he found the garden in chaos; the monkey puzzle tree among the many of the previous day's planting uprooted. They lay scattered about the garden.

He grimaced and began replacing them.

The owner listened to the man explaining his encounter at the Plough. He determined to take the offenders to court.

The landlord knew what had gone on in his pub and he named Mark Browning.

The court case took place.

The magistrates heard everything including the fact that all the plants were healthy.

Mark Browning's defence lawyer thereupon submitted that as the trees were growing successfully it surely must be the end of the matter.

The question of damage to the trees was raised. None had occurred.

The magistrates halted the case and considered the lawyer's submission.

It was a short interruption. Justice was about to be administered.

The chairman cautioned Browning and ordered him to be discharged.

The owner was flabbergasted – justice favouring a common troublemaker?

Mark Browning felt vindicated. Henfield men could look after themselves against any outsider trying to take their work from them.

The magistrates moved on to another Henfield case; damage to a property in Nep Town. Two of the perpetrators were before them.

Charges were put. First, Frederick Botting did maliciously injure an outhouse by throwing brickbats at it.

The only witness was called to give evidence, Abel Shoulders, the next door householder. He seemed reluctant to speak about events but his evidence was crucial.

On the evening of the 22nd May, he saw Frederick Botting throw something at the privy of an empty house belonging to Dr. Morgan.

He did not know what was thrown. Other young boys were there as well. He ordered them away and they went.

P.C. Goldring explained that he inspected the place the following morning having heard of the throwing and found a brickbat lying in the closet. It had damaged the doorpost to the extent of one penny.

There being no more evidence, the chairman of the bench summed up. He admonished Botting for throwing stones, warned of the consequences and discharged him.

Frederick made for his father, the Woods Mill miller, sitting in court anxiously watching proceedings.

The second defendant was a bigger boy, 13 year old Thomas Cain from one of the tenements further down the lane. He was accused of going into the garden of the empty cottage and pulling up several turnips, the property of Dr. Morgan, that had been left growing for seed.

Thomas Cain pleaded not guilty.

This time the witness was John Stenning, one of the smaller boys, who stated that Thomas Cain had got the turnips and thrown them at the other boys. The charge was proved.

The magistrates considered the case too serious for mere admonishment. Thomas Cain was fined 5s 0d with 11s 6d costs; in default he would be sent to prison at Petworth for three weeks hard labour.

Thomas Cain was on his own. He had no money but could get some from his father by the next day.

The chairman refused. There had been too much of such behaviour going on in Henfield and it was necessary to make an example of the defendant.

Thomas Cain paled. Go to prison?

Miller John Botting resolved the matter. He stepped forward and produced the money – which expressed his opinion of Dr. Morgan bringing charges over so petty a matter. Thomas Cain could go home.

The Steyning Union had a complaint that in no way could be considered a petty matter.

They had advertised for clothing tenders:-

STEYNING UNION. – To Drapers
THE BOARD OF GUARDIANS of this Union are
Desirous of receiving Tenders for supplying the whole
or any part of the following articles to the Union Workhouse,
at Shoreham, viz: -
Men's Cloth Jackets, sizes 4 to 7, at per dozen.
Ditto Vests, (waistcoats) ditto, ditto
Men's Corduroy Trousers, ditto, ditto.
Boys' Cloth Jackets, 8 to 13, at per dozen.
Ditto Vests, ditto, ditto.
Ditto Corduroy Trousers, ditto, ditto.
Men's Felt Hats, at per dozen.
Boys' Cloth Caps, ditto.
Men's Round Frocks, ditto. Boys', ditto. [3]

Samples of the articles could be seen on application at the workhouse. The goods supplied had to be of the same quality delivered in three weeks for approval by the Board.

Henry Longley gained the order.

When he sent in the first quota, the items were rejected out of hand; size wrong and quality poor.

Henry was asked to attend the next Board meeting. There the articles he had provided were laid alongside the workhouse sample garments.

He could do no more than accept he had supplied inferior quality clothing.

Acceptable replacements were sent.

None but he and the Union Board need know of his error.

Henry Longley kept his good name in the village by placing a notice in the window of his shop that the whole of the drapery and outfitting establishment would be closed on Easter Monday to enable his assistants to enjoy the holiday.

Others could follow his example if they chose.

Chapter 34

An arsonist – The Prosecuting Society – A ferocious bull

In August, Henry Longley attended a talk given to the Mechanics' Institute by Mr. Edmund Fry who had travelled down from London especially for the meeting.

The number of members able to attend was unfortunately low because the exceptionally fine weather meant many farmers were busy with harvest.

Mr. Fry's subject was the ongoing American Civil War, the most disastrous conflict unequalled in the history of the world, raging in its second year.

He gave a blow by blow account explaining how the southern Confederate States had declared themselves a new nation determined to keep their cotton trade with Europe and their employment of African slaves in opposition to the Northern Unionists' determination to keep the states as the United States.

A blood bath of fighting followed and even whilst he spoke, battles were raging on land and sea way across the Atlantic Ocean. The wonders of photographic pictures showed the suffering. Which way the conflict would swing and who would be victorious he could not say. President Abraham Lincoln was a strong leader; he should succeed in the end but how many years of destructive conflict were still to come? [1]

As the speaker concluded, members showed their intense appreciation. They had never had such a lecture.

That October, Henfield suffered destructive conflagration in the village.

Late on a Saturday night, fire was seen south of the common near enough the windmill for it to silhouette against the flames. A haystack and outbuilding were alight.

Fortunately the night was calm and enough people were on hand to save the building and a fair portion of the stack.

People hardly had time to congratulate each other when another fire was seen near the common corner.

The fire fighters moved at speed. They found a mass of flames engulfing a shed of grocer Widow Harwood. Nothing could be done to save it.

People knew mischief was afoot.

Moments later they knew where; just a couple of hundred yards away – more flames behind Widow Longley's Vine Cottage.

Fire fighters rushed again. This time it was a summer house and they were able to stop the flames spreading further – but not to prevent a lot of damage to the summer house.

People were sent hither and thither in pairs in case more fires were beginning. None were. The arsonist had gone to ground. [2]

A parish meeting was held at the White Hart. A reward of £50 would be offered. Bills announcing it were to be sent throughout the area. Opinion was rock solid in abhorring such actions carried out against widows and a gentleman of such quiet and unassuming manner as Mr. Stephens.

Notices were posted.

Nobody offered information. No more fires were started.

One inhabitant of Henfield, an obedient servant and payer of Police Rates, wrote to the press complaining about the midnight depredations of the most wanton and mischievous kind being so constantly committed there by a set of daring, drivelling drunkards. When turned out of the public houses, particularly on Saturdays, they caused the more respectable inhabitants to go to bed quite dreading the onslaughts the vagabonds might make. He did not expect the policeman could cleanse the streets but it did seem strange that the paid functionary should never be able to bring any one of the blackguards to justice, especially as the offences had continued for so many months.

The next week's paper included a letter from A POOR PUBLICAN;

> Sir, I can only say, as far as I am concerned, I never have the trouble of turning out drivelling drunkards from my house on a Saturday night any more than on any other night, and as regards the more respectable inhabitants of the place, the licensed victuallers have proved themselves one of the most respectable and liberal classes of men in England.

A letter from HEAR THE OTHER SIDE declared there had hardly been a drunkard on the streets since the railway was finished. Some of the mischief complained of like pulling up flowers and wrenching off gates had been proved to have been done before ten o'clock by a party much too sober to get caught whose object seemed to be to annoy the policeman.

Everybody agreed on one aspect. Regardless of differing opinions, the offenders needed to be caught.

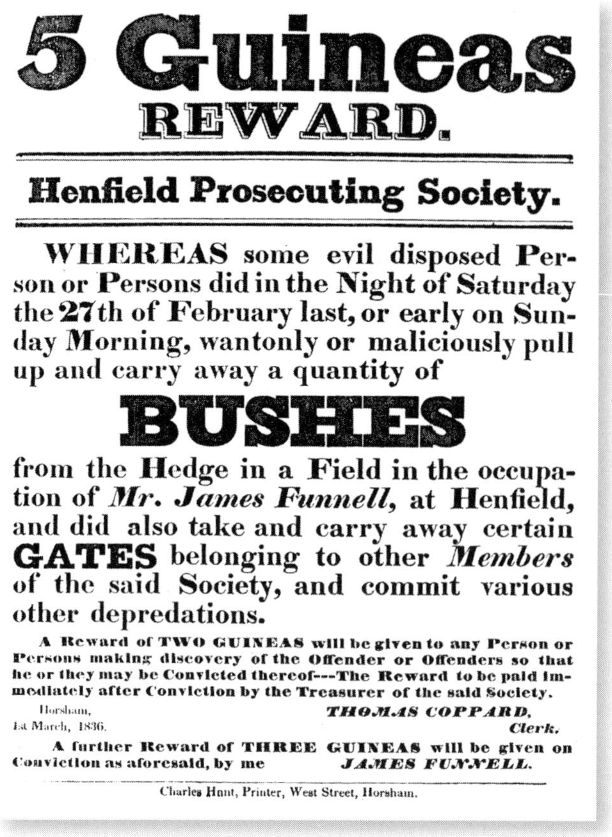
5 Guineas

REWARD.

Henfield Prosecuting Society.

WHEREAS some evil disposed Person or Persons did in the Night of Saturday the 27th of February last, or early on Sunday Morning, wantonly or maliciously pull up and carry away a quantity of

BUSHES

from the Hedge in a Field in the occupation of *Mr. James Funnell*, at Henfield, and did also take and carry away certain GATES belonging to other *Members* of the said Society, and commit various other depredations.

A Reward of TWO GUINEAS will be given to any Person or Persons making discovery of the Offender or Offenders so that he or they may be Convicted thereof---The Reward to be paid immediately after Conviction by the Treasurer of the said Society.

Horsham,
1st March, 1836.

THOMAS COPPARD,
Clerk.

A further Reward of THREE GUINEAS will be given on Conviction as aforesaid, by me *JAMES FUNNELL.*

Charles Hunt, Printer, West Street, Horsham.

Henfield Prosecuting Society [3]

No more depredations occurred. Henfield life went its quiet way until Christmas Eve arrived.

Mark Browning, the village defender against intrusive monkey puzzle gardeners, met some of his mates for a drink at the Plough. They enjoyed their pint and had another. That, too, was enjoyable.

By turning out time they had consumed copious enjoyment shared affably and loudly with all the Plough's customers, like it or not.

At 11.30, landlord Hider called time. Mark Browning's group called back. They were indeed having a very good time; let it continue.

The landlord felt obliged to call in P.C. Goldring.

Goldring went in and found the good time had become fight time. He managed to get one of them out into the street.

When he went in again, Mark Browning constantly moved in front of him to prevent him carrying out his duty. He told Browning to leave. When Browning refused, Goldring began to guide him out.

Browning reacted. He collared Goldring, tripped him up and threw his helmet into the street.

P.C. Goldring had been gentle enough. He became officious. The Plough was cleared.

At the first January Petty Sessions, Mark Browning described being roughly handled by the constable.

P.C. Goldring related how the defendant was constantly insulting him and on one occasion trod on his toe.

"Accidentally!" called Browning.

The interruption was ignored; the Superintendent of Police was about to speak.

He explained that Henfield was within his area. There were a lot of rough young men there of whom he believed the prisoner to be a leader.

The magistrates took him at his word.

The chairman explained that the bench were determined to put a stop to such riotous proceedings. Instead of setting the normal fine they were sentencing the defendant at once to 21 days' imprisonment to hard labour.

Mark Browning endured a long hangover at Petworth.

The vestry held another White Hart meeting to appoint an assistant overseer to help sustain decorum.

Grocer Charles Longley took the chair as parish churchwarden.

Farmer Thomas Williams, vicar's churchwarden, proposed Mr. John Fairs Martin, landlord of the White Hart and sergeant in the 18th Rifles. Fellow farmer Sydney Street seconded the motion and it was carried unanimously.

There could not be a better choice, a man able to influence young bloods on two fronts – the bar of his inn and the three stripes of his military standing.

The following month, Sydney Street himself was sworn in at the Petty Sessions as a fourth overseer. He was a conscientious parishioner who had already served both as waywarden and as parochial constable.

He had come to the end of his lease of Kidders out at Mock Bridge and now farmed Brookside, twice the size, with its fields beside Rye Farm bisected by the railway.

Sydney Street was respected as a farmer, a quiet, unassuming man but his neighbour at Rye disliked the Brookside bull considering it entirely untrustworthy, almost dangerous.

The two men did not fall out over the issue. Sydney knew his animal was of mean mien and took precautions to keep the better side of it.

Brookside was a small household, just Sydney, his wife and their 12 year old granddaughter Caroline who had been with them several years.

He employed two men but Caroline was his happy helpmate when not at school.

The two of them set off early one Sunday morning to move a cow to join others with the bull in one of the brooks near Rye. Their way took them under the railway at the dip in the farm road so shallow there was hardly head height for a man.

When they were still well clear of the bull's field, Sydney told Caroline to go home. The animal had been difficult those past days and he wanted his granddaughter well clear of the area.

She made off up the hill.

Caroline turned at the railway and saw the bull with the cows. Her grandfather was leaving the field, almost at the gate. She carried on home.

Across at Rye, the servant was feeding the hens. She saw the farmer with the cow enter his brook and a few moments later walking rather fast back near the gate with the bull about six yards behind him very quiet. She carried on feeding the hens.

The Rye Farm bailiff inspected his stock that morning and he came across Sydney Street lying face up between two brook gates, both wide open.

The bailiff's first thoughts were of the bull; far too dangerous an animal for any man. He straightway shut the gates.

Beyond them he saw the bull. It walked towards him quietly but bellowed and pawed the ground throwing up dirt.

The bailiff turned to Sydney, lying seemingly lifeless, and set off for help.

He announced the news at Brookside Farmhouse. Caroline was sent to fetch Dr. Caudle. The bailiff and a labourer took a cart down to the brook and lifted the body into it.

When the doctor arrived he confirmed what they already knew.

Word of the tragedy spread. Several 18th Rifles volunteers collected their weapons and set off for the brooks.

There, the bull was calm; a standing target.

Shots rang out, the bull crumpled to the ground and Sergeant Martin pulled the final trigger. Farmer Street was avenged. [4]

The next day an inquest was held at the farmhouse. Dr. Caudle explained that there was bruising in the small of the back of the man and on the chin. Post-mortem examination highlighted the heart being diseased and fatty whilst a cavity in one lung had tubercular deposit round it. Any excitement could have caused death.

The others gave their evidence. The coroner summed up and the jury retired to consider their verdict.

A few minutes later they returned to announce their findings. Sydney Street came to his death by injuries received in the back from a very ferocious bull.

Chapter 35

A maimed dog – School treat – The excise officer intervenes

There was animal trouble up at Chestham.

Mrs. Lucretia Wood had let the estate to a keen sportsman Captain Constable whose sport was shooting game. It meant an end to the free run of the extensive Chestham lawn for Alfred Smith's beagle hounds that were kennelled across the road.

In the Captain's opinion, the hounds were not kept under proper control. They destroyed game to the detriment of hunting.

Alfred Smith took note, improved his kennelling and had stricter watch kept over the hounds.

Captain Constable instructed his coachman to keep his gun handy.

Conflict was triggered when a hound, four year old Commodore, leapt the iron fencing around Chestham and headed for the scullery outbuildings.

Coachman Howell was to hand.

There was a single shot.

The howling of the maimed dog continued for seven or eight minutes. It was dispatched by a heavy blow.

Coachman Howell left Chestham and moved to London.

It took some time for Alfred Smith to trace the man's whereabouts. That done, P.C. Goldring travelled up and arrested him.

At court the facts were revealed.

Captain Constable related the damage done by Smith's hounds.

George Howell claimed he had been obeying his master's orders when he shot the dog.

Alfred Smith could not put a value on Commodore but he would never have sold the hound even for £10.

Defence counsel stressed there was a complete lack of identification that the dead dog was Mr. Smith's hound Commodore, which made the charge groundless.

The magistrates considered the death of the dog sufficient. They found the coachman guilty to the sum of £6 12s 6d.

Captain Constable felt it his duty to pay. He wrote a cheque to settle the matter.

Mrs. Constable had a far pleasanter duty to carry out, attendance at the annual treat for the children of the National Schools, being provided that year by Mr. Piper at Henfield Place.

Rev. Glubb had carried out his inspection the month before and sent his report to the bishop. It was an encouraging one for the teachers.

At the Boys' School Mr. Randle was proving an efficient master labouring without help or sympathy in accomplishing all that he could in so large a school of 121 pupils. His only assistance was from the boy monitors who received 4d each week.

The classes were fairly up to their work in arithmetic, reading, geography, writing and a small part of English History. They were well up in their catechism, prayers and hymns and knowledge of the scriptures and were very orderly in their conduct and movement.

Rev. Glubb felt a word of commendation and encouragement from his Lordship would greatly encourage the teacher.

The Girls' School was under the charge of an excellent mistress helped by an assistant teacher.

The Schoolboys at their best

The girls completed a good examination on the maps of England, Europe, Palestine and the travels of St. Paul. They were satisfactorily mending their own clothes and those of their parents. The school had given Rev. Glubb much satisfaction.

School Treat Day proved one of unbroken sunshine from dawn to dusk.

Morning was normal lessons with the children dressed in their best; 'passed down' and mended as needs must.

Afternoon was very different. The Hurst Band lined up on the common. Behind them were ranked the boys, armed with flags. The band struck up with "Cheer Boys Cheer" and the treat was under way across the common and into the High Street.

In Cagefoot Lane the girls were ready, each with her flag, waiting behind a magnificent banner intricately sewn by the mistress of the school.

The band breasted the hill and as the last of the boys passed by, the girls joined the parade and together they marched down the street past parents and bystanders lining the pavements. At Church Street the parade turned left to Mr. Piper's large field beyond the church.

There the children were regaled with bread, cheese and small beer. Faces beamed as food and drink disappeared.

Afterwards there was cricket or football for the boys; stoolball for the girls.

Sports for everyone followed.

Determined competitors leapt in sacks across the front lawn, hopped, were cheerfully blindfolded for wheel barrow racing, chose partners to be tied for three-legged tumbles, skipped in heavy shoed rhythm and ran their very hearts out.

The guests gained almost as much pleasure as the children; the endeavour, the amusing incident and the unbidden remark. It was indeed an entertaining occasion.

Late in the afternoon a halt was called and the children were seated in a large circle on the lawn in front of the house ready for tea.

Mrs. Constable happily assisted as one of the ladies graciously acting as waitresses. They served their young guests plates of bread and butter followed by more laden with cakes. Cups of tea were carefully handed round and refilled as many times as the child wished.

The children ate to their gunwales; such food would not appear again for many a month.

Onlookers smiled; one could hardly expect drawing room etiquette.

Henfield Place, near the church

Afterwards, the children moved back to the field for informal games plus the fun of scrambling for gingerbreads and sweetmeats.

Mrs. Piper and her adult guests retired to the house for their own tea; a polite occasion of society etiquette and conversation exchanging their understanding observations of the village children.

As the sun began to sink, the younger guests reappeared for prize-giving and the closing ceremony.

The girls received carefuly chosen useful awards. For the boys there were bats and balls.

When the final prize had been received, three cheers were given for Mr. and Mrs. Piper, for Rev. O'Brien and for Mr. Henry Longley, now superintendent of the schools.

To end their day, the children joined in the National Anthem and sang the special hymn learnt by them all at school; "Sun of my soul;"

Sun of my soul! Thou Saviour dear,
It is not night if Thou be near:
O may no earth-born cloud arise
To hide Thee from Thy servant's eyes.

Guests listened quietly.

When the sixth and final verse finished, Rev. O'Brien thanked the children and they were dismissed to set off for home with stories to unfold to any listening parent.

Rev. O'Brien turned his attention to other parish duties.

He and the churchwardens had a rather delicate matter to consider.

John Browning, son of 'Oyster Cottage' Thomas along the lane up to Burning Mountain would be putting in a request for a public house licence at the next Petty Sessions.

John had ensured a regular income for his family by opening a beerhouse. With all Nep Town in its orbit, the future was secure. His ambition now was for the beerhouse to become a public house – The Gardeners' Arms.

His neighbour, tailor William Gardener, was not keen to have a pub next door to him; and certainly not one named as if it was something to do with him. He had five children; four of them from his wife's first marriage, which had left her widowed, and their own little daughter, just one year old. He wished to bring his family up in a peaceful neighbourhood.

The vicar and his churchwardens also disliked the idea of yet another pub. They consulted the gentlemen of the village and agreed on joint action.

The hearing at the Petty Sessions was short. John had omitted to take proof of having posted his application. He would have to apply at the following Monday's Shoreham Sessions.

At Shoreham, John's application was supported by Mr. Runnacles who stated that his client accepted his premises were small but if the licence was granted his plans to greatly enlarge them would be carried out.

Mr. Lamb represented those opposed to the licence. He produced a written statement from them stating there were already six licensed houses in the parish which contained only 1500 inhabitants. They did not think another was necessary, particularly as the location was not on a public road but on one that was impassable in winter.

Mr. Lamb revealed the names of the signatories; Rev. J. O'Brien, his churchwardens and most of the respectable inhabitants of the parish.

The bench refused the application. [1]

Rev. O'Brien was pleased to achieve so practical a result for the benefit of his parishioners. Less pleasing was his indisposition which came back to prevent him attending the important meeting at the Girls' School being held on behalf of the Mission to Central Africa in connection with Dr. Livingstone's discoveries.

Such a meeting was a diary event.

Most of the gentry and clergy attended plus a few of the tradesman and middle class.

The guest speaker was the professor of modern history at Oxford, a central figure in the mission. He told of the ongoing achievements of Dr. Livingstone introducing Christianity and working for the freedom of the many still enslaved in Africa. Nobody knew exactly where he was but he was somewhere in those vast, untamed lands on official exploration.

His listeners were impressed. Dr. Livingstone's reputation they knew. To be with somebody so closely concerned with the great man's work was a true privilege.

They showed their appreciation and returned home.

Dr. Morgan, whose reputation was confined to Henfield, had to deal with a case of cruelty to a 7 year old girl – a woman's stepchild, Louisa Banfield.

Louisa's father was a day labourer on John Thorns' farm at Oreham Common. He related his woes to John Thorns who took it upon himself to alert Dr. Morgan.

The doctor's assistant, Mr. Lloyd, examined the child. Her condition was so wretched that Dr. Morgan reported it to the police.

They took the woman to court.

She attended with a baby in her arms, healthy and well enough nourished.

Louisa had to attend as evidence. She was unable to walk, her feet swathed in bandages covering neglected chilblains. Her aunt took her.

Mr. Lloyd gave his evidence:

"I examined the child and found it in a very emaciated state with marks of corporal chastisement. It had also a black eye. There was a scar on the child. It appeared not to have had proper food. I asked the mother about it and she said the child was dirty in its habits. She admitted she had beaten the child."

When the mother began her defence she accepted her error;

"I admit I have flogged the child because it was dirty, and I am sorry for it."

The magistrates were sorry, too, and sentenced her to six weeks' hard labour. Her baby went with her.

Louisa went to a brighter future with her aunt.

Mr. Challen, in his capacity as registrar of births and deaths, had to take one of the Henfield blacksmiths to court for neglecting to have his child vaccinated.

The blacksmith, John Summersell, pleaded not guilty.

Mr. Challen explained that the child was born on the 18th October and the birth was registered on the 28th November when he gave the parents the notice required by the Act of Parliament that the child should be vaccinated within four months of the birth or a penalty of 20s 0d would be incurred.

John Summersell claimed his wife had done the vaccination. She had then taken the child to Mr. Lloyd who said it was successful and offered to sign the certificate.

Mary Summersell confirmed she had done so when the baby was five or six months old. Mr. Lloyd had seen the scar and told her he would sign the paper if she took it to him.

Mr. Challen accepted her statement and explained that Mr. Lloyd had seen him about it and then said he could not sign the certificate unless he had vaccinated the child himself.

With the evidence and magistrates' decision completed, the chairman spoke to blacksmith Summersell;

"That the baby has been successfully vaccinated, nobody will dispute for the scar is plain to see. However, the Act of Parliament has not been complied with and the magistrates must therefore convict you. Under the circumstances they are only putting the small fine of 6d upon you instead of the stipulated 20s 0d. There are also 11s 0d costs of the case to be paid by you as the defendant."

Blacksmith Summersell was appalled. What! Pay money like that for not having done anything wrong? Not he. He would go to prison rather than do such a thing.

His wife knew her husband. She smoothed troubled waters and paid the money; they could go home together and continue caring for their family. [2]

Charles Stoner encountered troubled waters at the George when his wife became ill and failed to respond to the doctor's medication.

He grieved the loss of her not only as a wife but also as a skilful cook in providing for guests who always praised the dinners served them.

As a business man he had to continue a good standard of catering for his visitors and ensure he was providing all they required.

The Bakers and Millers' Society of Brighton chose Henfield for their annual outing. They booked their meal and entertainment at the George.

50 members arrived by train, walked the half mile to the High Street and ascended the stairs to the Assembly Room for a 1 o'clock dinner.

Their extended meal was followed by the main entertainment – cricket again, on the Town Field.

The afternoon was hot. Charles Stoner had taken care to ensure he had ample ale, wine and spirits available in the refreshments tent for such a number of men.

Guests and visitors took full advantage of refreshments at such reasonable prices. The bartender had constant custom.

Charles' son Alfred from the Station Hotel took over. There was no let up.

He served yet another glass of brandy.

"How much?" asked the customer.

"Sixpence."

The man paid his money and began conversation by introducing himself;

"I am John Stephen Buzza, officer of excise. Does the landlord have a licence?"

Alfred claimed uncertainty and directed him to the George.

The man made his way there and Alfred knew trouble was in the air.

The bakers and millers continued their day unaware and returned home content; another excellent day thanks to their hospitable host, Mr. Stoner.

Charles Nathan Stoner was far from happy. Excise officer Buzza had served him with a penalty notice of £50. A court appearance at the Petty Sessions was pending.

The day came. Prosecuting and defence counsels presented their varying interpretations of what went on.

Defence explained the exorbitant rent Mr. Stoner paid for the Town Field and how it was his friends he was entertaining.

Prosecuting counsel expressed surprise because the landlord had admitted the offence.

When they finished, the magistrates conferred and issued their verdict. Guilty, but with the mitigated penalty of £12 10s, being the lowest they could impose. They showed where their sympathies lay by suggesting the Board of Inland Revenue should consider a yet lower sum. [3]

Mr. Stoner returned home thankful that within the non-negotiable pitfalls of the law the magistrates had tried to administer justice.

By contrast, the Monday of the big FESTAL DAY OF THE MOBILITY OF BRIGHTON on Henfield Common saw Mr. Stoner right behind the arm of the law. The managers of the Ragged Schools of Brighton had decided on an outing for their pupils at Henfield. A special train had been booked.

Arrangements were made at Henfield for the common to have amusement shows, booths for refreshments, donkeys for children's rides and a band to enliven the day.

On the Monday morning, Brighton station was thronged with not only the children but also relatives, friends and followers.

The children were kept together leaving the others to fill the rest of the carriages. When the train reached Henfield, friends and followers alighted in their hundreds, the guard's whistle blew and the train departed for Southwater taking the children with it. The managers had taken evasive action.

The platform crowd were told of the alterations and that amusements were ready for them on the common.

Not entirely happy, they made their way to the village determined they would make the most of their day come what may.

A few became restive. Garden blooms disappeared, petty disturbances happened and Henfield residents quickly became less than happy.

At the George there was a squabble and in the ensuing commotion an unfortunate young boy had his thigh broken.

Dr. Adolphus Caudle dealt with the child but recrimination between friends threatened to overspill from foul language into fights.

Village worthies sensed riotous behaviour about to break out. A telegraph message was sent to Steyning requesting extra police.

The incident calmed. Just the noise remained.

The majority of visitors passed through to reach the common for the pleasures of the afternoon.

Donkeys had no rest and amusements enjoyed constant custom. The cheerful tunes of the band ensured general happiness.

All the attractions were kept busy until the crowd were suddenly informed they just had time to make straight for the station or miss their train.

The common emptied. Visitors hurried through the High Street to the station where they had more than enough time to regain their breath before the train was due. [4]

At last it arrived.

Reunited with the children, they returned to Brighton.

CHAPTER 36

Gas lighting – A General Election – Cattle murrain

The railway was destined to bring an end to the turnpike trusts and to barges on the Adur.

The Cowfold and Henfield Turnpike Trust reduced its toll charges and cut the percentage return for investors.

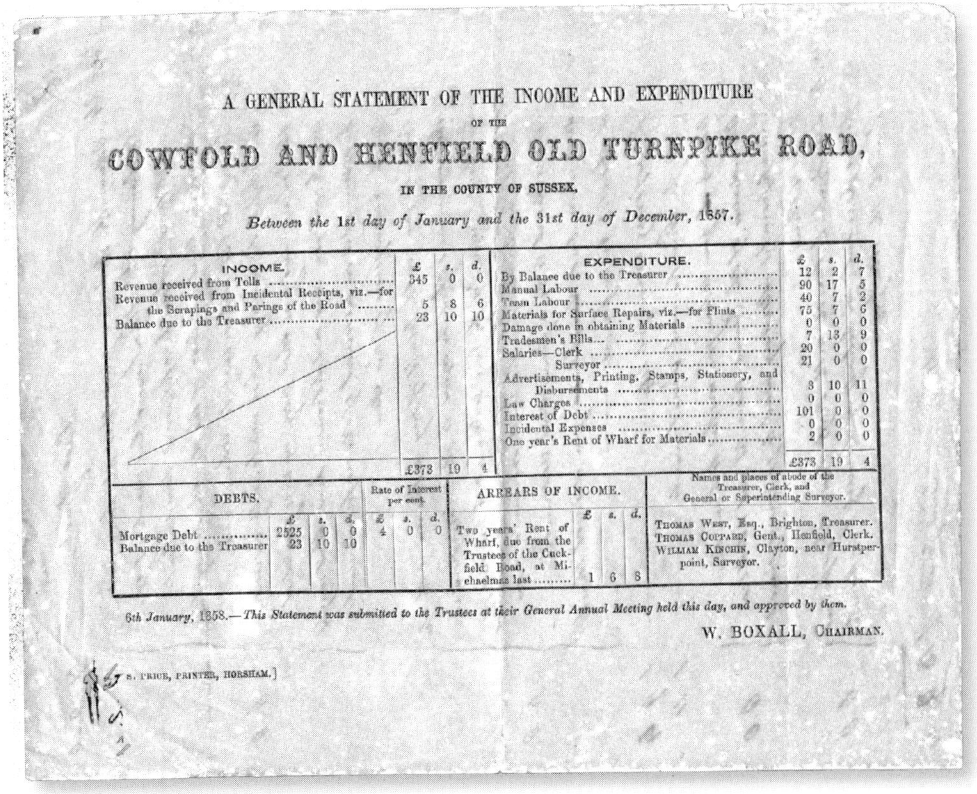

A GENERAL STATEMENT OF THE INCOME AND EXPENDITURE

OF THE

COWFOLD AND HENFIELD OLD TURNPIKE ROAD,

IN THE COUNTY OF SUSSEX,

Between the 1st day of January and the 31st day of December, 1857.

INCOME.	£	s.	d.
Revenue received from Tolls	345	0	0
Revenue received from Incidental Receipts, viz.—for the Scrapings and Parings of the Road	5	8	6
Balance due to the Treasurer	23	10	10
	£373	19	4

EXPENDITURE.	£	s.	d.
By Balance due to the Treasurer	12	2	7
Manual Labour	90	17	5
Team Labour	40	7	2
Materials for Surface Repairs, viz.—for Flints	75	7	6
Damage done in obtaining Materials	0	0	0
Tradesmen's Bills	7	13	9
Salaries—Clerk	20	0	0
Surveyor	21	0	0
Advertisements, Printing, Stamps, Stationery, and Disbursements	3	10	11
Law Charges	0	0	0
Interest of Debt	101	0	0
Incidental Expenses	0	0	0
One year's Rent of Wharf for Materials	2	0	0
	£373	19	4

DEBTS.	£	s.	d.	Rate of Interest per cent. £	s.	d.
Mortgage Debt	2525	0	0	4	0	0
Balance due to the Treasurer	23	10	10			

ARREARS OF INCOME.	£	s.	d.
Two years' Rent of Wharf, due from the Trustees of the Cuckfield Road, at Michaelmas last	1	6	8

Names and places of abode of the Treasurer, Clerk, and General or Superintending Surveyor.

THOMAS WEST, Esq., Brighton, Treasurer.
THOMAS COPPARD, Gent., Henfield, Clerk.
WILLIAM KINCHIN, Clayton, near Hurstperpoint, Surveyor.

6th January, 1858.—This Statement was submitted to the Trustees at their General Annual Meeting held this day, and approved by them.

W. BOXALL, CHAIRMAN.

[S. PRICE, PRINTER, HORSHAM.]

The Cowfold/Henfield Turnpike Trust annual account

The Adur Authorities ordered their water bailiff to repair the Mock Bridge Lock and ensure a clear waterway.

Of more immediate effect was the transport by rail of coal in bulk.

A dependable coal supply meant the manufacture of gas was viable to provide modernised lighting in the village. The oil lamps along the road would become a thing of the past.

Meetings were held. Interest was high with people pleased at the opportunity to improve their house lighting. The vestry was willing to introduce updated street lamps.

A committee was formed to agree the way forward.

Soon the search was on to find a suitable site for a gasworks. Thomas Faulkoner offered the perfect place just south of the station.

A Brighton company undertook to build and run the gasworks and to install all the necessary pipework.

Henfield solicitor Thomas Coppard was appointed as their secretary.

Building work and laying pipes up to the village took months.

Whilst it slowly progressed, the vestry created an Inspectors' Committee led by Registrar William Challen to liaise with the company on a price for supplying the gas.

Each lamp would have a patent burner set to use five feet of gas per hour. A price of £50 was agreed for the year.

The vestry set a lighting rate of 1s 0d in the £ on houses and 4d on land lying back from the road to cover building costs and gas supply. Future years would be cheaper having to cover only supply.

Finally everything was ready. [1]

A new man was appointed as lamplighter and gas took over from oil.

People remarked on the brightness of the lamps. No longer were there uncomfortably dark patches along the High Street.

Not quite everyone was enamoured.

At about 11 p.m. one night, the younger Peter Cragg at home in Church Street heard the sound of breaking glass in the street.

He went out and saw a man throwing stones at a street lamp.

Seven stones were hurled in quick succession.

Peter shouted. The man dropped a stone and ran. Peter Cragg knew him – the well known figure of displaced lamplighter, Jonathan Sayers.

It could have been the end of things except the vestry stepped in.

Sayers had served them conscientiously for many years keeping the oil lamps in a good state of repair and being assiduous in lighting and extinguishing them. That was accepted as exemplary but breaking lamps was out of order and had to be halted. They took legal advice.

Jonathan Sayers was summonsed to appear at the Petty Sessions.

When the charge of breaking a lamp was put he explained that he had not damaged any of the new gas lamps at all. It was just one of the old unused oil lamps that he used to light and look after.

He felt that nobody on the bench understood him; how he was as good a working man as any, what his job had meant to him, the pride he had taken in his work and how gas had destroyed his livelihood.

The bench were faced with a prisoner who had destroyed parish property.

Penalty £1 2s damage and 14s 0d costs; in default one month hard labour.

Jonathan Sayers knew they just did not want to understand. Because his work had been taken away, he did not have sufficient money. [2]

He took his thoughts to Petworth; a bitter and broken man.

The more fortunate men of Henfield had the opportunity to attend a lecture at the Boys' School entitled "Benefit Societies, Their Failures and the Causes." The speaker, Mr. Lawrence, had travelled down by train from Horsham where he was secretary of The Horsham or County Club.

For the working man, a Friendly Society was his safeguard against bad times. Why should anybody speak against them?

The audience listened intently as the speaker considered the failings of public house clubs; the sharing out from funds, the small amount members paid compared with the benefits, young members paying as much as the old and the fines which fell hardest on the labouring classes.

Mr. Lawrence pointed out that none of the evils applied to the Horsham and County Club where any man from 14 to 50 could join with younger members paying less. All local members received medical attention from Henfield's new doctor, Dr. Lewis.

The criticism seemed to apply to the Henfield Friendly Societies yet they were all flourishing if the annual feasts were anything to go by.

People went home wondering. Had the speaker given a sincere lecture or was he conducting a recruitment drive?

The answer came one sunny afternoon about 2 p.m.

A small fleet of vehicles arrived from Horsham and were met at the White Hart by the band of the 18th Sussex Rifle Volunteers.

Mr. Lawrence and friends from various branches of The Horsham and County had brought some of their club regalia with them to be paraded up the High Street.

They lined up. The band played and the parade was under way.

It was a short march, just as far as the George where they halted and met would-be members from within Henfield for lunch provided by Mr Stoner.

After a leisurely meal, they crossed over the road for cricket and various games on the Town Field under a blazing sun.

Mr. Stoner's bell summoned them back for tea and conversation before returning to the field for dancing.

In the evening it was time for formalities.

First, the health of Secretary Lawrence was drunk.

He in turn declared the District of Henfield open with schoolmaster Mr. Randle as clerk and Dr. Lewis the surgeon. He welcomed Henfield's members to The Horsham and County Club. Finally he called for three cheers for Mr. Stoner.

Mr. Lawrence's lecture had attracted 14 fresh members.

In July, attention turned to the more serious matter of a General Election. Sir Percy Burrell was standing again as one of the two Conservative candidates for Shoreham which encompassed all the Rape of Bramber.

Sir Percy's seat was pretty safe as far as the few voters of Henfield were concerned but there was also a candidate, James Hannen, for the in-power Liberal Party of Lord Palmerston.

James Hannen's agent, Mr Prichard, decided an electioneering centre was needed in Henfield. He wrote to Mr. Stoner who saw the opportunity for good business at the George and agreed to meet him.

Mr Prichard travelled up from Shoreham by train. William Rhodes was waiting at the station with a fly and drove him to the George.

There, Mr Prichard detailed his needs; the large hall for lectures if needed, two bedrooms and a committee room for ten days from the 4th of July. In addition they would like to put election notices on the outside wall of the building.

The agreement was made. All was set for a Liberal onslaught on Henfield.

Mr. Prichard's men plastered the front of the George with large notices. Every passer-by would know JAMES HANNEN was the man to vote for.

Apart from that, the election kept low key.

Mr. Prichard decided to change his sleeping room to a third bedroom. The Assembly Room remained reserved for his campaign but unused.

The small committee room remained locked until polling day when everything came to life. Mr. Prichard and his men occupied it and an agent kept them updated throughout the day with the Henfield poll figures.

Mr. Stoner provided the team a constant supply of wine and sandwiches.

Voters from outlying districts arrived by carriage.

Mr. Stoner catered for them as well with a satisfying dinner, free, plus wine for any man needing food and time to rest before his return home.

The day itself proved quite hectic. At its end, Mr. Prichard's team retired to bed fully aware that in Henfield the voting figures favoured the Conservatives. They could only hope that elsewhere the Rape of Bramber had voted Liberal.

The election result was soon revealed. 1542 votes had been cast through the Rape, predominantly Conservative. James Hannen had been left trailing with just 24% favouring him.

He and his team were able to put disappointment aside and rejoice. Lord Palmerston's Liberals were returned to Parliament with an increased majority.

Mr. Stoner was left with an unsightly bill-plastered frontage to his inn. It took two men armed with scrubbing brushes, soap and water a full two days to remove all traces of **JAMES HANNEN**.

The thorough scrubbing also ruined the paintwork requiring landlords Messrs. Tamplin to repaint their inn.

Mr. Stoner turned his attention to recouping his money, a total of £71 10s.

The bill was sent in.

Mr. Prichard studied it. Some of the charges were completely out of order; £25 for the market room, £3 for voters' dinners and £1 10s sandwiches and wine in the committee room.

He sent £41 in full payment of what he considered to be the correct charges and explained his objections to the remainder which would not be paid. The market room agreement was for when it was actually used. The voters' dinners had not been sanctioned by him because to do so would have been an offence under election rules of bribery by offering an incentive to voters. The sandwiches and wine to the committee room had not been ordered.

Mr. Stoner received the reply.

A long exchange of views commenced and came to a head with landlord Stoner having to take the matter to court.

There the learned lord heard the evidence and came to the conclusion which to him was patently clear. James Hannen's agent had paid fully for all legitimate charges. It remained for the plaintive, Mr. Stoner, to pay the costs of the case. [3]

Mr. Stoner did not feel in singing mood for several weeks.

Henfield's farmers were not in the mood for song either. Cattle murrain was sweeping through England; diseased animals dying, herds put down.

Farmers were very wary of buying suckling calves in case of introducing the disease. Milk normally destined for the calves was being used for extra butter making.

One of Henfield's farmers wrote to the Sussex Express explaining that if such a severe calamity was viewed in its proper light it would be admitted by all thinking men that there was none other than that of the finger of God in it brought upon the nation for some wise end and purpose.

Most men kept their feet on the ground. The disease must have arrived with imported cattle brought in under Government legislation and spread by beasts transported to new regions by train.

J.P. Mr. Goring gave a recipe for protecting cows; doses of a pint of charcoal and an ounce of nitre dissolved in water. Animals' noses washed daily with vinegar and water. Hovels and sheds having tar burnt on hot irons and regularly washed with dilute sulphuric acid and chloride of lime. Prevention was important.

The disease continued to spread. Livestock could not be sold on at market. Beasts for meat had to be slaughtered and skinned before being moved by the butchers.

The High Street butchers continued to kill their own beef in their slaughter houses and the refuse continued to flow along the drains but nothing came from Steyning, Horsham or Haywards Heath.

A practical farmer advocated isolation with gates locked at night. Not even people should have free access. He also warned farmers presently free of the disease to move manure out of their yards rather than risk losing it all by contamination if any animal became infected.

The Government felt obliged to step in. The movement of cattle by train was banned. A certificate had to be obtained before moving beasts between farms. The responsibility for ensuring compliance was vested in the county Quarter Sessions as being familiar with local conditions.

A Brighton farmer complained because he had a calf scheduled to be moved to a farm in Henfield where it was to be raised. It had been examined and was free of any disease yet he was still refused a certificate. He complained in vain.

Despite all the efforts of farmers, butchers and legislators, the disease continued with official countrywide figures showing over 62000 cases; 14000 killed, 41000 died and 7000 recovered.

In all the trouble, a Henfield farmer came up with a positive idea. Once things had settled down, re-establish a stock market in the village. The common had good turf and the Town Field could hold thousands of stock with the railway to facilitate their movement. It just needed the murrain itself to die out. [4]

Other facets of Henfield life continued regardless. A very special wedding celebration was to take place.

In preparation, five triumphal arches were erected across the roads leading from Barrow Hill House to St. Peter's Church. Each arch was decorated with evergreens and flowers. Interwoven were mottoes, flags, and congratulatory messages.

On the morning of the event, society ladies, dressed in their very best, and gentlemen in more reserved suits converged on the church.

Inside were tasteful decorations highlighted by cloth of a beautiful pink tinge strewn across the altar and its surrounds.

All assembled ready for one more arrival, that of Mr. Eardley Hall with his daughter Elizabeth. Awaiting her stood Mr. Henry West of Brighton.

Father and bride walked down the aisle attended by six bridesmaids to music sensitively played by organist Ernest Pattenden.

At the conclusion of the service, the organ sounded aloud as husband and wife walked back along the aisle hand in hand to emerge into sunshine and celebratory peals of the church bells.

Celebrations continued at Barrow Hill before the couple left, accompanied by an assortment of old shoes, for a three week honeymoon through the picturesque parts of England and Wales.

The couple missed out on the big day at Barrow Hill House.

Mr. Hall had generously offered to host Henfield's very own day, Flower

Show Day, which had become an essential part of the village calendar.

The event now attracted entries from a wide part of the county because the London, Brighton and South Coast Railway was allowing free transport for any exhibit.

The show itself was held in a spacious marquee, erected and tastefully ornamented under the special superintendence of Messrs Stoner. [6]

Not far off, but in an unobtrusive corner, was another small marquee. There the cottagers would be assembled later in the afternoon to receive their prizes.

The rest of the gardens were thrown open for all to wander through. Thanks to the generosity of Mr. Hall, the schoolchildren were being allowed in to both garden and show – with teachers in commanding control.

Invitations had gone far and wide:- Horsham, Cuckfield, Brighton, Burpham, Wivelsfield, Lancing and nearer to hand; Hurst, Cowfold, Steyning, Edburton, Ashurst and Newtimber. Rev. Nathaniel Woodard had provided lunch for 30 guests at Martyn Lodge.

Never had so many carriages been seen arriving, proof indeed of the attraction of Henfield's Horticultural and Floricultural Show.

The afternoon ceremonial began outside the White Hart where the Brighton Brass Band lined up in their eye catching bright uniforms. At their head was the superintendent of the show, none other than Charles Nathan Stoner the man of many Henfield hats who always seemed ready to try another.

They stepped out for Barrow Hill playing a rousing rendition of The Drinking Song from Verdi's "La traviata"; perfect for landlord Stoner.

Throughout the afternoon the band played a selection of waltzes, polkas and quadrilles as visitors wondered at exhibits or wandered the grounds.

Many paused on entry to the marquee to admire the intricate baskets and flower stands of blind basket maker Michael Martin.

Henry Longley showed a strange curiosity, an arbutus tree from the isles of Lake Killarney. It gained a lot of attention although more went to Charles Fowler's five feet high pyramid of flowers perfect in shape and with the colours beautifully blended.

Eardley Hall himself exhibited potted grape vines bearing ripe fruit ready for eating. Mrs. Hall had an equally mouth watering display, a 50 lbs globe of remarkably clear honey.

Charles Stoner also exhibited having a display of enormous potatoes.

The cottagers could not produce such exhibits although James Goacher was awarded a first prize for his honey – neither the purity nor quantity of Mrs. Hall's but nevertheless worthy of recognition. William Blake's show of grapes, hardly comparable with those of Mr. Hall, was also good enough for a special prize.

Among the amateurs, one man stood way ahead with a magnificent display of cut flowers and of fuchsias, geraniums and balsams. It was 'Lossam', Charles Ward. That day he could feel at ease. His prowess as flower grower at Hope Cottage was there for all to see.

The show remained open until 7 o'clock enabling labourers' families to enjoy it for a nominal penny each. It had been an outstanding event; visitor numbers up, income up and more prizes than ever before.

Giving the awards for the cottagers in the little tent was a success perhaps marred by an apparent lack of politeness on the part of a few who seemed unable to give thanks in the appropriate way. It was accepted as probable shyness and confusion caused by the occasion rather than any real want of manners.

Two children received thrilling prizes. 11 year old Ann Ward won a work box for the best device of flowers by a schoolgirl. 13 year old James Foreman, stepson of the GARDENERS' ARMS neighbour William Gardener, won a cricket bat for his wild flowers. His thrill was clear, a cricket bat of his very own.

The joy of owning a bat – cricket at the Boys' School [5]

A few of the cottagers gained prizes for imaginative items. Alfred Collins had artificial flowers formed from turnips and carrots. Richard Brownings displayed seedling peaches. He outdid all the cottagers and gained a large reference bible as winner of most cottage class prizes.

The prizes for best gardens were practical. Henry Fairs received a wheelbarrow for his Little Betley garden. As runner up, Henry Hill gained an excellent set of garden tools.

Just two hopes were held for future improvement. The cottagers' prizes were sufficient in number but the pecuniary award was not enough. Perhaps they might be a little more in line with those of amateur and professional.

Secondly, the exclusion of ladies from the committee was a great mistake. Several had worked indefatigably but in a subordinate role. It was both unwise and ungallant because a finer tone and finish would be given to everything connected with the show by the admittance of ladies as honorary members of the committee. They had certainly contributed greatly to the smooth running of the day. [6]

Henry Fair's 'Best Cultivated Garden' card of merit

Charles Stoner had made valuable contributions to the success of the flower show over the years.

He was now about to start a new chapter in his life, sharing it with his fiancée, Miss Hilton of London.

A month almost to the day after the marriage of Mr. and Mrs. West, the bells of St. Peter's rang their wedding peal for Mr. and Mrs. Stoner as the happy newly-weds made their way home.

The wedding breakfast was at the George.

50 of the aged poor were invited to the feast prepared especially for them in the Assembly Room; roast beef, boiled beef, plum pudding and beer. For those whose infirmity prevented them coming to the feast, the food was taken to them.

After the meal came the singing.

Mr. Stoner was prevailed upon to give a song. He chose "The Fine Old English Gentleman" which all agreed was quite appropriate.

The old folk chose the other numbers and sang until time came to give three cheers for the happy couple setting off for their honeymoon at Southsea.

Charles Nathan Stoner had already made his arrangements for the future. He would become the fine old English Gentleman leaving Messrs Tamplin to find another landlord for the George.

Chapter 37

Pig in a bag – Lottery luck – The lights go out

A sad departure occurred at Golden Square. One of Henfield's ladies of independent means, Ann Gander, was busying herself with household affairs in her Prospect Cottage when the servant heard her call out for help saying how ill she suddenly felt.

Almost immediately she collapsed. The servant failed to rouse her and the doctor was called.

He had seen such cases and understood what was happening. During the evening Ann Gander passed away.

Everyone knew Miss Gander. For years she had nursed her widowed mother and yet always managed to find time to help others.

She had been a zealous Sunday School Teacher seeking to sow the seeds of faith in children. She supported good works, visited the needy and was as kind a benefactor to the poor as her means allowed.

People knew they had lost a very good friend.

The influence of women such as her was extolled at a meeting in the Girls' School. Rev. Divie Robertson introduced the guest speaker, Mrs. Inglis.

People listened intently as she commenced her lecture.

She continued for nearly two hours, her listeners enthralled as she told of women from history guiding events, being courageous heroines, wise counsellors, dedicated nurses and gifted writers all to the benefit of mankind.

When she finished, Rev. George Hall thanked her; a graceful lady giving an evening that would not quickly be forgotten. The audience showed agreement with heartfelt applause. [1]

Even kind hearted ladies encountered occasional disquieting times, certainly if they were living cheek by jowl in Nep Town like Sarah Browning and Jane Naldrett. They were next door or opposite each other depending on the interpretation of what was the Brownings' yard with its pig sty and what was the Naldretts' garden.

Sarah was wife of John Browning who was still dreaming of gaining a licence and opening his Gardeners' Arms. She managed to find enough money to pay Mrs. Bonniface to come in from a few doors down the road and do the washing for her.

To Eve Bonniface it was a blessing. Seven children to bring up on an agricultural labourer's wage needed every possible extra penny.

Eve was busy at Sarah Browning's washboard one Tuesday when her little girl rushed in saying that Mrs. Naldrett was being cruel to one of the pigs.

The noise of a squealing piglet sent Sarah rushing out.

Sure enough, Jane Naldrett was in her yard, a squealing bag in her hand.

Eve followed and saw her mistress take hold of the bag with one hand, Mrs. Naldretts' wrist with the other and kindly ask her to give up the pig. When Mrs. Naldrett kept hold of the bag, Sarah Browning asked Eve to assist her open the lady's hand.

The noise of squealing pig had also brought next door neighbour Mrs. Gardener rushing to her door. She was in time to see Sarah Browning hit Mrs. Naldrett left handed on the side of the face and then seize her by the top of her dress. Mrs. Naldrett was holding a bag in her right hand. Mrs. Boniface and old Mrs. Thomas Browning helped get it from her.

As Mrs. Gardener was going back indoors, there was more noise in the yard. She turned in time to see the bag thrown out of Browning's house and John Browning put his hand on Jane Naldrett.

It all led to a Petty Sessions assault case against both John and Sarah Browning.

Jane Naldrett was first witness;

"I am the wife of Charles Naldrett, and live at Henfield, near the defendants. On Tuesday, 19th September, some of the defendant's pigs got into my husband's garden. It had frequently happened before and I had cautioned them about it. On that day, I caught one of the pigs and put it in a bag and was about to take it to the pound in the High Street when Sarah Browning came out and struck me on the face and scratched me. Mrs. Boniface helped her take the bag away from me. I then went into their yard after my bag when John Browning caught hold of me by the neck and pushed me violently. The bag was then thrown out of the door at me. I told Browning not to touch me He pushed me again twice and got me out of the yard. He hurt me very much. Our house is opposite to his."

The versions of Eve Bonniface, Mrs. Gardener and the Brownings followed.

When the magistrates had listened to all the evidence they conferred and returned to inform the court they had decided to hear a second charge concerning the case before they dispensed justice.

The charge was that Sarah Browning did obstruct Mrs. Naldrett by preventing her taking a pig to the parish pound and did forcibly release the same on land in the occupation of Charles Naldrett.

At last Mr. Naldrett was brought into the picture. The magistrates asked him who the garden fence belonged to. He said it was his.

It proved the deciding factor.

The magistrates retired again and this time returned to give their verdict.

They had given the case great consideration. Because the witnesses' evidence was so conflicting they had decided to dismiss both cases.

There was one condition. Charles Naldrett must put his fence in good repair and keep it so. [2]

John and Sarah Browning returned home somewhat mollified.

Charles and Jane Naldrett knew they had been wronged but all they could now do was go home and make their fence a pig proof barrier.

John Browning received a bonus at the next Petty Sessions. He was granted a licence for his public house. His beerhouse would become the Gardeners' Arms as soon as he was back in Nep Town.

The magistrates made one rule patently clear. Browning could now keep his premises open an hour longer until 11.00 p.m. but any drinks served after closing time would result in court action and loss of his licence.

John Browning returned home in buoyant mood. The future looked good.

That November, Rev. O'Brien announced a new venture, Penny Readings, which were proving popular in Sussex – an evening of recitation and music taking place at the Boys' School.

The schoolroom was fairly well filled for the first evening. Choir master William Hodges chose a boating song to start proceedings which the choir were credited with singing very well considering the short time they had for practice. Rev. Divie Robertson had the audience engrossed with his rendering of "The Pied Piper of Hamelin". Extracts from Shakespeare and "Paradise Lost" read by Eardley Hall provided a more serious balance.

At the end of the evening's entertainment the vicar announced that the readings had proved so popular they would happen fortnightly through the winter. [3]

Word of the Penny Readings' success spread. At the next one, many of the audience had to stand.

Rev. Divie Robertson was up to form with Dicken's Mr. Pickwick. Eardley Hall almost brought tears to the eyes of sensitive ladies with Tennyson's "May Queen". Charles Stoner brightened the evening with his wedding song "The Fine Old English Gentleman" and Henry Longley proved himself very competent playing the harmonium. The vicar was able to enthuse again

Henry Longley also provided entertainment for the customers at his drapery during the weeks leading up to Christmas. They could try a light hearted flutter on his lottery; a box of many tickets which might or might not be inscribed with the name of a shop article.

It was not cheap. People paid a shilling per try.

One very regular customer was Lieutenant Bulkley who always purchased tickets. He insisted on one condition; any inscribed ticket should go to a particular assistant. Mr. Longley tried to persuade him to include the others but he was adamant; it had to be Miss Edith Henbest, the pleasant mannered young girl popular with everyone.

The shop was Edith's home from home. She lodged there and for one so young with only ten months service she earned a good wage, £16 per year.

Henry Longley was thoughtful towards his staff. On Christmas Eve, Edith was allowed home to her mother in Southampton for five days.

On her return she made a chance remark about a length of silk.

Henry Longley overheard and felt uncomfortable.

He asked the girl for the key to the private box she kept in her room.

When he opened the box he had a nasty surprise. Neatly stacked were a number of articles that must have come from the shop.

He took them out; a long length of black silk, seven pairs of kid gloves, five artificial flowers, a pair of muslin sleeves, seven pocket handkerchiefs, a black cloth jacket and several trifling items.

He asked her to explain herself.

Edith assured him that all the things really were hers except the silk. She was sorry about the silk. She had taken it because she had said she was going to have a silk dress and when she came back without it the rest of the staff teased her. She was going to pretend it was hers.

Henry Longley accepted her word for the moment. He would look into the matter.

One aspect worried him. Members of staff could buy articles in the shop at a 10% price reduction. For cash payments of a shilling or more the item was entered in the Day Book, a private trade mark was added and a duplicate ticket given to the purchaser. For credit sales, a description of the item was entered in the cashier's book and the amount was deducted from the next wages payment. Could it be that his assistants were enabling each other to avoid payment?

He questioned his staff. None seemed involved in any deception. He felt he had no alternative to calling in the police.

More enquires were carried out. Edith Henbest had to appear at the Petty Sessions and then at the Assizes.

There she again explained everything.

Witnesses were called.

One of the cashiers, no longer with the firm, recalled selling fancy items to her on many occasions for which she had always paid. She also had an occasional gift from a particular gentleman when he obtained an item in the Christmas Lottery. He was certain that one of the pairs of gloves displayed as coming from her box was of a two-buttoned type he had never seen for sale in the shop.

When he was cross-examined by the defence counsel, he recalled selling a piece of alpaca to her and some muslin for which no payment had been made but it had definitely been recorded in the book.

One of the dressmakers at the shop told how Miss Henbest had quite openly shown the silk to her in the show room.

Prosecuting counsel declared that the prisoner had failed to account for most of the items.

The defence lawyer urged the jury to give the prisoner the benefit of any doubt they might have.

His Honour the judge summed up pointing out that the only items definitely accounted for were the alpaca and muslin.

The jury found her guilty of stealing the muff, gloves, scarf and cloth jacket but innocent of stealing the silk. They recommended mercy on account of her youth.

His Honour declared he took full notice of the jury's recommendation and it was with reluctance and great pain that he was pronouncing sentence on one so young with a previously unblemished character. However, the offence was all the more grave because it had been committed against the man whose bread she had been eating and in whose employ she had been earning her livelihood. He could do no less than sentence her to two calendar months imprisonment with hard labour. [4]

Nobody was happy, not even Mr. Longley – and certainly not Lieutenant Bulkley.

Nep Town Christmas for John and Sarah Browning was an adult only celebration. The children were spending Christmas with their aunt in Brighton while relatives were down from London.

John had wasted no time since obtaining his licence. He had altered his premises into the Gardeners' Arms with a large club room upstairs.

Boxing Day they kept things going late into the evening. When next door neighbour William Gardener arrived home from his own celebrations at the Station Hotel there was still a racket coming from the club room.

William was one of the vestry's parochial constables for the year. People were for ever jibing him about failing to control the Gardeners' noise.

That night it was even worse – and way past closing hours. William decided there must have been complainants. He would act on their behalf.

He took up his truncheon, went to the front door of the pub and rapped loud and long on it demanding entrance.

After too long a wait, he heard John Browning ask who was at his door that late hour.

It irked William; a next door neighbour's voice was surely recognisable.

John refused to let him in and told him to go for his master.

William wanted to know who might be his master for he was a parochial constable.

John Browning's answer was abrupt; "P.C. Goldring."

William backed off and sent his wife for the policeman.

Goldring asked her the reason.

"There's an infernal row at that Gardeners' Arms again and they won't let my husband in."

P.C. Goldring walked round and found William there flourishing his truncheon and looking as if he himself was a bit tiddly.

"There is a party inside and they must come out. They have no business there," complained William.

Goldring knocked at the back door and eventually it was opened. John Browning took them upstairs to the club room.

People were seated round a table. On it was a plate of cake and one of apples and nuts. There was no sign of beer.

Sarah Browning explained;

"They are all lodgers and are staying the night here, Mr. Goldring. My children are with my sister in Brighton."

Goldring checked on the people, told William Gardener he must take any steps to bring charges and left. The disgruntled Gardeners went too.

Goldring kept watch for a couple of hours before returning home. Nobody left the Gardeners' Arms. No song disturbed the peace. That night, John and Sarah Browning were being law abiding citizens.

Two more people doing their best to be law abiding citizens were solicitor Thomas Coppard of the Gas Company and registrar William Challen of the Vestry Lighting Inspectors. Their paths crossed.

Immediately after Christmas one of the public notices on the church door announced a Vestry meeting for the 29th to pass the Lighting Inspectors' accounts and decide expenses for the coming year.

Mr. Coppard sent off the Gas Company's supply offer in time for inclusion at the meeting; £50 as before.

Mr. Challen sent the Vestry's reply to Mr. Coppard; £50 was too much.

He explained that the Inspectors had been assessing the probable total gas consumption. It was imperative that the lighting rate be kept as low as possible. During the past summer when the lamps were not being lit, extra standards had been erected at Cagefoot Lane and Church Street. Those outside the George and at Golden Square had been replaced with ones that included a meter to record the amount of gas being consumed. The average of regular readings through autumn was used to calculate the total consumption. It had been decided to limit the hours of lighting. At the beginning of each month from January to April, lighting up time would become a half hour later; from September to December a half hour earlier. Lamps would be extinguished at 11.00 p.m. instead of 11.30. They would not be lit on the four nights around each full moon. Price £41.

The two sides reached immediate deadlock. Neither would budge.

New Year's Day brought a surprise for almost everyone; not a single street lamp was alight that evening. People pondered the reason.

When it happened again the next night, people began asking serious questions. Had the gas works broken down?

Along by the railway goods yard the answer was obvious, the gasometer stood high, clearly with a full store of gas. There was no smell of a leak; no workers were digging holes to the piping.

The lamps were still out on Epiphany Sunday but that did not prevent people turning out for the evening service – Canon Woodard had issued an invitation for all attending it to go to his house afterwards for a celebration. Word had spread.

After the service, gentry with their families and labourers with theirs walked down the churchyard and along to Martyn Lodge; rich and poor together in the most affable and social manner possible, a mark of Canon Woodard's concern for everyone.

Martyn Lodge

People arrived there to find the entrance hall beautifully illuminated with Chinese lanterns. In the centre stood a Christmas Tree adorned with knick-knacks which were to be drawn for later in the evening, something for everyone.

The poor were conducted to the kitchen for a bountiful supper; goose, pies, plum pudding, cake, ale, punch and an abundance of other delights.

Plum pudding – what poor man's wife could include such ingredients in her recipes?

½lb currants - 1lb raisins -
¼lb sugar - 4 eggs - 1lb suet -
2 or 3 ounces bread crumbs -
lemon juice and peel - a wine glass of brandy.

Canon Woodard's guests indulged themselves.

Following the meal there were gifts; a choice of either a blanket or two hundredweight of coal and of a ¼ lb of tea or 2s 6d in money.

At 9.30 p.m. they returned to the Christmas Tree and had the draw for the knick-knacks.

Canon Woodard then bid his poorer guests goodnight and they walked off into the darkness. The rest of the company were conducted to the dining room for a magnificent banquet.

At its completion, Rev. Divie Robertson, amused them all as fortune-teller. Afterwards they gathered round the piano to sing Christmas Carols.

It was late when Canon Woodard bid his remaining guests goodnight. They, too, trod a dark way home.

The lack of lighting was completely ignored by the Rifle Corps. They were assembling three times a week in the drill room behind the White Hart preparing for the forthcoming Easter Monday Review.

There had been a discordant note among the 2nd Battalion struck by news from Horsham that their volunteers would not be attending because the Review had been allotted to Dover instead of Brighton. Henfield men were determined they would represent the battalion regardless of bad feeling.

Drill Sergeant Jones demanded simultaneous and precise response to his commands. The 18th would be under minute scrutiny at Dover; perfection was imperative.

Any lack of musketry skill would be set against them. Sergeant Jones was demanding in this as well; load the charge and bullet, ram it down the barrel, remove the ramrod, set the percussion cap, aim and fire.

Through January and February the 18th honed their musketry. Honour was at stake.

It was in February that parish constable William Gardener eventually had John Browning in court for keeping the Gardeners' Arms open Boxing Day for the sale of beer at unlawful hours. The magistrates wished to know why there had been such a delay in bringing proceedings.

William explained he was a tailor and had been at constant work through January completing a clothing contract for the Steyning Union.

The magistrates were satisfied and William gave his evidence.

Mr. Runnacles was once again defending John.

He remarked that the person who complained to the parochial constable had not been identified. How strange to have a mystery figure complaining of noise to a constable living right next door to the public house.

William insisted his version of events was correct.

P.C. Goldring doubted Gardener's sobriety on the night.

The magistrates declared they had heard enough nonsense, dismissed the case and charged the costs to William.

William was incensed; all those hours stitching clothes for Union Paupers only to have the money snatched away because he did his duty properly as parochial constable.

He vented his anger by complaining about P.C. Goldring. The magistrates ignored him. [5]

Chapter 38

4.00 a.m. bugle blast – Government grant – Kiss in the Ring

When March began, people had little thought for its proverbial coming in like a lamb or lion; it was arriving without lit lamps. Two months of darkness were too much to put up with.

An open meeting about the matter had been arranged at the George for the 2nd.

Disgruntled residents turned up to air their views and listen to the various reasons for the failure put forward by the disputing parties – the Gas Company and the Inspectors.

The chairman read the official reason for the meeting.

Mr. Coppard explained the situation with the Company's very fair offer to supply the gas at 33s 0d per lamp per year amounting to £50. People were invited to comment.

Complaints began:- no lights for over two months; repeated refusals by the Inspectors to accept the Company's price; the insertion of expensive meters on two lamps – meters that cost 25% of the year's lighting rate.

The points were carefully recorded but no helpful answers were forthcoming. The Inspectors had boycotted the meeting.

A lengthy report appeared in the Sussex Express.

The letters to the editor in the very next issue included one from VEREX replying for the Inspectors.

VEREX clarified matters. Henfield now had 30 public lamps erected. The lamps would be used for a set number of nights with exact times for lighting and extinguishing, plus cleaning, at a shilling a night by an employee of the Gas Company.

The cost was calculated on 129 nights lighting with gas used at 7s 6d per 1000 feet, a total of £41.

The news helped no one. The lamps remained unlit.

The Inspectors invited ratepayers to their monthly meeting on the 6th.

Nobody attended. The meeting was adjourned to the 15th at 7.00 p.m.

On the 10th Mr. Challen received another letter from Mr. Coppard. He replied at once;

Henfield March 10

Dear Sir,

Lighting Public Lamps

I have to acknowledge the receipt of the very kind offer of the Gas Company to allow the Lamps again to burn at such times as may be so very suitable to themselves. Have the Gas Company forgotten that in our offer dated 30th Decr last when we offered to burn by meter that we in our simplicity supposing it was our province, said that if that offer was accepted we would direct on what nights the lamps would be lighted? and we still believe it ours and not the Gas Company's province to do so. I think I may say that the Inspectors will have no objection whatever to burn till eleven oclock but as to being a party to having the lamps lighted when they are not wanted viz on moonlight nights. I think we ought not to be asked to make ourselves ridiculous simply to put money into the Gas Company's pockets. I think I can promise to burn liberally but not to the extent wished. I will consult my Brother Inspectors and give you their decision. [1]

To Thomas Coppard Esq.

More letters were exchanged with the final one from the Gas Company on the 15th finally agreeing to the Inspectors' rate of 7s 6d per 1000 feet of gas with the shilling for lighting, extinguishing, and cleaning.

That night the lights were on again – just in time for the Inspectors' adjourned meeting with ratepayers.

Nobody took advantage of the lamp lit streets to attend. Their needs had been met.

April brought snow. It began in the afternoon of the 12th and was still falling the next morning, Easter Sunday.

Slippery roads did not impede the large congregation gathering for the evening service, a fully choral one with the special anthem, "Christ our Passover."

The vicar preached and listeners could let their thoughts wander a few moments as their eyes took in the text above the altar, "Christ is Risen" wonderfully worked in daffodils on a foreground of primroses. The good ladies of the church had again proved their worth.

The service concluded with organist Ernest Pattenden playing Handel's "Hallelujah Chorus." Uplifted by the music, people made their way home with the street lamps lighting their way whether they were heading for Station Road or Barrow Hill. The Gas Company and the Inspectors had the well-being of everyone at heart.

While the worshippers returned home, the 18th were travelling to join with East Grinstead volunteers for a night under canvas and an early morning journey to the Dover Review.

By midnight all were tented and asleep. The bugler would rouse them at 5.00 a.m.

At 4.00 a.m. bugle blasts broke their slumber. The bugler had mistaken the hour.

The men were well in time for their train.

It started at six but did not reach Dover until well after 12.

The great March Past had begun promptly at noon. East Grinstead and the 18th were too late.

Instead they marched straight up the hill to join the mass attack and defence of Dover Castle by 25000 troops.

The attacking force was supported by a shelling bombardment from a naval squadron at sea. Out beyond the port, three modern paddle wheel steamers manoeuvred to fire their 28 guns. Two sailing brigs provided a further 20.

It proved a day of overpowering noise from sea and castle as the defenders repulsed repeated advances by the enemy.

By evening the invaders knew they were beaten. A general withdrawal was made. Dover Castle was safe.

At 8.00 p.m. the men were paraded back to the station.

Not until 11 did the 18th's journey home begin.

They travelled through the night to reach the South Eastern Railway's Tunbridge Wells station at 5.00 a.m.

From there they marched across the town to the London, Brighton and South Coast's station and arrived at Brighton in good time for the first Horsham train. At 8.30 a.m. they were finally home in Henfield. [2]

The 18th felt they had proved themselves worthy of their uniform.

For village people with time for entertainment, good reports were circulating of shows being put on for several days in a marquee on the Town Field.

The marquee housed a Marionette Theatre where well known plays were being presented to enthralled audiences. The dexterity with which the puppets were manipulated was fascinating – wonderful imitations of real life.

When the day's performance concluded, the marquee became a mini circus ring for a display by trained dogs; in all, a visit well worth making.

The new landlord at the George, Mr. Welling, had managed to book comedian musician Mr. Windebank for a performance in the Assembly Room.

If anybody was to attract a full house it was Mr. Windebank with his humour and flutina accordion. The room was packed.

Mr. Windebank proved in great form portraying twelve characters, each succeeding one even more amusing than the last. He did not have his accordion with him but he had brought along his seven year old son.

The boy sang and acted at intervals. His marvellous performancc brought applause almost equalling his father's. What a protégé.

Rev. Glubb was looking for outstanding performances in his June school inspections.

The schools no longer had to rely on funds raised by subscription, church sermons and the quarterly shilling from parents.

Under new legislation, the Government was paying an annual grant of four shillings per child for those attending more than 200 sessions. For each pupil passing the set examinations in reading, writing and arithmetic eight shillings was paid but for each section failed there was a 33% forfeit.

Rev. Glubb found all was as normal for June at the Boys' School; the older pupils having just left and younger ones kept at home for haying – the school with over 100 boys on the books yet only 45 present for inspection.

At the end of his visit he prepared a sobering report for the bishop;

> I was able to form a pretty correct estimate of the School. I think this and all our schools are getting more satisfied with a lower standard of education. This appears silently taking place through this Deanery and the Kingdom at large. My fear is that with the Government Inspectors making secular instruction the tests of their grants and the want of real heartfelt religion, the schools are not benefitting the community as they would if they were brought up religiously in the fear of God. [3]

The Rural Dean was a worried man.

Vicar Rev. O'Brien had a far greater worry. With new houses throughout the village, Henfield's ever increasing population meant St. Peter's Church was no longer large enough. Restoration and enlargement were needed.

A vestry meeting was arranged to consider plans for the work.

The vicar was again indisposed. Eardley Hall chaired the meeting and explained that there were more than 40 of the principal ratepayers and their households plus a further 40 rate paying cottagers and their families without seating. Throughout the whole church there were no more than four or five free seats for people who did not have reserved places. The galleries were no longer adequate.

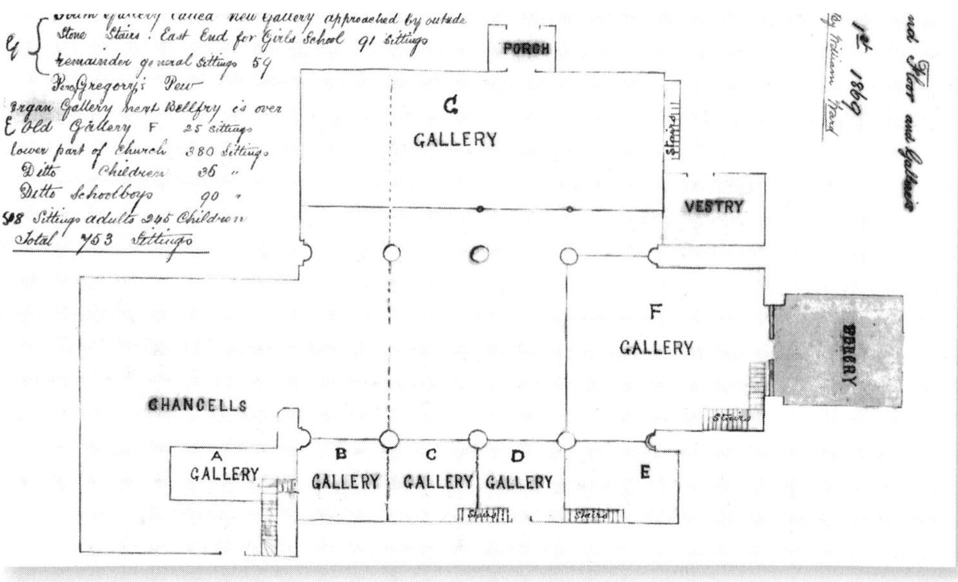

The church galleries [4]

Enlargement was essential to provide comfortable seating for all who may wish to reserve them and also to have considerably more free seats. Contributions towards the general costs were essential. The family of the late William Borrer Esq. had kindly offered to build a north aisle as a memorial to him.

The meeting expressed thanks for the Borrer family's generous offer. The architect's plans were accepted.

Work on St. Peter's would begin as soon as formalities were completed.

Meanwhile, the pub Friendly Societies each paraded to the church for the service at the start of their fete days.

The George Old Friendly Society was first. About fifty members marched and on their return to the pub they enjoyed landlord Welling's capital dinner. Charles Stoner was in the chair of honour and was able to announce that the funds were in good order.

He then proved his adaptability by leading the singing of all the old favourites chorused with increasing fervour as the drinks flowed.

The White Hart held their Whit Monday celebration marching to church for their service taken by the vicar who then had the pleasure of chairing the dinner. He declined the opportunity to join in the afternoon of dance and merry making but a large group of men from Brighton's Clifton Ville Working Men's Institute more than made up for his absence happy to drink with any sort of Friendly Society man.

The last two societies to hold their festivities were the Loyal Myrtle Lodge of Odd Fellows and the Foresters.

The Odd Fellows' day shone bright with the arrival by coach and four of the splendidly uniformed band of Sir Walter Burrell from Knepp Castle. A second coach and four brought Sir Walter himself and his son.

Headed by the band, the members made their annual march to the George and settled for a 2 o'clock dinner in the Assembly Room.

Henry Longley sat at the centre table as chairman. Charles Stoner, no longer with the Foresters, was vice-chair along with Dr. Adolphus Caudle.

After the meal came the loyal toasts followed by one from Henry Longley to the "Army, Navy and Volunteers" where he managed to include the gallant 18th with its energetic members from both Henfield and Sir Walter Burrell's West Grinstead.

Once the toasts were completed and the last of the wine finished, they crossed the road to the Town Field where the children were already enjoying the swings and goodies of the booths specially erected for them.

Cricket v The Town was the inevitable entertainment followed by an evening of dancing with Charles Stoner excelling as self appointed master of ceremonies until the setting sun ushered them all home.

The next week a hundred members of The Foresters met in front of the Station Hotel at 11.00 a.m. each with the insignia of the order at his chest.

The Arundel Band headed them but at the very front an honoured member held the Foresters' nostalgic new banner, a colourful depiction of Robin Hood's last shot in the Greenwood. Never had such a beautiful banner been displayed in Henfield.

Robin Hood headed them round the village with extended halts outside the houses of several gentry for the band to play a selection of cheerful tunes.

They were back at the Station Hotel in time for new landlord Knight's two o'clock dinner – medical officer Adolphus Caudle seated as chairman with chosen village traders in support.

Afternoon entertainment was ready in the field of Henfield Place with a large marquee erected for refreshments and shelter from sun or rain.

Happily it was sun.

There were team games of trap and bat, cricket and stoolball for adults; the fun of swings and booths with toys for the children.

Those not interested in team games could try their skill at archery, specially brought in from Brighton's Tivoli Gardens, or in shying sticks to knock Aunt Sally's well chipped head off its stand.

Alternatively, attractive trinket prizes were there to be won in 'three sticks a penny'. Throw the stick, knock the trinket off its stand onto the ground and win the prize. Simple, with three goes for just a penny.

Pennies were paid.

The trinkets fell time and again to hit the stand but just fail to topple over to the ground – such frustration.

More fun by far was to be had playing Kiss-in-the-Ring; the hopeful kisser circling behind the ring of participants to tap the chosen recipient and commence a chase round the ring to everyone's cheerful encouragement and laughter. A carefully measured maidenly run or madcap manly chase could win the kiss. Men and women young at heart and lung could have three goes or more without any penny and resort to the marquee afterwards for a refreshing drink and chat.

In the evening there was dancing for everyone, the band playing tune after tune until at last the final dance was called. [5]

Another season of society celebrations was over.

Chapter 39

The Snake House – 'Spinning Jenny' – Smallpox

Dr. Adolphus Caudle's next official appointment was as a member of Henfield cricket team for their match on the common against Broadwater, assisted by three county players, who had brought a pigeon with them to take home news of the result.

Some people had doubted the wisdom of facing such opposition but cricket as ever was cricket and Henfield bowled the opposition out for 46 replying with 82. Adolphus Caudle, hardly the most gifted of Henfield cricketers, was neither fortunate enough to make a catch nor called upon to bowl. His contribution came with the bat; 'nought not out' as number eleven.

The result was pencilled on a slip of paper, the paper was attached to the pigeon's leg and the bird was set free to wing its way home to Broadwater bearing the news that cricket had yet again proved a game of unlikely result.

Birds featured up at Mock Bridge where ten year old Alfred Knight decided to use a bit of initiative and a handful of corn to lure sparrows into a shed. With the birds happily pecking up the corn, Alfred closed the door and set about the sparrows.

His father was a farm labourer, his father's master a member of the Sparrows Club still functioning and rewarding the decease of sparrows and their ilk.

Alfred worked hard at his time consuming task to achieve the remarkable score of 84 – enough to gain pence from the farmer and a headline in the newspaper, SPARROW CATCH EXTRAORDINARY. [1]

Sparrows also made the news at Eardley Hall's Barrow Hill House.

The staff noticed that sparrows were constantly flying up with food to one of the house martins' mud cup nests on the eaves. It was obvious they had taken over the nest for their own brood.

The domestics decided the nest should be removed.

A ladder was placed against the wall.

One man held it steady while his mate climbed up to dislodge the nest.

He pushed the mud cup off easily enough but an unexpected length of something fell with it, hit the ground by the foot of the ladder and wriggled top speed into the bushes. A snake had been making its own clearance of nestling sparrows. Given another day or two it could have finished the lot.

The men were 'all shook up' and related their tale to the other domestics. The story was around Henfield days before the Brighton paper could report the news; too good a story to go without embellishment – Barrow Hill, the Snake House. [2]

By November, an even greater story was going round the farmers and butchers. Cattle murrain was on the wane. Markets could open fully again. Cattle could be transported by train.

The news was just a little too late for the first open Steyning Market but by the following week sellers and buyers were fully organised.

In December Rev. O'Brien began a second eight week season of fortnightly Penny Readings at the Boys' School.

The performers played to a packed schoolroom every occasion with standing room only for some and a few late comers finding there was no space for them at all.

The favourite reader soon became apparent; Rev. Divie Robertson whether he was relating Dickens' wonderful descriptions, or amusing pieces like Nelly Gray or The One-legged Goose.

With the approach of Lent, the vicar had to bring the readings to a close.

At the end of the final one, Rev. Divie Robertson made a jovial speech to the audience thanking all the ladies and gentleman who had provided such wonderful entertainment for Henfield people.

Penny Readings were fine entertainment for some but the general working man was happier with the comfortable familiarity of his pub.

Wheelwright Richard Reeves' choice was the George. He was a member of the club there and enjoyed the facilities offered by landlord Welling.

They included the opportunity for a light hearted game of Spinning Jenny played in the privacy of the smoking room well away from the public bar.

The game was simple; spin the jenny on a chequered cloth and hazard which of the red, white and black squares it would finish on. What gave it a touch of excitement was the light-hearted gamble – a little bit of money on the right square.

Richard Reeves was playing with William Balchin and two others when an argument arose and things began to go a bit wrong.

Reeves took up his money and said he would not play any more.

Balchin was on a winning streak and objected to it being ended.

He took off his jacket to sort things out.

Reeves declared he would not disgrace himself by fighting.

Balchin fetched him one to the head and he went down. When Balchin went in for another blow, Reeves thrust him away.

With that they really set to.

Reeves sent Balchin reeling, his head smashing into a hanging advert. They bundled into an armchair sending it crashing against the wall.

Reeves came of worse and realised he was hurt with blood on his chest.

The barmaid called to the landlord.

Mrs. Welling came. She asked for someone to stop the pair fighting.

Tailor James Galey responded with alacrity.

Reeves left in a hurry.

Shortly afterwards he was back again. He had forgotten his hat.

Mrs. Welling gave it to him and as soon as he was out of the door again she locked it. There had been trouble enough that night.

Balchin was not satisfied. He did not intend losing his winnings and went out through the window followed by Galey.

Balchin had another go at Reeves. Galey stepped in to separate them and in the process Reeves finished up with two black eyes.

He headed for home up in Nep Town. Once there he took to his bed. Next day his wife went for Doctor Caudle.

The doctor came and treated the wound on Reeves' chest.

Richard Reeves was in bed for a fortnight and off work for a further week. He had managed to keep hold of his gambling pence but Doctor Caudle's eventual bill was over £1. The Jenny had certainly not spun his way.

He took Galey to the County Court over the matter. It was another gamble that failed with more costs falling to him when the judge concluded it had been a drunken brawl caused by the landlord allowing gambling on his premises – something which would result in the loss of the George licence should the magistrates hear of it. [3]

There was a very different occasion at the Station Hotel. It concerned deaf Maurice Sayers who for many years had been very reliant on his ear trumpet.

He had been a labourer on the railway during its construction.

After changing his job, he still made use of the track as a convenient footpath.

He was walking home along the line just past the Steyning cutting one morning about the same time as the train from Brighton was gaining speed after the Steyning stop.

As the train steamed out of the cutting the driver saw Maurice and sounded his whistle.

Maurice kept walking.

The driver put his engine into reverse. The fireman applied the brake as fast as he could.

The noise of screeching brakes added to the blowing whistle.

At last Maurice noticed and turned to see the engine bearing down on him.

He twisted to leap clear only to be hit and thrown 25 yards through the air.

The train continued skidding to a halt.

Navvies working in the cutting ran to his aid. They ran in vain.

Maurice was dead. Near his body lay his ear trumpet.

At the inquest, the driver and one of the navvies explained what had happened. The jury returned the only verdict they could; "Accidentally killed." The coroner recorded it and the inquest was over.

Regardless of the accident, there was a lot of disquiet on the railway. Employees of the London, Brighton and South Coast were pressing for improved working conditions; hours were too long, safety was jeopardised.

Negotiations fell through and at the end of March a strike was called. Omnibuses were put on at Shoreham to carry passengers to stations on the Horsham line. The one replacing the early morning train came up Barrow Hill into the village, discharged its Henfield passengers and headed on to Partridge Green.

In Brighton the men were not whole hearted strikers. Drivers and firemen were turning to and trains were available. Two of the afternoon trains from Horsham failed to run and that was that. The omnibus horses were returned to their stables. [4]

In 1871 the government announced legislation that was welcomed by all working men; Easter Monday, Whit Monday, the first Monday in August and Boxing Day were to be holidays.

The news was welcomed by most people but 'Sunny' Woolgar, master basket-maker of Broadmare Common, was not enamoured. He was still prone to difficulties with his workers. A temporary employee had suddenly drawn his day's 2s 0d wage and left. The next morning 'Sunny' noticed that one of his knives was missing, an old one but still worth a good eight pence.

He explained the matter to P.C. Goldring.

Goldring set off in hot pursuit and discovered the man across the river at Ashurst enjoying a drink at the Fountain Inn with a couple of friends.

Goldring searched him and sure enough the knife was in his pocket.

He did not deny taking it and explained why;

"I didn't know it was any good. I took it to eat my grub with."

Goldring took him into custody.

The Petty Sessions would not be sitting for a week. The suspect remained confined awaiting his trial. Once it came, proceedings did not take long. The verdict had to be guilty. Just the outcome was in doubt.

The Chairman pronounced sentence; "One day's imprisonment."

'Sunny' Woolgar had his eightpenny knife back.

There were Woolgars aplenty in Henfield, over 60. Two of them, Stephen and Abraham, were keen members of the 18th Rifle Corps.

On a boisterously windy September Wednesday, the 18th played a cricket match on the common against the 7th Horsham Rifles.

Henfield batted first. Out strode opening batsmen Stephen and Abraham.

They coped with Horsham's speed bowlers and paved the way for the 18th to make a respectable 73 with Sergeant Martin of the White Hart batting last and hitting 15.

There was a delay between innings when the rising wind threatened to rip the canvas from the large refreshment marquee. The 18th and 7th formed a united fighting force. The canvas was safely removed and landlord Welling of the George could relax; his property and profits were safe.

The 7th Horsham then set about the Henfield bowlers with a second wicket stand that threatened to decide the match until Stephen Woolgar caught out the main danger man and Abraham clean bowled the partner.

Abraham took two catches, bowled another man and Horsham fell for 60.

The poles of the marquee were dismantled and riflemen became hospitable civilians. It had been a good day's cricket.

In October it was every rifleman for himself in proving his prowess at the Knepp Castle rifle range.

Ensign Stanford proved champion winning the Sir Percy Burrell silver cup for five shots at 400 and 800 yards. Assistant Surgeon Lewis scored a bull in a shoot off to prove best man at 500 yards and win a snuff box and a suckling pig kindly donated by Lady Burrell.

Private Hever won a saddle net and there were money prizes for seven privates including 10s 0d to Stephen Woolgar.

When the next battalion orders of the 2nd Sussex were received, they included an announcement that brought loud hurrahs from the 18th; 'The commanding officer has very great pleasure in pointing out as the best shot in the battalion, a most zealous and painstaking officer, Ensign Stanford of the 18th Sussex'.

At the end of October, they held their reunion at the White Hart with Ensign Stanford taking the chair in place of Captain Sir Percy Burrell unfortunately indisposed at Knepp Castle. Dr. Lewis kindly donated his prize suckling pig as a source of succulent pork. Sir Percy sent a brace of pheasants while someone else gave two brace of ducks. These with other meaty contributions became a sumptuous feast.

Rev. O'Brien said grace and the meal began.

At its end came the toasts with musical interludes between each; "The Queen", "Army, Navy and Volunteers," down through "The Town, Trade and Farmers of Henfield," and finally "The Ladies."

There being no lady present to reply to that toast, the lot fell to Corporal Thorns who almost found the task beyond him but finally managed a few appropriate words. His colleagues felt for his embarrassment.

Registrar Mr. Challen promptly took over with a song of the past rarely performed but thoroughly enjoyed for its sentiment; "My Faithful Fond Old Wife." The married rifleman could perhaps spare a thought for his wife, faithful in the house with the children.

More songs followed until Chairman Ensign Stanford vacated his seat, the signal for all to wend their way home.

In November there was an evening at the George where the marvellous acoustics of the Assembly Room would prove a boon. Two talented ladies were giving a pianoforte and vocal recital especially for those with a love of music.

People settled to enjoy selected pieces by classical and less renowned composers with informative sketches about the life of the better known.

The greatest applause went to the greatest works; Beethoven's "Pastoral" sonata, three of Mendelssohn's Songs without words and Mozart's "Voi che sapete" from Figaro. The singer put such intense feeling into her voice that the audience could but empathise as she did her utmost to perform with a cold that made it utterly impossible to achieve perfection.

Such slight shortcomings did not detract from the evening. People went home with glorious music still in their heads.

Within days there was fear in their heads. A virulent strain of smallpox had broken out. It spread to 23 people.

Such was the terror when the first person died that the men bringing the coffin to the house refused to go inside and handle the body. Registrar William Challen and the nurse had to do the task themselves.

William Challen's wife showed sympathy for the sufferers by making 40 gallons of beef tea for those recovering. They were thankful for the help and encouragement the restorative drink gave.

Chimney sweep James Humphrey had never got round to being vaccinated or ensuring his son James was.

They both fell victim and died within days of each other; young James on the 19th of December, his father on the 23rd.

Smallpox still dictated the procedure for their funerals. Both took place late on the night of the death in accordance with age old practice.

Chapter 40

Night attack – Roman Candles – A missing ramrod

In the New Year, the Rifle Volunteers announced they intended to stage a night attack on a supposed camp somewhere in Henfield on Wednesday 3rd of February. Members of the 2nd Sussex Battalion would be assisted by other corps. The public were invited to witness the event.

People knew the Easter Monday Brighton Reviews had been a spectacle worth seeing. Surely Henfield would put on a good show.

Sergeant Jones had several new recruits to bring up to scratch. Among them was 18 year old Henry, eldest son of millwright-machinist William Cooper with his modern workshops just beyond the chapel.

Military discipline could be the making of Henry. Teenage rebelliousness and associating with a girl his father did not approve of were causing discord in the family.

Sergeant Jones had the satisfaction of bringing the recruits to an acceptable level. The 18th were in good shape.

The evening of the 3rd arrived – daylight giving way to moonlit night; ideal conditions for secret manoeuvres carried out with an intrigued audience.

At 6.30 the bugler signalled the muster outside the White Hart.

Over 200 paraded with representatives from the 1st Sussex Artillery, the 2nd Sussex, 29th Middlesex, 43rd York, 2nd Gloucester and 1st Norfolk.

The 2nd Battalion were not among them. They had already been marched off to defend the camp – Mr. Stephens' windmill up on the rising ground south of the common. There they hoisted the National Flag and prepared their defences.

The assault troops, headed by a band, marched up the High Street and round the Common Corner to the lane on the north side. They would advance across the common and over the Brighton Road to the ditch and earth bank at the foot of the hill to their objective, the mill.

News of imminent attack reached the defenders. They lit a line of torches in front of their position and fired off a fusillade of rockets.

The attackers responded with more rockets. The sky lit bright. Both sides opened fire.

The artillery's guns boomed. Riflemen discharged their dated musket rifles, reloaded and fired again as fast as they could – gun powder charge and bullet in, ramrod down barrel and removed, new percussion cap on, aim and fire; the well drilled sequence.

For fully half an hour the noise of gunfire echoed round the village.

The light of the rockets dulled, the attackers ceased fire and in silence the men advanced across the common encountering unexpected bog patches.

At the road they reassembled and rifles were reloaded.

The command to attack was sounded.

The men gave a deafening cheer and charged up the hill.

The defenders replied with such withering fire the attack was repulsed in rapid retreat to the road.

Their captain reassembled them and tried a different tactic; a silent detour round by 'Lossam's' Hope Cottage in a flanking movement.

Again they were observed and driven back.

Once more the captain brought them to order and with a furious charge they stormed the defences, captured the flag and occupied the mill.

The battle was over.

Spectators made their way back to throng the High Street ready for the returning troops.

Victors and prisoners made their way from the mill and lined up on the road; a band at their head and another at their tail. Torches were handed out to each man.

The bands struck up and the march back to the White Hart began.

As they rounded Golden Square, coloured lights and Roman candles were handed out. The combined glare made the High Street gas lamps dim, the people multicoloured.

The crowd thrilled to it; never, ever had there been such a night in Henfield.

The troops marched on to the White Hart and halted. Safety checks on rifles were completed and the company dismissed.

For the men the night was not over. They gathered in the drill shed, long and roomy enough for them all, at the back of the inn where a good meat supper awaited them thanks to the generosity of Lady Burrell.

Captain of the 18th, Sir Percy Burrell, M.P., had the seat of honour, pleased to have been able to attend from Knepp Castle.

Grace was said. Men sat down.

Food was eaten, the cloth was removed and steaming bowls of punch were put on the tables.

It was time for the toasts, eventually ending with Henry Longley proposing the health of the visitors and the members of the different corps.

The band played Auld Lang Syne, Sir Percy Burrell vacated his chair and the day was over – the Henfield Review. [1]

Henry Cooper felt himself fully a man at the Review. He had previously had doubts about the effective use of firearms. If one had to shoot a man, where should one aim?

He had tried to discuss the matter with James Hole, one of his father's employees;

"Do you know the best place to shoot a man and kill him?"

James Hole had better things to think about;

"Don't ask me such silly questions as that, Harry, I don't know anything about it."

Henry was not to be put off:

"I was told the best place was through the arm. There is a place in the arm where you would kill a man directly if you hit it. I should have thought the best place to kill a man would be through the head."

James Hole was more interested in his work. He was a wheelwright, not a rifleman.

Henry still had doubts and was no nearer an answer when he attended the next 18th Rifles drill. Sergeant Jones put them through their paces as if another Review was scheduled.

About 9.00 p.m. he dismissed them. Three of the younger recruits asked to take their rifles home. Sergeant Jones agreed.

He checked the rifles were not loaded and were in a clean state. Any man returning one dirty would face unpleasant disciplinary action.

The men took their rifles and went home.

Sergeant Jones locked the armoury and the drill shed. He too set off but only as far as the White Hart bar; a drink after drilling the 18th was essential. He settled with his pint – the good natured chat and banter of friends a respite from the hobnailed-boot thumps of drilling riflemen.

About half an hour later, as one of Mr. Longley's employees was stabling a horse at the back of Mr. Cooper's yard he heard a gunshot followed by a screamed shout;

"Help! Help! Murder."

Mr. Cooper's yard beside the Congregational Church

As he hurried to find out what was happening, he saw a man run away by the wall of the yard. The moonlight was bright enough to show he was wearing light coloured clothes.

Chemist Mr. West was walking up the other side of the street. He was almost at his house when he heard the scream.

Moments later a man in volunteer uniform came running down by the Plough with a rifle in his hand.

He saw Mr. West and ran over to him gasping;

"I am lost. I am lost."

The man put his rifle down and put his hand to his head. "What's the matter? Have you lost your cap?"

"Yes, some man has knocked me down and stunned me and took my cap and rifle, loaded it and shot my father.

"Where is your father?"

There was no reply.

"For God's sake go for help and the doctor."

Mr. West went into his house leaving the man to fetch the doctor.

By this time somebody had rushed into the White Hart; "There's been a gunshot. Mr. Cooper's been injured in his shop."

The bar emptied.

A small group of men had gathered up by the chapel. Sergeant Jones joined them and saw Henry Cooper in front of his father's house, his rifle in his hand.

The sergeant went straight to him;

"Cooper, what have you been up to?"

Henry was in a state of shock;

"I was knocked down by a man in a black coat and a black hat, and he loaded my rifle and shot my father with it."

"Where's your cap and the rifle ramrod?"

"I don't know."

"Show me the place where you were knocked down."

Henry took him to the yard behind his father's workshops. There they searched for the cap and ramrod. The ramrod was nowhere to be seen but they did find the cap. Henry put it on.

Sergeant Jones told him to turn out his pouch. It was empty.

They went to Henry's house.

Dr. Lewis was there attending Mr. Cooper. A shot had entered at an angle high on his left arm, smashed the bone end exited near his shoulder. His pain was eased a little by a palliative draught. Dr. Lewis was binding the wounds.

Sergeant Jones left them. He took the rifle back to the armoury and inspected it. He lifted the hammer of the gun to discover a discharged percussion cap still in place – the rifle had been fired.

By the time P.C. Goldring reached the house, Dr. Lewis had finished treating the wound and had been to inspect the shop hoping to find what had passed through his patient's arm.

There he had seen bloodstains where Mr. Cooper had stood. On searching the far end of the shop he found indentations in the brickwork. On the floor was part of a ramrod.

Dr. Lewis showed the constable the broken ramrod. Goldring went to the shop and found the other part.

Henry Cooper was still in the street. Goldring questioned him and was told of the man in black.

Henry had a question for the constable;

"Have you found the ramrod?"

"Yes, we have."

"You are sure to find things out are you not?"

"We shall see tomorrow."

With that the men parted. Henry returned home to an uncomfortable night's rest.

The next morning the police superintendent from Steyning arrived. Henry was taken into custody charged with attempted murder.

P.C. Goldring made enquiries seeking witnesses or people with any information. Several had things they wanted to say.

James Hole told of Henry's words to him.

Apprentice George Hill told how earlier in the evening of the shooting Henry Cooper had asked him to go up to Mr. Tobitt's grocery for two pennyworth of gunpowder. He had done so and taken it to Henry in the Plough who had bought him a glass of ale for doing it.

Gunsmith Peter Ward described Henry entering the shop during the afternoon seeking a double-barrelled pistol but the shop not having one.

George Thorpe, an employee of Mr. Cooper, told of a conversation he and Henry had. Henry had wondered what would happen to the business if his father died. He was told not to think of such nonsense. Henry had reckoned he and his sister would have to go into service.

All of them had to attend when Henry was taken to appear before the Steyning magistrates. Each recounted his part in the affair.

First, Doctor Lewis described how he had inspected the pieces of ramrod microscopically and discovered blood stains.

Sergeant Jones explained his involvement.

In turn, the others told their part.

The Steyning superintendent provided one further piece of information. Footprints had been found at the site of the crime, the right differing from the left in the position of three nails and a pelt. The prisoner's boots had proved to have exactly the same differences.

Henry was taken to Petworth to await the next Assizes at Lewes.

At Lewes he pleaded guilty. The judge expressed horror at such a crime and passed sentence.

Transportation had been ended. Henry Cooper would serve 7 years penal servitude in England. [2]

For his father, the shock of what his son had done was worse than the pain he was suffering. It could never be forgotten.

His wounds mended and his business improved steadily to warrant the largest Henfield entry in the 1874 Post Office Directory: - Cooper William, millwright, engineer, machinist, brassfounder & appraiser; steam ploughing, steam threshing and seed-cleaning machinery for hire.

Chapter 41

H.M.S. Minotaur – The bag in a pond – 'Snow black' night

The Directory also had an amended entry for St. Peter's. The rebuilding programme was complete.

Mr. Borrer's extension for the schoolchildren had been torn away.

The church rebuilding under way, 1870

In the nave the galleries and ceiling had come crashing to the ground revealing the old roof timbers.

Worshippers' familiar box pews had gone, replaced by rows of lookalike seating.

The only remaining medieval stonework was around the old chapel between the chancel and the new north aisle. The extensions had walls of mortared flints carefully knapped and patterned together.

The chancel was higher and longer with a new eastern window behind the altar.

St Peter's was now appropriate for modern times.

With thanks to The Friends of Henfield Museum

The rebuilt St.Peter's of 1871 with its medieval chapel of stone walls

There was also a new vicar.

Rev. O'Brien, who seldom enjoyed good health, had died. People knew they had lost a deeply religious man who always did what he thought was best for his parishioners.

When their new vicar moved into the vicarage there was great rejoicing. It was Rev. Divie Robertson, a man blessed with a sense of humour.

The ordinary person's sense of humour was being catered for at the Assembly Room with a visit by one of the latest groups in show business, the Christy Minstrels.

Newspaper reviews acclaimed the show-stopping Christy Minstrel mix of song and humour about the freed slaves of America.

The Assembly Room was packed; the audience expectant.

The minstrels' blackened faces, their cleverly accentuated singing, hilarious contortions, grimaces and amusing side remarks proved great entertainment. [1]

At its close, many of the audience gave enthusiastic applause. For them, it had been an extremely funny show; an insight into the everyday life of the American Deep South. Who would have thought it without seeing the show?

Others saw it as distasteful music hall humour – clever but coarse.

The cricket club concentrated on life within the parish. In future the Henfield team would all be Henfield men. No man from outside would be allowed to play for the club however skilled he was.

An all Storrington team visited for a match on the common.

Both teams had bowlers using the new method of swinging the arm full height above the shoulder. Batsmen seemed to prefer it and the game was played in a far friendlier manner than many where star players were involved. The result was a draw; honours even and no ill blood.

The season proved Henfield able to hold their own with captain Richard Fillery leading the team to six victories in their eight fixtures. He also topped the batting averages at 28.7 for his 13 innings.

At the end of the season, the non-club cricketers of Nep Town played a Marrieds v Singles match on the Town Field.

The Marrieds batted first opening with their two sailors, Fred Hampton and Tom Bowline, on leave from Portsmouth where they were proud to be serving on H.M.S. Minotaur the navy's new state of the art steam powered ironclad fitted with five masts in case of engine failure and muzzle loaded guns because the innovative breach loading system had proved inadequate.

The sailors' batting was not quite adequate either with each being out for four. Landlord John Browning did less being out for one and the next five scored even less than him. Mr. Standing came to the team's rescue with 13, half his team's total.

The Singles were well past that when the break for lunch was called.

The teams crossed the Town Field and walked left up the bridleway to Nep Town where John Browning's wife provided a hearty meal in the Gardeners' Arms which was followed by restorative pots of beer.

The afternoon's revitalised cricket saw plenty of mighty whacks bringing the day's runs to over 200 with victory going to the Singles.

Cricket completed, they all made their way back to the pub, bought their beers and settled to an evening of song highlighted by some uproarious contributions from sailor Tom Bowline.

Turning right from the Gardeners' Arms along the Town Field bridleway brought people to Potwell House now occupied by Miss Borrer – almost a hundred years after her grandfather had left the place plagued by the foul aromas of the Tanyard.

The Tanyard itself no longer existed. Her brother had levelled the pits and dismantled most of the buildings. The pond remained.

Benjamin Blann was passing it on his way to work early morning when he noticed a strange object protruding from the water.

Miss Borrer's coachman retrieved it; a sort of bag made from carpet material with twine bound round, heavy.

They put it on the bank, cut the twine and took a pace back; a ghastly stench rose from the bag.

The coachman tipped it over. Out came two bricks and a baby's body.

When the men got over their shock they informed Miss Borrer. The police were called.

The body was taken to the George Inn Stable where Dr. Caudle undertook a post-mortem examination.

At the inquest Dr. Caudle stated the body was of a healthy, fully developed boy. He believed from the state of the lungs and general appearance that the baby had breathed. A slight indentation on the head had probably been made after death by the bricks although he could not be certain because the corpse was so decomposed. It had been in the water about two weeks.

Proceedings were then delayed while the police enquired after the murderer.

They had little to go on. The bag had been fashioned from a material made for church purposes only; an unusual design of crimson patterned with black fleur-de-lis and edged with a Greek border. It was taken to shops in Henfield, Brighton and Worthing. No shopkeeper could help.

Police constables carried out further enquiries throughout the village and surrounding area hoping to find somebody who might have been induced to carry out such a crime.

At the adjourned inquest the police reported on their enquiries.

All had proved blank. They could find no trace of any likely suspect. The carpet had probably been obtained from a London warehouse.

The coroner summed up for the jury. Their finding was immediate;

"Wilful murder against some person or persons unknown." [2]

The coroner thanked Dr. Caudle. The inquest was over.

Dr. Caudle had earned the reputation of being an equitable man intent on helping everyone regardless of status.

In October, he was called upon to assess the health of his friend Dr.

Morgan who was trying to enjoy a well earned retirement in his new home, Russ House.

It was proving impossible because of the nuisance caused by market gardener George Greenfield whose ground abutted his.

The man kept his pigs there. They were dirty and the pigsty stank to high heaven, the smell completely overpowering outside the house and on some days even penetrating it.

Dr. Morgan had spoken to his neighbour several times but the nuisance continued until he felt he had no alternative to forwarding a complaint to the Steyning Union.

The Union attempted to deal with it under the government's Nuisances Regulations enacted to deal with the cholera outbreaks.

George Greenfield made some effort to improve the cleanliness of the sty but the odour of pig remained.

Court action had to be taken.

There, Dr. Morgan explained the position and state of the sty assuring the court of the accuracy of his description gained by placing a box against the garden wall to obtain the perfect view.

His statement brought wry laughter.

Dr. Caudle was called.

He gave his considered medical opinion that Dr. Morgan's deteriorating health was a direct result of the unwholesome conditions arising from his neighbour's pigs.

It was time for the defence lawyer. He claimed the keeping of pigs was important and that his client kept them in good order. The case arose entirely from the fanciful ideas of the complainant who had failed to show the pigs created any nuisance. He suggested Dr. Morgan had a hole in the garden wall allowing sewage to flow into his neighbour's property.

Dr. Morgan refuted the idea.

Captain Thomas Wisden said had seen the pigs that morning and was certain they did not constitute a nuisance. They were on ground owned by his father who would never allow a tenant to have pigs in an offensive condition.

George Greenfield's other neighbours were called. They too considered the pigs were kept in a clean state that did not cause offence.

It was time for the magistrates to pass judgement. They were in complete agreement that care should be taken to keep animals clean. Having listened to the evidence of both sides they were unanimous in their decision – case dismissed. [3]

Dr. Caudle's good intentions had floundered.

People's attention turned to the forthcoming national event, Guy Fawkes; a day for the lads of the village.

The event was to be much bigger than usual. A recent inhabitant arriving from East Sussex had given sound advice on the best way to celebrate the occasion.

Costumes were made, bonfires built and a goodly stock of rockets laid by.

The careful preparations proved well worth while.

Costumed revellers paraded the streets, bonfires blazed, fireworks spluttered and fizzed colourfully and rockets zoomed.

Around the summits of the Downs, red and orange pinpricks showed other celebratory fires recording the providential frustration of Popish plots.

At the end of November, it was time for the annual programme of Penny Readings at the Boys' School.

HENFIELD.—PENNY READINGS.—A penny reading was held at the boys' school room, on Wednesday last. We append the programme :—

Glee.........“ O, who will o'er the Downs so free.
Reading ...(“ Horatius”) by Lord Macaulay ...Rev. D. Robertson.
Glee.........Hark ! hark ! the lark at heaven's gate sings.
Reading ..The convicts return (Chas. Dickens) Eardley Hall, Esq.
Song ......“ King time” ....Mr. W. Hodges.
Reading ...An extract from Nicholas Nickleby
(Chas. Dickens) ....Rev. D. Robertson.
Round ......“ Winde gentle evergreen” ....
Reading ...Brutus and Cassius ....(from Shakespeare).
Rev. F. Gambier and J. S. Teulon, Esq.
Reading ...“ How they brought the good news
from Ghent to Aix,”..................Rev. D. Robertson.
National Anthem.

The 'Penny Readings' programme

The second Penny Readings was just before Christmas. The choir sang “Good King Wenceslas”. Rev. Divie Robertson read extracts from Dickens' “Christmas Stories”.

Across at Barrow Hill House, Mr. Hall, very aware of seasonable benevolence, gave money to be shared among the children of the National Schools. It was to be spent on useful articles of clothing.

Boys were considered as in greatest need at 5s 0d; the girls having 4s 0d and infants 2s 6d.

With over 300 children on the school registers it cost him upwards of £60; huge money in the working man's mind, a gentleman's Christmas largesse in Eardley Hall's.

On Christmas Eve he attended the Boys' School breaking up celebration. That day, 123 boys made sure they attended.

They sang 'Hark, hark the herald Angels sing', listened to Rev. Robertson encourage them for the future and were reminded of their debt to Mr. Borrer. 24 of the boys gained prizes of a useful book. Plum cake and oranges were eaten by them all, sweets scrambled for.

Finally Mr. Eardley Hall presented the school with a new football.

Christmas Day brought its seasonal peace and time of friendly gatherings around the village for most people, but not all. Some were among the Union inmates at Shoreham Workhouse where Mr. and Mrs. Seaborne were still in charge.

The workhouse Christmas Day treat of roast beef and plum pudding had widened to include nuts and oranges for the children and tea, tobacco, snuff and beer for the old folk.

Among those old folk were the High Street tailor/hairdresser, William Vinall, and his wife, Sarah. Both had been born in the village.

They had led hard-working, law abiding lives bringing up their children decently with help from the income of William's small beerhouse.

Through the years, he had been listed in the County Directories 'tailor and hairdresser' but as he grew older less work had come his way.

His final census entry read 'tailor out of employment'.

They moved from their rented house into lodgings and aged as gracefully as they could. When they were finally unable to look after themselves they were obliged to accept the unthinkable, removal to the workhouse.

Widower William Piper, one time railway labourer whose geese had so upset old 'Lossam', hit such bad times that he was forced to go in from his tenement at the back of the common where he had lived with his housekeeper, granddaughter Harriett Dale – herself born in the workhouse but not returning to it.

Spinster shopkeeper Mary Stringer, who had confronted the two ill mannered men in her Berlin Wool Shop, had relied on her savings in later life until there was nothing left and she, too, had been forced to accept workhouse life.

For them, the beef and plum pudding were a brief respite; Boxing Day was just another workhouse day.

For people in their own homes, the Boxing Day holiday allowed time to recover and relax a little before the onslaught of January.

The New Year onslaught of 1881 came as cold as ever with ice-covered floods, frozen fields and frozen roads.

On a mid month Monday, a slight thaw set in.

That evening, barometers showed pressure falling rapidly. The wind veered to the south east.

During the night the temperature plummeted. By dawn, fallen snow was forming drifts.

The snow fell faster.

Roads became impassable. In the fields, sheep disappeared from view.

The morning train from Horsham arrived more or less on time. As it steamed through the drifts along the cutting to the station, sheets of snow were thrown to each side.

The station stop was minimal. The train headed on for Steyning.

Wind and snow continued unabated.

The last train from Brighton reached Henfield exceedingly late.

Nobody alighted; nobody joined.

The guard waved his flag. The driver restarted the train.

Steamy smoke rose along the cutting. Snow sprayed thick each side.

Halfway to Partridge Green, where the railway crossed the river at Betley Farm, a drift lay deep between the iron sheeting along the sides of the bridge.

The engine ploughed into the snow, slowed and stopped. [4]

Snowflakes spattered the carriage windows. The few passengers huddled into their clothing.

Driver and fireman climbed down from the engine, shovels in hand, and began clearing the line.

They shovelled snow for more than an hour.

At last there seemed a chance of moving.

They clambered aboard again, sounded the whistle and set the engine in motion.

The train moved slowly forward towards the unfrequented future of the twentieth century.

References

KEY: B = EAST SUSSEX RECORDS OFFICE *C = HENFIELD CRICKET CLUB*
K = KEW NATIONAL ARCHIVES *M = HENFIELD MUSEUM*
W = WEST SUSSEX RECORDS OFFICE
NEWSPAPERS:
2 = BRIGHTON GAZETTE *3 = BRIGHTON GUARDIAN* *4 = BRIGHTON HERALD*
5 = LONDON GAZETTE *6 = LONDON DAILY NEWS* *7 = SUSSEX ADVERTISER*
8 = SUSSEX EXPRESS *9 = SUSSEX DAILY NEWS* *10=WEST SUSSEX GAZETTE*

Introduction
1 People *(from left to right)*: Jim White, William Browning, Jim Browning, Tom Browning, Harry Gander, David Paine, William Barnet, Alfred Smith.
Glossary
1 8 22-9-1838
Chapter 1
1 Par 100/36/1
2 7 5-5-1825
3 7 7-6-1800
4 W Par 100/37/8
Chapter 2
1 M fol 2-1
2 4 28-3-1807
3 7 4-7 1800
4 W Par 100/37/8
5 7 31-3-1800
6 7 5-9-1812
Chapter 3
1 W MP 2605
2 W Par 100/4/3
3 3 3-6-1841
4 7 21-7-1800
5 K AMS 6981/1
6 M School
7 7 14-9-1812
8 7 14-9-1812
Chapter 4
1 7 24-6-1815
2 W Epvi/48
3 W Par 100/7/44
4 K Asss 94/1798
5 W Par 100/7/1
Chapter 5
1 W Epvi/46
2 2 29/3/1827
3 W Epvi/46
4 2 25-5-1843
5 W Epvi/42/4
6 7 11-6-1827
Chapter 6
1 2 25/11/1830
2 2 9-3-1831
3 2 24-2-1831
4 W Epvi/46
Chapter 7
1 W Par 100/30/2
2 W Par 100/37/4
3 W Par100/37/8/1
Chapter 8
1 7 27-4-1835
2 W G9 MF145
3 7 20-8-1835
4 2 17-9-1835
Chapter 9
1 3 13-9-1835
2 2 17-9-1835
3 3 13-9-1835
Chapter 10
1 W Par 100/4/5
2 2 29-12-1836
3 K HH/12/13099
4 2 14-1-1836
5 2 24-12-1836
6 2 25-5-1843
7 C Pavilion
8 8 21-7-1836
Chapter 11
1 B AMS 6981/1
2 W Par 100/7/44
3 8 24-7-1842
4 8 16-2-1843
5 8 3-6-1843
6 8 30-11-1849
Chapter 12
1 2 13-6-1841
2 8 2-12-1843
3 2 18-4-1844
Chapter 13
1 8 16-4-1842
2 K HW/1/10/2
3 8 19-8-1843
4 8 20-9-1845
Chapter 14
1 8 7-9-1844
2 8 21-5-1842
3 7 17-5-1845
4 8 9-2-1842
5 8 11-4-1846
6 8 20-5-1846
7 8 17-8-1844
Chapter 15
1 2 9-3-1843
2 W Epvi42/4
3 8 14-2-1843
Chapter 16
1 7 5-10-1843
2 C Pavilion
3 2 3-6-1841
4 8 26-6-1841
5 W Par 100/7/44
Chapter 17
1 8 25-5-1844
2 8 15-8-1842
3 8 2-6-1838
4 3 22-7-1840
5 8 5-9-1846
6 7 25-5-1846
Chapter 18
1 W QRW/827
2 8 7-4-1846
3 8 6-3-1847
Chapter 19
1 W G9 MF 146
2 8 29-12-1849
3 W Ep/vi/42/5
Chapter 20
1 8 7-6-1845
2 8 19-6-1855
3 W QR/W834
Chapter 21
1 8 1-8-1848
2 8 4-8-1849
3 7 20-12-1853
Chapter 22
1 8 23-7-1850
2 8 7-12-1850
3 8 5-9-1857
Chapter 23
1 6 21-12-1849
2 7 19-2-1855
3 7 16-9-1851
4 8 21-6-1858
Chapter 24
1 8 6- 9-1856
2 8 16-10-1855
3 8 17-8-1852
4 W Epvi42/4
5 7 11-3-1856
Chapter 25
1 8 13-9-1856
2 8 19-12-1857
3 8 10-4-1858
4 8 22-5 1858
5 8 25-7-1857
Chapter 26
1 7 13-10-1857
2 8 26-12-1857
3 8 16-4-1858
4 8 31-7-1858
Chapter 27
1 10 24-2-1860
2 7 29-12-1858
3 8 15-1-1859
4 8 29-3-1859
Chapter 28
1 7 18-10-1859
2 5 19-6-1860
3 8 24-5-1860
Chapter 29
1 Ep/11/40
2 2 1-5-1866
3 7 21-8-1860
4 7 14-8-1860
Chapter 30
1 10 1-11-1860
2 7 28-10-1860
3 10 1-3-1860
4 7 6-11-1860
5 7 29-1-1861
6 7 12-2-1861
Chapter 31
1 7 9-4 1861
2 7 2-4-1861
3 8 27-4-1861
4 7 18-6-1861
5 8 24-7-1861
Chapter 32
1 4 13-7-1861
2 7 17-8-1861
3 8 1-6-1861
4 7 13-3-1862
Chapter 33
1 10 20-3-1862
2 8 24-1-1862
3 8 4-9-1869
Chapter 34
1 8 26-8-1862
2 8 11-10-1862
3 W MP 934
4 8 16-7-1864
Chapter 35
1 7 1-9-1863
2 7 9-6-1863
3 7 1-9-1863
4 8 24-7-1866
Chapter 36
1 W Par 100/43/1
2 7 3-1-1863
3 8 2-10-1867
4 8 25-11-1865
5 B AMS 6981/1
6 8 12-9-1865
Chapter 37
1 7 31-3-1863
2 8 21-10-1865
3 8 13-12-1864
4 8 7-3-1874
5 8 10-2 1866
Chapter 38
1 W Par 100/43/1
2 8 27-4-1867
3 W Ep11/40/6
4 Par 100/4/17
5 8 17-7-1866
Chapter 39
1 8 14-7-1866
2 8 21-8-1866
3 8 2-3-1867
4 2 28-3-1867
Chapter 40
1 8 13-2-1869
2 4 6-3-1869
Chapter 41
1 8 23-3-1869
2 8 17-6-1873
3 8 24-10-1871
4 9 20-1-1881

Index

This selective index gives the first mention in a chapter for four sections; GENERAL, HENFIELD LOCATIONS, PEOPLE and OTHER PLACES.

GENERAL

A

Accident 78, 218, 223, 244, 266
Animals 2, 5, 14, 5, 70, 89, 99, 111, 114, 180, 234, 241, 256, 258, 266, 279, 300, 312
Archery 294
Army 14, 59, 103, 192, 209
Arson 62, 252
Assizes 27, 62, 282
Assault 116, 144

B

Ballad 127
Band 36, 39, 147, 178, 214, 234, 238, 260, 269, 293, 303
Bank Holiday 299
Bankrupt 21, 31, 109, 138, 141, 162, 208
Barge 5, 83, 131, 207, 267
Basketry 14, 107, 166
Beadle 56
Beef tea 301
Beerhouse 34, 125
Begging, 126
Betting 9
Blacksmith 1
Boxing Day 225
Brewery 1, 32, 137, 140, 225
Brick making 12, 31, 243
Bridlway 2
Brooks 2, 60

C

Cattle murrain 272, 296
Chain Pier 238
Chalk 5
Chess 231
Child cruelty 96, 263
Chimneysweep 6, 103, 301
Cholera 136, 312
Christmas 68, 151, 178, 198, 225, 244, 283, 314
Christy Minstrels 309
Church 18, 44, 64, 79, 89, 120, 133, 137, 155, 227, 230, 245, 289, 308
Clothing 6, 25, 84, 88, 94, 130, 250, 305
Coal 4
Coastguard 59
Cock fighting 9
Conditional Surrender 35
Conservative 270
Copyhold 45, 73
Copyhold Act 175
Corn market 189
Corn Law 23, 121
Corn mill 52
Counterfeit 219
Cricket 16, 21, 71, 115, 146, 174, 196, 215, 293, 295, 310
Curate 11, 44, 78

D

Dance 11, 17, 215, 293
Debtor's gaol 2, 4
Desertion 143
Distress warrant 45
Drink 9, 137, 219, 231, 248, 272, 293
Drover 101
Drunkeness 253

E

Easter 109, 270
Easter Monday 228, 230
Education 11, 17, 21, 53, 95, 118, 120, 178, 197, 212, 259, 290, 314
Election 109, 270
Emigration 86
Evacuation 14

F

Faggots 5
Famine 133
Farming 19, 29, 32, 98, 100, 121, 132, 136, 150, 169, 170, 197, 207, 216, 272
Fellmonger 12
Fighting 81
Fire 12, 60, 150, 170
Fire engine 150
Floods 100, 200, 216, 225, 244
Flower Show 177, 182, 217, 238, 274
Food 6, 22, 27, 39, 66, 85, 89, 98, 111, 126, 129, 135, 157, 190, 197, 205, 231, 245, 260, 274, 285, 300, 304, 314
Football 215
Freehold 13, 31, 169
Friendly Soc 9, 16, 35, 78, 83, 160, 177, 214, 243, 269, 292
Fruit 33, 178, 218
Furniture 35, 65, 98

G

Gambling 297
Gamekeeper 111
Game Law 24
Games 260, 294
Gas 267, 284, 288
Government 45
Grand Review 230, 290, 302
Gravel 5
Guardians 50, 56, 92, 93
Guns 73, 97, 111, 114, 134, 176, 230, 258, 290, 300, 303
Guy Fawkes 313

H

Hard Labour 68, 96, 132
Harriers 16, 174
Heriot 33
High Sheriff 12, 17
Highway rate 77
Hindu 120, 183
Home 6, 45, 87, 98, 130
Hops 61
Horse race 173
House 45, 107, 157
House of Correction 6, 91
Hulk 28, 112
Hunt 16

I

Illness 79, 115, 244
Incendiary fire 62
Inland Revenue 265
Inquest 69, 78, 93, 207, 298, 311

J

Justitia 28

L

Labourer 3, 27, 37, 46, 64, 84
Lady Day 38
Liberal 270
Library 251
Lottery 281

M

Magic Lantern 245
Manor Court 22, 31, 139
Market 101, 296
Medical Attention 14, 29, 52, 85
Merchant Navy 143
Michaelmas 18, 38, 78
Militia 1, 14
Morse 236
Mortgage 139
Murder 311
Music 11, 180, 197, 223
Musical box 198
Muslim 120, 183
Mutiny 183

N

Napoleon 231
Navy 40, 209, 290, 310
Needlework 11
New Year 70, 82
Night Watch 81
Nuisances 137, 242

O

Occupation 2, 10, 21, 32, 44, 53, 101, 108, 151
Oakum 94
Oil lamps 81, 268
Ordinary 10, 16, 21
Organist 227, 245
Overseer 3, 44

P

Parish Pound 279
Parliament 19
Pauper Grave 69
Penny Reading, 280, 296, 313
Petty Sessions 37, 68, 97, 111, 126, 152, 166, 192, 226, 265, 299
Photograph 198
Ploughing Match 171
Poaching 111
Poison 128, 226
Police Gazette 102
Poor Rate 44, 124, 177, 203
Pope 155
Postal service 111
Potato blight 135
Prosecuting Society 254

Q

Quarter Sessions 2, 15, 24, 47, 81, 89, 132, 191
Queen's Bench 242
Queen Victoria 136
Quit rent 35

R

Railway 70, 110, 148, 161, 187, 194, 200, 205, 224, 230, 236, 246, 273, 290, 298, 315
Rates of pay 38
Reeve 32, 42
Relief 57
Removal 47, 88
Rifle Corps.(18th) 209, 216, 228, 230, 256, 269, 286, 290, 299, 302
Riot 58
Roads 246
Robbery 101, 130
Round frock 63, 138
Rough Music 232

S

Settlement 47, 165
Sewer 242, 312
Sheep theft 27
Sheriff 17, 100
Shops 1, 33, 101, 108, 125, 140, 164, 183
Singing 83, 146, 196, 203, 212, 223, 227, 245, 261, 277, 278, 289, 292, 313
Skating 226
Slate 5, 39
Smallpox 127, 301
Snake House 296
Snow 70, 226, 289, 315
Solitary Confinement 85, 92
Sparrows Club 133, 295
Spinning Jenny 297
Starvation 135
Stocks 1, 127
Stoolball 215, 294
Street lights 81, 285, 288
Strike 298
Suicide 93
Swindle 239

T

Tamplin 31, 151
Tanning 12
Taxation 1, 203
Telegraph 236, 266
Thatch 13
Tipnoke 15
Tithes 122, 136, 245
Tobacco 9
Toll 5, 76, 265
Tonic Sol Fa 247
Transportation 92, 112, 132
Trap and Bat 215, 294
Tree (timber) 5, 13, 40, 78, 104, 248
Turf 42
Turnpike 1, 40

U

Union 50, 108, 129, 135, 242, 250, 287, 312
Useful Knowledge Soc. 163, 179, 183, 200, 231, 252

V

Vaccination 127, 264
Vehicle 2, 14, 22, 33, 40, 58, 75, 110, 150, 153, 227, 234, 298
Vestry 37, 44, 64, 88, 108

W

Wages 37
Weather 70, 115
Wedding 273, 276
Wharf 5
Whipped 85
Whit Monday 16
Windmill 2, 24, 34, 53, 61, 190, 201, 223, 252, 302
Workhouse 2, 29, 44, 50, 56, 65, 78, 88, 94, 135, 171

HENFIELD LOCATIONS

A

Adur 1, 70, 83, 99, 188, 200, 207, 265
Alder Wood 112
Assembly Room 244, 265, 279, 275, 309

B

Barrow Hill 13, 17, 38, 91, 101, 115, 178, 246, 273, 290, 295, 313
'Bee Hive' 2, 31, 45, 76
Bineham Bridge 99
Betley 172, 238, 275
Bramlands Lane 77
Broadmare Common 12, 17, 22, 31, 100, 107, 124, 164, 299
Brooks 2, 29, 34, 99
Brookside 99, 157, 201
Browns Land 60
Buckwish 60
Bull Inn 97, 215, 224
Burning Mountain 2, 58

C

Cagefoot Lane 11, 79, 260, 284
Chestham 39, 136, 216, 258
Church Street 1, 12, 205, 284
Common Mill 34, 190, 252, 302
Crouch Hill 5, 39, 74, 75, 219

D

Dagbrook Lane 100
Dogham Place 107, 115, 139, 143

E

Eastout 98
Elm Grove 11, 17, 21
Eton's Farm 5

F

Fieldsland 216
Forges 22, 139, 214
Frogs Hole 130

G

Gardeners' Arms 262, 275, 279, 310
George Inn 1, 10, 16, 22, 31, 39, 50, 73, 115, 136, 151, 153, 170, 177, 214, 222, 232, 244, 264, 270, 284, 288, 296, 311
Golden Square 1, 22, 45, 76, 93, 137, 150, 278, 303
Great Betley 130
Grinstead Lane 12

H

Haycroft 1, 33, 64, 99, 108
Henfield Common 4, 16, 37, 73, 76, 107, 114, 137, 143, 150 , 190, 266, 302
Henfield Place 247, 259
High Street 1, 34, 40, 45, 81, 108, 150, 154, 179, 197, 208, 215, 224, 234, 244, 265, 268, 279, 302
Holedean 199
Hope Cottage 108, 115, 275, 303
Horn lane 77

K

Kentons 171, 215, 222
Kidders 126, 215, 255

L

Lashmars 129
Lipride 105
Lyyds 23

M

Martyn Lodge 274, 285
Middle Field 114
Mill House 124
Mock Bridge 4, 40, 73, 76, 126, 131, 150, 224, 255, 265, 295

N

Nep Town 2, 12, 57, 89, 107, 160, 165, 175, 201, 223, 249, 262, 280, 297, 310
NepTown Mill 2, 24, 31, 61, 201, 223
New Hall 41, 61, 150, 174
New Inn 46, 83, 100, 129, 164
Nymans 40

O

Oreham 27, 41, 60, 77, 151
Oreham Place 132
Oyster Cottage 58, 262

P

Parish Pound 2, 279
Parsonage Farm 18, 89, 170
Plough Inn 1, 9, 78, 110, 158, 183, 231, 248, 254
Pokerlee 22, 33, 78, 99, 201, 206, 224
Potwell 12, 90, 197, 310
Prospect Cottage 1, 17, 278

R

Red Oaks 121, 197
Russ House 312
Rye 29, 34, 85, 99, 157, 215, 225, 238, 255

S

St Peter's 1, 45, 79, 273
Shiprods 192
South Worms 105
Station Hotel 229, 242, 293, 297
Station Rd 290
Stonepit Lane 130
Streatham Manor 12, 22, 31, 39, 115
Stretham 201

T

Tanyard 1, 12, 89, 311
Terry's Cross 76
Town Field 2, 39, 90, 115, 215, 228, 265, 270, 293, 310

V

Vine cottage 253

W

Wantley 103
West End 75, 101, 129, 195
West Mill 168
White Hart 1, 9, 16, 31, 81, 123, 134, 150, 154, 164, 180, 207, 253, 274, 293, 299, 302
Windmill Lane 2, 175
Woods Mill 77, 168, 249

PEOPLE

A

Alfrey 124
Ashton Rev 80

B

Bailey 34, 128
Baines 105
Baldwin 140
Banfield 172, 263
Baron de la Zouche 25, 41, 65, 124, 136
Barnett 6
Barringer 191
Batchelor 72
Beard 11
Beckett 123
Bignell 72, 115
Blake 275
Blaker 72
Blann 311
Blondin 238
Blower 3
Borrer 12, 17, 21, 31, 38, 50, 56, 64, 77, 101, 120, 140, 178, 182, 231, 246, 292, 310
Botting 6, 168, 249
Bound 12
Bowline 310
Brooker 217
Brooks 194
Brown 153, 205
Browning 58, 158, 172, 181, 185, 248, 254, 262, 278, 310
Brownings 102, 175
Buck 244
Buckmaster 121
Buckwell P.C. 114, 126, 131, 153, 165, 171
Budgen 191
Bulkley Lieut 281
Burrell 187, 241, 270, 293, 300, 303
Burtenshaw 90, 101, 215
Bushby 111, 117, 147, 174, 177
Buzza 265

C

Cain 6, 27, 97, 250
Caplin 68
Carpenter 175
Caudle, Dr 52, 83, 150, 180, 207, 219, 223, 232, 244, 256, 266, 293, 295, 311
Challen 93, 124, 187, 264, 268, 284, 289, 300
Chate 27
Cheeseman 96
Clarke 150
Colgate 142, 164
Collins 275
Constable 258
Cooley 175
Cooper 302
Coppard 18, 47, 145, 187, 234, 242, 268, 284, 288
Cordy 76
Corke 140
Cornford 17
Cosslet 225
Cragg 107, 166, 191, 199, 268
Crichton Rev 244
Curzon 136
Cutress 104, 164, 202

D

Dalavanti 244
Dale 108, 127, 191, 314
Davey 215
Dear 219
Debney 248
Dennett 112, 114, 122, 245
Dowell 131
Duke of Norfolk 122
Duke of Richmond 52, 99, 122
Dunlop 79, 118, 120, 133, 136, 155, 238

E

Earl of Egremont 122
Earl of Sheffield 122
Easom 239
Ede 41, 54, 56, 61, 67
Egerton P.C. 181, 184, 192, 205
Ellman 122
Elmalie 217
Embling 31

F

Fairs 275
Faulkoner 50, 61, 268
Fillery 72, 310
Flint 159
Florance 31
Foreman 218, 223, 275
Fowler 274
Franks 47
Freeman 172
French 206
Frost 164
Fry 252

G

Galey 297
Gander 1, 17, 217, 278
Gardener 205, 262, 275, 279
Garrett 140
Gilbert 138, 175
Glubb Rev 178, 212, 259, 290
Goacher 274
Goddard 27
Godley 25, 118
Godman 20, 44, 50
Goldring P.C. 211, 217, 249, 254, 283, 299, 306
Golds 29, 54
Goring Rev 42, 58, 187, 194, 226, 258
Greenfield 144, 312
Gregory 1, 13, 22, 31, 41, 64, 107, 114, 139, 214
Guy Rev 11, 63, 137

H

Hall 25, 58, 120, 144, 273, 278, 291, 295, 313
Hall, Rev 46, 89, 123, 135, 163, 180, 200, 231, 278
Hamilton 156, 179
Hammond 117, 147
Hampton 310
Handmore 151
Hannen 270
Harding, 114
Harmes 112, 191
Harwood 33, 46, 139, 214, 253
Hawley 50, 67, 96, 129
Hayler 54, 58
Hedgecock 2, 18, 22, 31, 139
Heisch 210
Henblest 281
Herrington 72
Hever 300
Hill 275, 307
Hills 182
Hilton 275
Hitchens 123
Hoadley 86, 98, 104
Hodges 280
Holcombe 91
Hole 226, 304
Holden 56
Holland Rev 200
Hughes 5, 73
Humphrey 107, 151, 301
Hunter 97

I

Ingles 278
Ingram 91

J

James 126
Johnny Broome 205, 210
Jones 286, 302
Joyce 202
Jupp 56

K

Kennedy 162
Kensett 104
Keywood 75, 100, 164
Kinchcin 77
Knapp 160
Knight 72, 84, 294, 295

L

Lake 142, 161
Lamb 262
Lanaway 12, 72
Lashmar 108, 224
Lawrence 269
Lee 58
Leeves
Legg 56
Lelliott 5, 201, 208
Lewis, Dr 245, 269, 300, 316
Liffen 18
Lloyd 35, 192, 263
Loase 2, 22, 31
Lock 2
Loder 209
Longley 21, 137, 163, 179, 185, 194, 210, 215, 231, 247, 252, 261, 274, 281, 292

Lord de la Zouche 25, 41, 65, 124, 245
Lossam 25, 108, 144, 303, 314
Luard Col 234
Luxford 191

M

Marchant 111
Marshall 138
Martin 27, 46, 96, 101, 160, 218, 223, 232, 255, 274, 299
Mason 34, 109
McVey 211
Melvil 182
Mitchell 123, 170
Moon 54, 58
Morgan, Dr 15, 39, 50, 85, 108, 112, 127, 136, 187, 202, 233, 249, 263, 312
Morley 124, 226
Morrison, Dr 137
Murphy 117
Muzzall 45, 75, 101, 130

N

Naldrett 278
Newland 107, 115, 143, 217
Nightingale 177
Nye 27

O

O'Brien 156, 178, 187, 198, 228, 261, 280, 292, 296, 308

P

Pagden 174
Pannett 192
Parsons 57, 127, 182, 217
Patching 2, 40, 46, 137
Pattenden 3, 10, 22, 31, 45, 152, 226, 245, 273
Paul 205
Payne 130, 175
Penfold 2
Penikett 148, 174, 196
Perkins 142, 161
Pesterfield 172
Peters 46, 87
Phillips 10, 21
Pierce 112
Picknell 174
Piper 61, 78, 102, 145, 171, 200, 247, 260, 314
Poiney P.C. 131
Porter 15
Pritchard 220
Puttock 52, 56, 92, 93

R

Randall 60, 189
Randle 144, 171, 199, 215, 222, 270
Reeves 296
Rhodes 220
Richardson 165
Roberts 244
Robertson Rev 278, 296, 308
Runnacles 262

S

Sandham 58
Saunders 27, 85
Sayers 67, 81, 96, 112, 190, 268
Scott 61, 194
Seaborne 54, 67, 96, 314
Sebur 84
Shallcross 47
Sharp 77, 140
Sharpe 131
Shepherd 53, 69
Short P.C. 81, 90
Shoulders 68, 87, 94, 249
Silverson 112
Simmonds 170, 177, 201
Skinner 147
Smith 31, 73, 103, 110, 118, 122, 134, 173, 180, 190, 203, 217, 245, 258
Songhurst 72, 117
Sowter 12
Stammer 100, 157
Standing 101, 310
Stapley 89
Steadman 221
Stenning 250
Stephens 191, 196, 302
Stillaway 103, 127, 233
Stoner 26, 126, 134, 151, 170, 177, 182, 196, 215, 222, 228, 242, 245, 264, 270, 293
Street 216, 255
Stringer 27, 183, 314
Summersell 264

T

Talbot 221
Tamplin 32, 140, 151, 218, 222, 271
Taylor 117
Thomsitt 133
Thorns 132, 196, 217, 222, 241, 245, 263, 300
Thorpe 307
Tidy 184
Tidey 104
Tobitt 164, 307
Tribe 59
Trower 46, 129
Trussler 165
Tugwell 99, 218
Tuppen 21

V

Vallance 72, 169
Verrall 23
Vinall 6, 27, 44, 70, 81, 124, 314
Viscount Gage 122

W

Walker 55
Waller 56
Wallinger, Rev 80
Ward 14, 25, 73, 78, 108, 114, 125, 164, 206, 218, 224, 242, 275, 303
Warden 129
Ware 34
Weekes, Dr 99, 104
Welling 290, 299
West 62, 83, 207, 244, 273, 305
Weston 111
White 158
Whiteman 58
Wigney 25, 110
Williams 72, 255, 296
Wilson 103
Windebank 196, 223, 290
Winsor 229
Wisden 12, 77, 133, 150, 216, 312
Wood 16, 39, 79, 103, 136, 150, 158, 182, 224
Woodard 285
Woolgar 61, 105, 107, 124, 130, 166, 199, 206, 217, 299
Woolven 5, 41, 72

Y

Yeates 108, 224, 242

OTHER PLACES

A

Adelaide 86
Africa 120, 252, 262
Albourne 172
America 252, 309
Arundel 16, 80
Ashurst 16, 99, 188, 274, 299
Atlantic 227

B

Beeding 5, 68, 102, 131, 185, 198, 208, 226
Blackstone 125
Bolney 48
Boulogne 14
Bramber 2, 18, 70, 206
Brighton 3, 10, 14, 21, 34, 40, 58, 70, 75, 87, 108, 115, 126, 138, 151, 167, 170, 181, 195, 208, 214, 222, 230, 237, 248, 266, 268, 298, 311
Broadwater 295
Brussels 156
Burpham 274
Bury St Edmunds 76

C

Calcutta 143
Cambridge 87
Canterbury 14, 179
Cawnpore 183
Chalvington 117
Chatham 40, 107
Chichester 11, 42, 6
Cowfold 76, 181, 194, 220, 267, 274
Crimea 177
Crystal Palace 238
Cuckfield 10, 274

D

Ditchling, 75
Dorking, 187
Dover 286
Downs 14, 76, 313
Dyke 4

E

Eastboune 148
East Grinstead 290
Edburton 234, 274

F

France 1
Fulking 61

G

Goodwood 52, 99
Guildhall 163

H

Hampshire 48, 230
Handcross 209
Hassocks Gate 111
Hastings 80
Haywards Heath 272
Hereford 95
Hickstead 34, 76
Horsham 14, 22, 40, 77, 187, 194, 208, 236, 269, 274, 299
Hove 153, 173
Hurstpierpoint 12, 20, 31, 72, 87, 222, 260, 274

I

India 182, 192
Ireland 39, 133, 135, 156
Isle of Wight 237
Ixworth 76

K

Kent 107, 179, 230
Knepp Castle 187, 194, 241, 293, 300
Killarney 274

L

Lancing 274
Leicester 22
Lewes 10, 40, 48, 112, 174, 307
London 21, 34, 40, 48, 65, 75, 138, 141, 161, 187, 194, 208, 236, 258, 311
Lindfield 10
Loughborough 22
Lower Beeding, 220

M

Madras 18
Maidstone 151
Millbank 92
Moscow 20

N

Newcastle 5
Newtimber 274 New Zealand 120
Niagara Falls 238

O

Ovingdean 230
Oxford 4, 22, 263

P

Parham House 65, 136, 245
Partridge Green 208, 237, 298
Petworth 6, 15, 58, 91, 96, 102, 126, 132, 154, 166, 174, 181, 191, 200, 210, 227, 234, 255, 268, 307
Portslade 76
Portsmouth 40, 237, 310
Poynings 4, 138, 145
Putney 80

R

Rome 155
Rudgwick 117
Russia 20, 209
Rustington 100

S

Saddlescombe 4
San Francisco 143
Shermanbury 37, 160
Shepherd & Dog 61
Shoreham 1, 16, 40, 53, 56, 65, 88, 93, 108, 131, 143, 149, 169, 185, 194, 226, 230, 237, 298
SmallDole 138
Southampton 99, 281
Southsea 148
Southwick 25
Steventon 111
Steyning 2, 16, 37, 50, 56, 67, 99, 111, 121, 131, 138, 140, 149, 165, 181, 187, 203, 206, 266, 272, 298
Storrinton 16, 58, 117, 138, 147, 310
Suffolk 179
Sunderland 5
Surrey 230
Sussex 40, 77

T

Terry's Cross 76, 181
Thames 86, 92
Tunbridge Wells 140
Twineham 76

U

United States 227

V

Valenciennes 18
Van Diemen's Land 92

W

Wales 223
Waterloo 20, 35, 44
Weald 1
West Grinstead 187, 201, 206, 227, 241
West Hoathley 191
Westminster Hall 89
West Stoke 11, 64, 79, 137
Windsor 4
Wiston 187, 194
Withdean 63
Withyham 164
Wivelsfield 274
Woodmancote 16, 37, 112, 172
Woolwich 40, 44
Worthing 186, 311

Y

Yapton 52

From the 1895 OS map showing the development of the village.
Scale 6 inches to mile (approx).